All Roads Lead to Congress

The $300 Billion Fight over Highway Funding

Costas Panagopoulos
Fordham University

Joshua Schank
Bipartisan Policy Center

DISCARD

CQ PRESS

A Division of Congressional Quarterly Inc.
Washington, D.C.

CQ Press
1255 22nd Street, NW, Suite 400
Washington, DC 20037

Phone: 202-729-1900; toll-free, 1-866-4CQ-PRESS (1-866-427-7737)

Web: www.cqpress.com

Cover design: Kimberly Glyder

Images: cover, John Atkins/Corbis; 2, AP Images; 18,
www.ourdocuments.gov; 28, 53 (all), Scott J. Ferrell, *CQ Weekly;*
160, Jason Reed/Reuters/Landov; 179, *Parade* magazine, Alaska Department of
Transportation

♾ The paper used in this publication exceeds the requirements of the American National Standard for Information Sciences—Permanence of Paper for
Printed Library Materials, ANSI Z39.48-1992.

Printed and bound in the United States of America

11   10   09   08   07   1   2   3   4   5

Library of Congress Cataloging-in-Publication Data

Panagopoulos, Costas.
    All roads lead to Congress : the $300 billion fight over highway funding / by
Costas Panagopoulos, Joshua Schank.
        p. cm.
    Includes bibliographical references and index.
    ISBN 978-0-87289-461-7 (alk. paper)
        1. Legislation—United States.   2. Legislative bodies—United States.
3. Transportation and state—United States.   I. Schank, Joshua.   II. Title.

    KF4945.P36 2008
    328.73'077—dc22   2007034371

For M. Ruggiero
—C. P.

For Max Schank
—J. L. S.

DATE DUE

CONTENTS

TABLES, FIGURES, MAPS, AND BOXES

PREFACE

Transportation is one of those issues that many people don't think about until the system breaks down. On August 7, 2007, the relevance of transportation policy to our daily lives was thrust into the nation's consciousness as we surveyed the devastation and tragic loss of life brought about by the collapse of the Interstate 35W bridge that spanned the Mississippi River in Minneapolis, Minnesota. The aftershock of that catastrophe, as much as any single event in recent memory, forced road planners, road builders, and highway users to consider the magnitude of issues related to transportation policy, and to question the federal government's role in safeguarding and expanding our transportation infrastructure. A policy area that often exists in relative obscurity took on epic dimensions as the nation struggled to explain the disaster, to learn from it, and to take steps to prevent anything like it from reoccurring.

We may never know for sure if any actions taken by Congress, or by other lawmaking bodies or elected officials, could have prevented the Minneapolis bridge collapse. But what we do know—and what the nation was reminded of in the wake of the disaster—is that the federal government, in partnership with state and local governments, is charged with legislating policies and directing funds to sustain adequate maintenance for transportation infrastructure across the country. Since the creation of the interstate highway system a half-century ago, Congress has been tasked with, and gladly taken on, the responsibility of overseeing the mammoth construction requirements—and commensurate funding needs—of federal highways in all fifty states and the District of Columbia.

In this book we tell the story of how Congress and its members carry out that awesome responsibility. We do this in the classic "case study" manner; we describe the day-to-day, month-to-month, and year-to-year details of the most recent highway and mass transit legislation, a reauthorization of surface transportation laws that made its way through Congress between 2003 and 2005 (see timeline in Box P.1). The book came about because the two of us were working as fellows in the office of Sen. Hillary Rodham Clinton, D-N.Y. As academics, we both recalled sifting our way through countless texts about Congress and the legislative process during our educational careers. But few books had prepared us for the reality we observed and experienced working behind the scenes on Capitol Hill. The tasks we performed, the events we witnessed, and the relationships we built were like nothing we had ever read about, and we wanted to pass them along to students of government in such a way as to retain their inherently entertaining nature while providing the academic depth that is essential to useful scholarship.

Our case study exhibits usually unseen aspects of the lawmaking process and demonstrates how policy interacts with the power structures, institutional arrangements, and electoral incentives in Congress in the quest to be enacted into law. We aim to give readers a detailed, comprehensive, and impartial glimpse into what really happens behind the scenes of a major bill in Congress—told from the vantage point of two interloping academics who experienced this process firsthand—but then also outline some of the theoretical implications of the process we track. This is not a view easily found elsewhere.

We approach our account from two very different perspectives. One of us (Costas Panagopoulos) is a political scientist who studies Congress, lawmaking, voting behavior, and elections. The other (Joshua Schank) is an urban planner by training and profession who has lived and breathed transportation policy his entire career. (Panagopoulos served in Senator Clinton's office as a legislative fellow; Schank was Senator Clinton's transportation fellow, brought in from Columbia University specifically to work on the legislation discussed in this book.) We believe that these two perspectives combine to provide a deep understanding of both transportation policy issues and the function of the federal government.

The book begins by setting the context of a Capitol Hill staffer's existence. The first chapter discusses a staff aide's life on the Hill and the often thankless, but surprisingly influential, work that occurs behind the scenes in anticipation of such a large bill as surface transportation reauthorization. Jockeying for position starts before there is even a bill over which to fight.

In Chapter 2, we follow the bill as it is "marked up" in House and Senate committees. That is where the chess moves become even more complex and the staff starts working overtime. The bill moves on to the floors of the House and Senate in Chapter 3, where suddenly everything becomes more public and the fights are brought into the open for all to see. Chapter 4 describes the black hole of Congress known as the "conference committee," in which much of the previous work on a bill can soon come to naught. In this case, it does. The bill dies, only to be resurrected under a newly elected Congress. Chapter 5 shows what the bill goes through the second time around, and how legislative priorities and political passions can look and feel quite different when people are exhausted with the process. Finally, Chapter 6 serves as an epilogue for the entire story, looking at some of the consequences of the legislation and drawing some conclusions about the whole process.

Although the book is meant to be observational rather than judgmental, there are some obvious truths about transportation policy that emerge from our insider's view that we believe are directly relevant to the daily lives of most Americans. The reality is that there has not been a visionary, large-scale change in transportation policy in this country since the birth of the interstate system in 1956. The bill as described in this book is one with more "earmarks"—pork-barrel projects—and less policy than any transportation bill in history, and the fight we witnessed and describe here is often little more than a squabble over the leftovers. That precious taxpayer dollars are used almost exclusively for new construction rather than repair of existing facilities is the undeniable reality, and the inescapable results are what can lead to crumbling infrastructure, such as occurred in Minneapolis.

This is not meant to imply that the flaws in the transportation bill, as opposed to possible flaws in the bridge's construction, are the reason that I-35W collapsed. The mistakes that led to its demise were in all likelihood primarily technical rather than financial. However, we do maintain that transportation policy in the United States needs vision and direction. The bridge disaster in Minneapolis was everything we all want to avoid. Unfortunately, it often takes such fateful wakeup calls to overcome the powerful electoral and political incentives that preoccupy our nation's leaders, and to jostle them into remedial action. We can only hope that the giant has been stirred.

ACKNOWLEDGMENTS

There are many people whose actions led to the creation of this book, even though they themselves might not be aware of it. In Congress, special thanks are extended first and foremost to Senator Clinton. Her leadership, commitment, and attention to policy details served as an inspiration to us, and without her neither of us would have been able to benefit from the unique experience of working in the Senate.

Panagopoulos came to Capitol Hill as an American Political Science Association Congressional Fellow. Each year, APSA selects a handful of political scientists to spend a year in Washington to observe the policy-making process firsthand. Jeff Biggs, APSA Congressional Fellowship Program director, labors tirelessly to make the fellowship experience top rate. His efforts are much appreciated. Special thanks go to the other 2004–2005 CFP fellows whose insights, knowledge, and friendship helped to make the experience especially rich.

Panagopoulos is also grateful to the Hon. John Brademas, D-Ind., a former majority whip in the U.S. House of Representatives (1977–1981), for encouraging him to spend time as a "fly on the wall" in Congress and for recommending him to the program. Dr. Brademas also read the complete book manuscript meticulously and offered thoughtful comments and suggestions. Discussions with former CFP fellows Jon Bond, Jim Campbell, Dave Dulio, Paul Herrnson, Robin Kolodny, Thad Kousser, Frances Lee, Paul Light, Dave Magleby, Forrest Maltzman, Thomas Mann, David Mayhew, Norm Ornstein, and James Thurber generated insights that are doubtlessly reflected in the pages that follow.

Panagopoulos also acknowledges colleagues at Yale University and in the Department of Political Science at Fordham University for intellectual debts, and is thankful for their support and generosity. Jeffrey Cohen, Diana Evans, Richard Fleisher, and Donald Green deserve special appreciation for their mentorship, guidance, and support.

In Senator Clinton's office, Panagopoulos also thanks Kris Balderson, Tamera Luzzatto, Laurie McHugh, and Michael Szymanski.

For Schank, the greatest help came from Lee Bollinger, president of Columbia University, who sponsored his work in the Clinton office and made the entire experience possible. Elliott Sclar, Schank's undergraduate professor, mentor, and doctoral adviser, suggested to Mr. Bollinger that Schank might be a good fit for the job. Ellen Smith, who serves in government relations for Columbia, was also instrumental in making the experience happen.

In the Clinton Washington office, there were many people who helped Schank along. Tamera Luzzatto brought him back to the staff after his fellowship was over to help out when the transportation bill was resurrected. Sean Sweeney was Schank's partner in crime in the bill's first life and showed him the ropes on Capitol Hill and transportation policy, and Sean O'Shea was a great partner the second time around, one who knew how to exploit Schank's previous knowledge of the situation to the fullest. Sean Conway, Melissa Ho, Shalini Matani, and Ben Souede all helped crystallize the experience of working in that office by listening to and even caring about the inner workings of transportation policy.

Also extremely helpful were those who allowed Schank to use company resources and time to work on this book project. They include Sergio Ostria of ICF International and Robert Brownstein of PB Consult, who not only encouraged work on our book but also provided useful discussions concerning the content. Mort Downey, Jeff Ensor, Emil Frankel, Steve Lockwood, and Pepper Santalucia also proved very helpful with their thoughts on the key policy issues in this book. We also thank our reviewers John Forren, Miami University; Gerald Gryski, Auburn University; Mark Joslyn, University of Kansas; and Gary Mucciaroni, Temple University.

We would also like to thank those who agreed to be interviewed. Ruth Van Mark, who was the deputy staff director for the Senate Environment and Public Works Committee when this was all happening, made time in her schedule and even agreed to be recorded for the purposes of this book. Her insights into what happened after the fact were usually much clearer than what may have been perceived by the authors previously. Amy Chiang, who was the deputy chief of staff for Rep. Sherwood Boehlert, R-N.Y., provided an interview from China and much of the information on House side machinations. Jeff Squires, who was minority deputy staff director for the Senate Environment and Public Works Committee, also provided an interview and great additional insight from the Democratic perspective. And though she did not participate directly in its creation, the entire experience of working on the Hill would have been far less interesting, and this book far less entertaining, without the actions and personality of Dawn Levy.

Most of all, Panagopoulos thanks his family for their unending love and support: Mark, Tim, George, and Vasiliki. Schank would like to thank his wife, Lindsey Schank, for always supporting him and believing in his writing more than anyone else on Earth. That dinner at 1789 was special and delicious.

Lastly, although certainly not least in any way, we thank our colleagues at CQ Press for their strong support of this project. Charisse Kiino helped to inspire the project and then shepherded it and us throughout, offering constant encouragement, support, and keen insights. David Rapp, our esteemed editor, was patient and kind and shared his expertise generously. And the CQ Press production crew, led by Steve Pazdan and team members Talia Greenberg, Allyson Rudolph, and Allison McKay, produced a marvelous volume. Any errors of omission or commission remain our own.

May 14, 2003	Administration's SAFETEA 2003 introduced in House (HR 2088).
May 15, 2003	Administration's SAFETEA 2003 introduced in Senate (S 1072).
September 30, 2003	TEA-21 expires; Bush signs five-month extension (#1).
November 12, 2003	Full committee consideration and markup held by the Senate Environment and Public Works Committee; committee reports S 1072 favorably to full Senate (as amended) (17–2).
November 20, 2003	TEA-LU (HR 3550) companion measure introduced in House.
December 9, 2003	108th Congress, Session 1, adjourns.
January 9, 2004	S 1072 reported to the full Senate by the Senate Environment and Public Works Committee and placed on the Senate Calendar.
January 20, 2004	108th Congress, Session 2, begins.
January 28, 2004– February 12, 2004	Senate considers S 1072 (SAFETEA) bill on the floor.
February 12, 2004	Senate passes SAFETEA bill (76–21).
February 29, 2004	Bush signs sixty-day extension (#2).
March 24, 2004	Full committee consideration and markup held by the House Transportation and Infrastructure Committee; reported favorably to the full House by voice vote.
March 29, 2004	Reported to the House as amended by the House Transportation and Infrastructure Committee; referred to the House Education and the Workforce, Energy and Commerce, Judiciary, Resources, and Science Committees to consider provisions that fall within their jurisdictions; all committees discharged and placed on the Union Calendar.
March 30, 2004– April 1, 2004	Full committee consideration and markup held by the House Rules Committee. Rule for floor action reported.
April 1–2, 2004	House considers measure and amendments.
April 2, 2004	House passes reauthorization bill (HR 3550) (357–65).
April 8, 2004	House bill received in Senate.
April 30, 2004	Bush signs sixty-day extension (#3).

May 19, 2004	Senate insists on its amendments and requests a conference; chair authorized to appoint Senate conferees with a ratio of eleven Republicans to ten Democrats.
May 20, 2004	Senate names conferees.
June 3, 2004	House disagrees with Senate amendments; agrees to a conference. House names conferees.
June 9, 2004,	Conference committee proceedings held.
June 30, 2004	Bush signs thirty-day extension (#4).
July 30, 2004	Bush signs sixty-day extension (#5).
September 30, 2004	Bush signs eight-month extension (#6).
November 2, 2004	2004 presidential election. President George W. Bush reelected. Republicans retain control of House and Senate.
December 8, 2004	108th Congress adjourns. No action on transportation reauthorization.
January 4, 2005	109th Congress, Session 1, begins.
February 9, 2005	House reintroduces TEA-LU (HR 3). Referred to House Transportation and Infrastructure, House Rules Committees.
March 2, 2005	Full committee consideration and markup held by the House Transportation and Infrastructure Committee.
March 7, 2005	Bill reported to the House as amended by the House Transportation and Infrastructure Committee and placed on House Calendar.
March 8, 2005	Full committee consideration and markup held by the House Rules Committee. Reports rule to House.
March 9, 2005	House adopts rule; considers and amends bill.
March 10, 2005	House passes HR 3 (417–9).
April 6, 2005	Senate introduces companion measure (S 732) SAFETEA.
April 26, 2005– May 17, 2005	Senate floor considers and amends SAFETEA.
May 17, 2005	Senate passes SAFETEA (89–11) (total $295B).

May 26, 2005	House disagrees with Senate amendments and requests a conference; House names conferees; Senate disagrees with House amendments. Senate agrees to a conference and names conferees.
May 31, 2005	Bush signs thirty-day extension (#7).
June 9, 2005	Conference committee proceeding held.
July 1, 2005	Bush signs eighteen-day extension (#8).
July 19, 2005	Bush signs two-day extension (#9).
July 21, 2005	Bush signs six-day extension (#10).
July 27, 2005	Bush signs three-day extension (#11).
July 28, 2005	Conference report filed (total $286.5B).
July 29, 2005	House adopts conference report (412–8); Senate adopts conference report (91–4); measure cleared for president.
July 30, 2005	Bush signs fifteen-day extension (#12).
August 10, 2005	SAFETEA-LU signed by President Bush, becoming Public Law, PL 109–59.

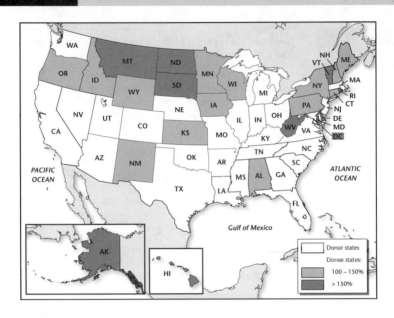

MAP P.1 — Transportation Equity Act for the 21st Century, Donor/Donee States

Donor states
Donee states:
100 – 150%
> 150%

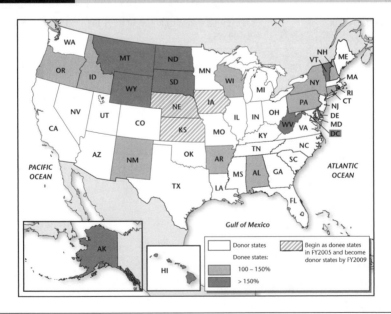

MAP P.2 — Safe, Accountable, Flexible, and Efficient Transportation Equity Act, Donor/Donee States

Donor states
Donee states:
100 – 150%
> 150%
Begin as donee states in FY2005 and become donor states by FY2009

Source: Compiled by authors using data available from the Federal Highway Administration.

CHAPTER 1

HOW A BILL BECOMES LAW

POWERS BEHIND THE THRONE

Dawn Levy, a smart, confident, and ambitious woman from Brooklyn in New York City, was a living legend in the small but rarified world of transportation policy on Capitol Hill. As a senior staff aide to Max Baucus, senator from Montana and the senior Democrat on the Senate Finance Committee, her specialty was transportation. She advised the senator on multiple issues related to the committee's work, but transportation was where she had the most extensive experience and reputation.

By 2003, Levy was Baucus's primary advisor on transportation finance. And in that insider's role, she was a force to be reckoned with; even staffers older in age or seniority but farther down in the pecking order would visibly shiver upon hearing her name. Her clout was unusual in that she worked for a conservative Democrat from a rural state, which meant she and her boss were often aligned with Republicans from other rural states, putting them in opposition to urban members from their own political party. This was especially so on the topic of transportation, where Montana's interests were very different from densely populated New York, Massachusetts, and Connecticut, states where Democrats also commanded seats in the Senate. Other Democratic staffers knew that if Baucus, at Levy's urging, aligned with majority Republicans on a transportation bill, their states were more than likely to be the first casualties.

Sen. Max Baucus, D-Mont., ranking Democratic member of the Senate Finance Committee, appears with fellow senator Bryan Dorgan, D.-N.D., at an April 2005 press conference.

Levy had worked in transportation for years, and she knew the players and the landscape well. She also had learned some of the essential techniques for getting her way in the rough-and-tumble legislative factory on Capitol Hill. She knew her subject cold, worked long hours, pursued her goals with relentless energy, and never took no for an answer. She also had no qualms about completely switching her position when it was advantageous to her (and her boss). In other words, she was a consummate Senate staffer.

Indeed, staff aides like Dawn Levy are the grease that makes the wheels of Congress work. They clear a path for what little incremental movement the legislative branch of the U.S. government achieves in any month, year, or biennial session—or decade, for that matter. Her boss, Baucus, had been in Congress since 1979, and had served as either chairman or ranking minority member of the Finance Committee since 2001 (depending on which party controlled the Senate). The Finance

Committee is responsible for the entire tax code as well as Social Security, Medicare, and welfare laws, all of which came under Baucus's purview. In addition, Baucus was a member of two other committees in the Senate—the Agriculture, Nutrition, and Forestry Committee, and the Environment and Public Works Committee—so his attention was spread, like all senators, over all manner of public policy issues. But when the nation's surface transportation laws came up for renewal in 2003, Baucus was in a pivotal position, both as senior Democrat on the tax-writing Finance Committee, as a key swing vote on the Environment and Public Works Committee, and as a representative of an expansive but sparsely populated rural state. So to make sure that he and his constituents' interests were protected on the so-called highway bill, Baucus would rely heavily on Levy, his top surrogate on transportation policy with a vital say on how to write the new bill.

And Levy, for her part, had to know not just how to craft a bill to her boss's liking, but how to get it approved in the committees of jurisdiction, how to get it passed in the Senate, and how to craft a final compromise with the other body of Congress, the House of Representatives, so that it could garner the final approval of President George W. Bush, who held ultimate veto power. More important, perhaps, Levy had to make sure that the opposition—whoever they may be and in whatever form they took—did not succeed in getting their way at the expense of Baucus and Montana. In short, she not only had to know how the system worked, but also how to *work* the system.

Levy managed to accomplish such a feat through a clever combination of chutzpah, legerdemain, and none-too-subtle gamesmanship. As we will detail in subsequent chapters, she used her position to convene meetings of other staffers, control the agenda of those meetings, and even change the subject when it suited her purposes. She crafted a novel financing plan that served to shake up political alliances and alter the legislative dynamic, without ever actually putting the idea on paper for anyone else to parse. And she kept her boss at the center of the action without requiring him to expend his own political capital in the early stages of the process. In the end, a $300 billion bill to extend and revise the nation's transportation policies for another six years had Dawn Levy's stamp on it but none of her fingerprints.

Senator Baucus, who always had his difficulties getting reelected in a state that favors conservative Republicans, came out a big winner in his fight for highway funds. Yet few people outside of Montana—indeed, few inside the state either—have ever heard Dawn Levy's name mentioned in conjunction with Montana's good fortune. Such anonymity among the voting public is also the mark of a successful staffer—Job No. 1 is to make sure the boss always gets the credit.

In fact, just about every legislator who is worth his or her salt has at least one staff member like Dawn Levy to rely on. This is the stark reality of our representative system of government that is rarely, if ever, discussed in the traditional treatises on "How a Bill Becomes Law." The power of invisible and unelected staff aides, though central to that process, is also not the only departure from the textbook norms of legislative procedure. Indeed, to fully understand and appreciate the inner workings of Congress and the White House, one must look beyond the civic lessons and the television news reports to see how an institution of lawmakers creates our nation of laws. It's been called the legislative equivalent of a sausage factory—but in this case, there is good reason to watch how it's being made.

SETTING THE STAGE

Article I of the U.S. Constitution gives Congress the sole power to write and pass laws. The Constitution also established two legislative chambers: a House of Representatives, whose membership is proportional to the populations of the respective states; and a Senate, where each state has two members regardless of its population. The two chambers must agree on the exact wording of each and every bill they present to the president for his enacting signature. While the Constitution provides no direct legislative role for the president, it does allow him or her to make recommendations to Congress, and it does give to the president the power to veto bills presented to him, though Congress can still override a veto if proponents can muster two-thirds majority votes in each chamber.

Beyond those specific prescriptions, however, Congress is pretty much left to its own devices as to how to fashion legislation and move it through the various stages of enactment. And over the years, the two chambers gradually arrived at fairly similar legislative procedures to follow, though with sharply divergent rules and characteristics. Any member of the House or

Senate may introduce a bill for consideration by the respective chamber, but both chambers' rules stipulate that every bill must immediately be referred to a standing committee with express jurisdiction over the subject matter covered by the bill. Committee chairs, in turn, have sole authority to decide which bills will be considered by their panels. If a majority of a committee decides to order a bill "reported" to the floor for consideration by the full Senate or full House, then the majority leaders of each chamber have sole authority to decide which bills will be brought to the members for a vote. If both chambers pass different versions of the same bill—variations of even one word or comma are not permitted—they must reconcile the differences, either by one chamber conceding to the other chamber's wording, or by convening a House-Senate "conference committee," where negotiators meet to hammer out a final version. Both chambers must then vote to approve the conference agreement before it can be sent to the president. (See Figure 1.1.)

That's how a bill becomes law—in theory, at least. But it rarely goes according to that simple plan (and if it does, experienced observers become suspicious!). Indeed, the rules allow for as many variations on this process as the human imagination can create, and if nothing else, members of Congress—and their staffs—have quite fertile imaginations.

The keys to following the legislative dance are fairly simple and even obvious, though each one requires some complex and artful footwork. They can be summed up as the "Four Ps," as follows:

- **Power**—who has it, by what public or private sanction do they exercise it, what institutional or political tools are available to them, and how far can they go to get what they want.

- **Process**—using perquisites of power, such as seniority, committee jurisdiction, variations in House and Senate rules, and relationships with the executive branch to get what you want.

- **Policy**—the actual substance of the legislative debate, developed over years and sometimes decades, usually dependent on legislative and legal precedents, constitutional law, ideology, partisanship, persuasive abilities, and (not least) public opinion.

- **Pots of Money (Price)**—what it costs, how will it be paid for, and at what political price.

FIGURE 1.1   **How a Bill Becomes Law**

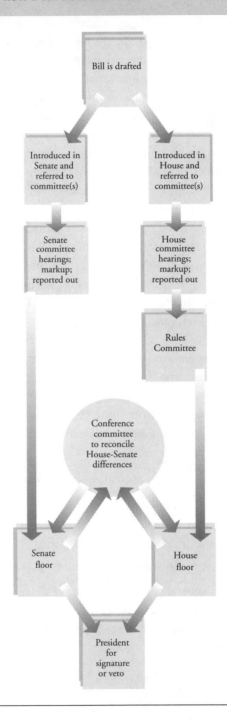

This book will use the case study method to examine how each of the Four Ps come to play in the way a bill becomes law. We have chosen to follow the most recent reauthorization of the nation's highway and mass transit programs, formally titled the "Safe, Accountable, Flexible, and Efficient Transportation Equity Act—A Legacy for Users" (SAFETEA-LU), because it demonstrates quite vividly each of these operative aspects over the months and years it was moving through Congress. Transportation policy in and of itself may not be very gripping, though it does affect people's daily lives in very tangible ways, from the quality of the roads we drive, to the taxes we pay at the gas pump, to the ability to get to work each day in an efficient and affordable manner. Transportation also affects energy policy, environmental regulations, and even public health. Nevertheless, transportation rarely registers in national public opinion surveys as an especially important issue in influencing voters' preferences for president or members of Congress.

At the same time, the surface transportation bill is relatively easy and straightforward to understand. Though it is only revisited every six years, the completion of the interstate highway system in the mid-1990s has left little reason or incentive for Congress to make substantial changes in federal transportation policy, so there are few debates over arcane policy questions. Even so, the bill does provide telling insights into two fundamental crosscurrents of American politics—partisanship, or the ideological battle between Democrats and Republicans; and regionalism, the ongoing contest for resources among the fifty states. The real challenge in formulating the legislation now comes from the long, never-ending fight among the states over a finite pot of money. The amount of funding authorized in the bill, slightly less than $300 billion, made for some serious power struggles among members of Congress and the White House, and among their respective staffs. The battles effectively decided how much money states and localities would receive to build highways and mass transit systems. The battles also determined how much money we all pay at the gas pump in the form of federal taxes, how large the federal deficit will be, and how safe our cars and trucks will be. And finally, they can influence the fate of each member's reelection prospects, and thus the balance of power in both the House and Senate. During an era when majority control of each chamber is held precariously from one biennial election to another, any bill that carries a $300 billion price tag will have both winners and losers, and thus could conceivably turn any number of incumbents out of office. For that reason alone, the transportation bill carried fateful consequences for the political direction of the entire country.

After outlining some of the basic principles and watchwords for observing the process, this book will follow the path of this legislation chronologically from its inception, as a bill introduced in the House and Senate, to its enactment upon the president's signature. We will focus particular attention on the action in the Senate, where coauthors Joshua Schank served on staff as a transportation policy advisor and Costas Panagopoulos was a legislative fellow for Sen. Hillary Rodham Clinton, Democrat of New York, and thus was able to observe firsthand the meetings and machinations of the bill's many authors. The Senate provides special interest on this bill because jurisdiction for the bill is divided among several committees and thus several competing centers of power. The Senate, where tiny Rhode Island has as many votes as mammoth Texas or California (two each), is also the locus of the regional infighting that characterizes highway funding, so it provides a unique window into that critical aspect of American politics. Ultimately, our purpose is to show, not just tell, how a bill really becomes law.

POWER: HOW TO GET IT, HOW TO USE IT

Why do members of Congress do what they do? Why does Congress pass certain pieces of legislation and not others? To explain congressional action—and inaction—we must try to understand the basic goals of the 435 voting members of the House and 100 members of the Senate, and then understand how they interact with their constituents, with various interest groups, political party strategists, and campaign contributors that compete for their attention, and with each other.

Theories of legislative behavior commonly assume that legislators, such as members of the U.S. Congress, are motivated by the desire to stay in office. David Mayhew's seminal book on Congress argues that members are, first and foremost, "single minded seekers of reelection."[1] That is to say, they may care about other things, like policy and ideology, but what they care most about and what drives their daily actions in Congress is their commitment to keeping their jobs. In another seminal study, Richard Fenno argues that members of Congress actually pursue three goals—power, policy, and reelection—but even so, the overarching preoccupation with reelection looms large in the minds of legislators.[2]

Because legislators are so preoccupied with holding onto their seats, we can view their actions and activities as being fueled primarily by this aim. The things they do and the choices they make must contribute to, in one way or another, their reelection agenda. Mayhew argues that members of Congress pursue this goal by engaging in three activities: *position taking, credit claiming,* and *advertising.*[3]

Position taking involves making public statements about public policy and governmental action that reflect the preferences of the member's constituency while, at the same time, reflecting positively on the member. Such statements are viewed as indications that members care about the things that their constituents care about and help the members go on the record for sharing views with the people they represent in Congress. Oftentimes, position taking is only symbolic, and members do little more than offer expressions of support for certain policy options. Still, members appear to view position taking as a helpful approach to remaining popular with constituents.

Credit claiming is another popular tactic that members employ to curry favor with constituents. Politicians like to associate themselves with projects or other benefits directed to their constituencies, and they will work hard to make sure their electors know that they were responsible for delivering these benefits to their districts.

Indeed, far from being ashamed of a practice that many critics deride as "pork barrel" politics, members of Congress will often advertise their success in providing these local benefits, at least implicitly making the argument that the benefits would not have been forthcoming without their personal efforts.

The Power of Incumbency

To some extent, there is good reason to believe members' efforts are convincing and successful in keeping their constituents happy. Even as public approval of Congress overall is generally low, approval of respondents' individual representatives is often considerably higher. Moreover, the reelection

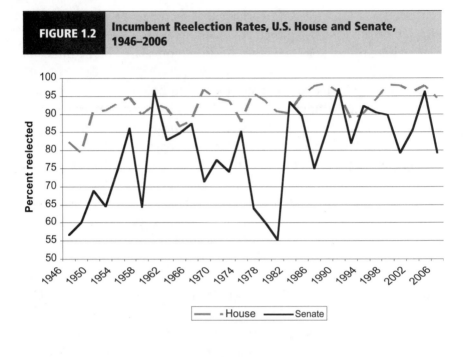

FIGURE 1.2   Incumbent Reelection Rates, U.S. House and Senate, 1946–2006

Source: Harold W. Stanley and Richard G. Niemi, *Vital Statistics on American Politics, 2007–2008* (Washington, D.C.: CQ Press, 2008), 53.

rates for members of Congress have routinely exceeded 90 percent for members of the U.S. House since 1964. (See Figure 1.2.) In 2006, 95 percent of incumbent members of the House who were seeking reelection retained their offices; 79 percent of U.S. senators seeking reelection won in that year.

Scholars have put forth a variety of explanations for the sources of the apparent electoral advantages of incumbency. Bruce Cain, John Ferejohn, and Morris Fiorina find that members' success in cultivating a *personal vote* by providing constituent services has contributed to this phenomenon.[4] Others observe that incumbents' ability to raise more funds relative to their opponents, especially from special interest groups, helps at election time.[5] Moreover, structural benefits accrue to incumbents from heavily gerrymandered districts that offer protection to officeholders. Still another possibility, however, is that constituents are basically pleased with their members and want to reward them with reelection.

To maximize the likelihood of reelection, therefore, members aim to maximize the benefits they direct toward their districts. Even if the empirical evidence to support this relationship is murky at best,[6] what is important is that members perceive it to be true. "The lore," argues Mayhew, "is that [district benefits] count—furthermore, given home expectations, that they must be supplied in regular quantities for a member to stay electorally even with the board."[7] Consequently, legislators feel they have strong incentives to pursue particularized benefits, broadly defined to include benefits directed to a specific individual, group, or geographic constituency, in such a way that allows a single congressman to be recognized as the claimant for the benefit.[8] "Here, the congressman fills the traditional role of supplier of goods to the home district," writes Mayhew.[9] The perception is that securing such benefits is especially helpful in advancing the reelection goal. In the words of a Democratic member, "They've got to see something: it's the bread and butter issues that count—the dams, the post office and the other public buildings, the highways. They want to know what you've been doing."[10]

The Politics of Pork

Given the importance of particularized benefits in pursuing reelection, it should be no surprise if legislation that permits members of Congress to "bring home the bacon" becomes especially attractive to many members of Congress. Some scholars find that the institutional peculiarities that have evolved in Congress respond directly to members' desire to pursue these "distributive politics efficiently."[11] In recent years, attention has turned to addressing the growing number of congressional "earmarks," or special provisions inserted into bills, or (more often) into a bill's accompanying committee report, directing a federal agency to allocate funds to specific local initiatives, such as a research grant, a "pilot" program, or a "special demonstration project." These earmarks, the basic fodder of pork-barrel projects, have long been regarded by scholars as part of a broader package of particularized benefits bestowed by members of Congress upon their districts. But even though earmarks are an age-old process, the past twenty years or so have witnessed an exponential rise in earmarking practices. Critics deride the practice as ad hoc policymaking at best and illegal graft at worst. But many members of Congress are just as adamant in their support of the practice, maintaining that they are better judges of what would benefit their districts and states than an unelected bureaucrat toiling away in an impersonal government agency in Washington, D.C.

Another, more enlightening way to look at earmarks, however, is as a manifestation of the continuing power struggle between the executive and legislative branches of government. As the executive branch has grown over the past half century, presidential administrations have assumed ever-greater degrees of power over how money and resources are allocated to states and localities. The New Deal of Franklin Delano Roosevelt and the Great Society of Lyndon Baines Johnson created hundreds of federal programs governed by funding "formulas" for distributing the federal largesse. Congress wrote the formulas, to be sure, but most if not all of the interpretations for how those formulas would be meted out were left to the agencies themselves. In the parlance of Mayhew, members of Congress were finding themselves increasingly distanced from the "credit" that comes with delivering particularized benefits to their constituents.

The one avenue an individual member can take to counter this executive branch hegemony is through the practice of earmarks—that is, by inserting a specific directive to the agency to funnel a specific amount of money to a specific project for his or her specific constituency. In the past, this practice was most prevalent when the White House was controlled by a conservative Republican, and one or both chambers of Congress were under majority rule of Democrats. During the 1980s, for instance, President Ronald Reagan successfully resisted Democratic initiatives for new social programs, but he was virtually powerless to avoid signing "must-pass" spending bills to fund basic operations of the government, to provide emergency support payments to farmers, and to fund local roads and highways (in fact, Reagan vetoed the transportation bill and the veto was overridden by Congress). As a result, Democrats began larding those bills with earmarks—or more often, they would insert earmark language into the accompanying committee reports that explain Congress's legislative intentions. Committee reports are technically non-binding on the agencies, but few agency directors are willing to risk the ire of a congressional oversight committee whose express desires are purposely ignored. So Reagan was effectively stymied in his cost-cutting efforts. In his 1988 State of the Union Address, the Great Communicator famously slammed down on his lectern two bills totaling more than a thousand pages that he had just signed under such duress, and warned the assembled joint meeting of the House and Senate that he would never do so again. It was a brilliant public relations ploy, and had a momentary effect on members' appetite for earmarking, but it was ultimately a hollow gesture. Earmarking has only grown more widespread since Reagan's day.

Ironically, the practice has literally exploded under the GOP administration of George W. Bush, working with a predominately GOP Congress. When Democrats won control of the House and Senate in the 2006 midterm elections, Bush tried to deflect the blame to the opposition party, but the facts he cited from a Congressional Research Service study actually applied to members of his own party when they were in majority control.

In his 2007 State of the Union message, Bush urged members of the newly elected Democratic majority in Congress to reduce earmarks. "What we need to do is impose spending discipline in Washington, D.C.," pressed Bush. He continued:

> [T]here is the matter of earmarks. These special interest items are often slipped into bills at the last hour—when not even C-SPAN is watching. In 2005 alone, the number of earmarks grew to over 13,000 and totaled nearly $18 billion. Even worse, over 90 percent of earmarks never make it to the floor of the House and Senate—they are dropped into committee reports that are not even part of the bill that arrives on my desk. You didn't vote them into law. I didn't sign them into law. Yet, they're treated as if they have the force of law. The time has come to end this practice. So let us work together to reform the budget process, expose every earmark to the light of day and to a vote in Congress, and cut the number and cost of earmarks at least in half by the end of this session.

Calls to cut back on pork-barrel projects have never been in short supply on both sides of the aisle and throughout U.S. history. These cries are mostly rhetorical, however, and given the importance that legislators themselves place on delivering particularized benefits, reductions of earmarks are unlikely to be seriously considered. This is a classic example of a *tragedy of the commons* problem. Since individual members have few incentives to think about the big picture, such as the overall budget, the public's perceptions of Congress, etc., they will only care about what's important to them or their individual districts. In the end, each member's indifference is not enough to be of consequence, but erosion of trust in Congress as an institution or ballooning deficits will ensue. Yet no one member can be held individually accountable. These incentives are so powerful that they drive congressional behavior. As Kenneth Shepsle argues, in Congress

> there is an attitude of live and let live. Each legislative agent seeks to obtain benefits for his constituency and, even in failure he can claim credit for having fought the good fight. Each agent behaves essentially this way and expects all others to behave similarly. Although there are some exceptions, the general rule does not impose sanctions on those who seek to place the distributive and regulatory powers of the state in the service of their constituents. That's the system.[12]

Partisanship and Special Interests

Scholars of American politics have detected a key shift in the political landscape in recent years—partisan polarization. Evidence of members of Congress separating into liberal and conservative camps is now abundant. Moderates in the nation's legislature have virtually disappeared. As Nolan McCarty, Keith Poole, and Howard Rosenthal argue, "[o]ver the past thirty years, the parties have deserted the center of the floor in favor of the wings."[13] Polarization is a potent force that affects congressional decision making in profound ways. One of the more devastating effects is that it can paralyze the process of public policy formation and lead to legislative failure.[14]

The legislative process we describe in this book cannot be told without reference to partisan polarization in Congress. Our story unfolds in an environment frequently characterized as one of the most polarized

Congresses of the postwar era.[15] To be sure, manifestations of the effects of partisanship and polarization pepper our account of the transportation reauthorization process, and these considerations are not absent from our analysis. But partisanship and polarization do not drive the fate of the legislation we track as much as they may influence other bills. By and large, the hurdles legislators struggled with on the highway bill were less ideological than they were political. For the most part, legislators on both sides of the aisle agreed they wanted more money and a larger share of the pie.

Similarly, special interest groups, which figure prominently in typical accounts of congressional lawmaking, are not featured center stage in this book's story. We do not intend for this to suggest that they were largely absent from the process, but simply that their goals, at least for those that were most powerful, coincided with the overall objective of the members: more money.

In this regard, the legislation we track is unique in that the process it follows highlights bargaining and debate that are fueled by localized, constituency-based, or regional interests more so than partisan or ideology-based bickering.

Spreading the Wealth

This may strike some readers as puzzling: Why wouldn't the majority party want to direct disproportionately more of the spoils to its members, especially if the party perceives there to be electoral benefit in doing so? Moreover, why would evidence of such a strategy be scarce in an environment that is as politically charged and polarized as it was in the Congresses we examine?

Scholars have debated these questions extensively. Early work on the Congress, including Mayhew's seminal book,[16] posited that distributive politics transcends partisanship. The conventional wisdom among scholars is that the distribution of particularized benefits is largely nonpartisan, although this view has been challenged by studies that detect partisan elements in the distribution of federal resources.[17]

For the most part, the transportation reauthorization process we describe in this book supports this notion of "universalism," in which members share broadly in the benefits.[18] As Melissa Collie puts it, legislators "avoid excluding minority interests from the benefits of distributive legislation."[19] The majority party's willingness to make concessions to the minority party with respect to distributive benefits has been explained variously.[20] One explanation for such behavior is that the majority party makes concessions to the minority party because it envisions a situation in the future when it is itself in the minority status and would prefer to be treated in this manner. Alternatively, Balla et al. suggest that the party in control cuts the out-party in on the action in order to "inoculate itself from criticism" of wasteful spending from the minority party. As we will see, there are few guarantees that the majority party will prevent such attacks despite its willingness to bring the minority party in on the action.

The Appeal of Transportation

Legislators' ability to include pork-barrel projects in just about any appropriations bill is virtually unlimited. But six-year authorization bills that include plentiful opportunities to secure particularized benefits don't come along every day. So when one does, it has special attractions to just about every member of Congress. The reauthorization of the surface transportation bill, negotiated during from 2003 through 2005, was just such an initiative. When finally completed, the price tag of the transportation bill signed by President Bush on August 10, 2005, was a record-breaking $286.4 billion and included over 6,300 earmarks totaling $24 billion, an increase in total earmarks of over 1,200 percent since the 1991 transportation bill.[21]

Most of those earmarks were designated for so-called "special demonstration projects," the purest form of earmark in that they are direct allocations to specific projects, which have had the sharpest growth. For example, in the 1982 highway bill (the Surface Transportation Assistance Act), there were ten earmarks for "special demonstration projects." In the 2005 reauthorization, there were over 5,500 such projects.[22]

HISTORY OF THE SURFACE TRANSPORTATION BILL

Congressional staffers typically refer to surface transportation legislation as the "highway" bill, and not just because the bulk of the funding in that bill goes for highways. The origins of the bill go back to the first efforts by the federal government in the 1920s to bring order and quality to the patchwork of roads that the forty-eight continental states were building for the nation's early fleets of cars and trucks. By 1940, Congress had helped the states build 150,000 miles of primary U.S. highways crisscrossing cities and counties in every state. It was the success of that network that propelled the states and federal government into an historic public works partnership, the interstate highway system. The 1956 National Interstate and Defense Highways Act created a vision of a standard, interconnected network of nationwide limited access highways, modeled in part after the German Autobahn. (See Box 1.1.) From a transportation planning perspective, this was the most monumental piece of legislation ever passed by Congress, with far-reaching implications for the development and economic growth of the United States.[23] From a legislative point of view, however, the 1956 bill created something more important—a funding mechanism.

The Highway Trust Fund

There is no shortage of legislative initiatives that languish in Congress because they lack an acceptable funding mechanism. Few initiatives are likely to pass without a clear funding plan. There are some laws in today's political environment that do not adhere to this rule, such as those authorizing defense spending or tax cuts; these are cases where very few members of Congress want to take a strong stance against the legislation, and certainly not members of the party in power. However, in the current political climate, very few members of Congress will want to stand up and support a bill that creates deficit spending unless it is for an extremely popular cause.

For these domestic spending bills, then, a corresponding funding mechanism is usually required. The interstate highway system was created with such a mechanism built in. At the time that legislation was being debated in the 1950s, tolls were the most typical method of paying for a major highway. The New Jersey, Ohio, Connecticut, and other state "turnpikes" were all built shortly before this era using toll revenues for financing. However, experts argued that tolls would not be able to pay for the interstate network because many of those roads would be traversing unpopulated areas with little demand. And in the congested urban areas, tollbooths slowed traffic. So a system was proposed whereby the road construction would be financed through the federal tax on gasoline. This

BOX 1.1	National Interstate and Defense Highways Act of 1956

Popularly known as the National Interstate and Defense Highways Act of 1956, the Federal-Aid Highway Act of 1956 established an interstate highway system in the United States. The movement behind the construction of a transcontinental superhighway started in the 1930s when President Franklin D. Roosevelt expressed interest in the construction of a network of toll superhighways that would provide more jobs for people in need of work during the Great Depression. The resulting legislation was the Federal-Aid Highway Act of 1938, which directed the chief of the Bureau of Public Roads (BPR) to study the feasibility of a six-route toll network. But with America on the verge of joining the war in Europe, the time for a massive highway program had not arrived. At the end of the war, the Federal-Aid Highway Act of 1944 funded highway improvements and established major new ground by authorizing and designating, in Section 7, the construction of 40,000 miles of a "National System of Interstate Highways."

When President Dwight D. Eisenhower took office in January 1953, however, the states had only completed 6,500 miles of the system improvements. Eisenhower had first realized the value of good highways in 1919, when he participated in the U.S. Army's first transcontinental motor convoy from Washington, D.C., to San Francisco. Again, during World War II, Eisenhower saw the German army's advantage that resulted from their Autobahn highway network, and he also noted the enhanced mobility of the Allies on those same highways when they fought their way into Germany. These experiences significantly shaped Eisenhower's views on highways and their role in national defense. During his State of the Union Address on January 7, 1954, Eisenhower made it clear that he was ready to turn his attention to the nation's highway problems. He considered it important to "protect the vital interest of every citizen in a safe and adequate highway system."

Between 1954 and 1956, there were several failed attempts to pass a national highway bill through Congress. The main controversy over the highway construction was the apportionment of the funding between the federal government and the states. Undaunted, the president renewed his call for a "modern, interstate highway system" in his 1956 State of the Union Address. Within a few months, after considerable debate and amendment in the Congress, the Federal-Aid Highway Act of 1956 emerged from the House-Senate conference committee. In the act, the interstate system was expanded to 41,000 miles, and to construct the network, $25 billion was authorized for fiscal years 1957 through 1969. During his recovery from a minor illness, Eisenhower signed the bill into law at Walter Reed Army Medical Center on June 29. Because of the 1956 law, and the subsequent Highway Act of 1958, the pattern of community development in America was fundamentally altered, henceforth based on the automobile.

method meant that all drivers would pay for the system indirectly, even if they did not use the system. It also meant that unpopulated areas with very little demand could have roads financed by drivers elsewhere.

To be clear, the gasoline tax was not created by the 1956 act. The federal gas tax was first levied in 1932 as a temporary measure to address a mounting fiscal crisis and to balance the federal budget. That first gas tax was supposed to lapse when the budget was back in balance, but in fact it was never repealed. Initially, revenues accrued in the general fund, and Congress could allocate the funds at its discretion. With the passage of the Federal-Aid Highway Act and Highway Revenue Act of 1956, federal gas tax revenues were earmarked for roadway spending, thereby creating a sustained cash flow for this purpose.[24]

The gasoline tax, originally set at one cent per gallon in 1932, increased to four cents per gallon in 1960 and remained at that level until the early 1980s. Revenues were deposited into an account called the Highway Trust Fund created by the 1956 act. The fund was initially designed as a "ceiling" rather than a "floor" for highway spending. In other words, Congress didn't want highway builders raiding the Treasury's general coffers for funding, but they reserved the right to raid the highway fund's coffers for whatever else they might deem necessary. The Highway Trust Fund turned out to be enormously successful as a funding mechanism. Demand for gasoline rose astronomically over the following decades, providing plentiful funding for the 45,000-mile interstate highway system that we enjoy today.

Over the next fifty years Congress made several changes to the trust fund. The primary change was that the fund is no longer designated exclusively for spending on highways. A portion of the federal gas tax is designated for the mass transit programs—a change first brought about in 1982.[25] In addition, a very small fraction of the trust fund goes directly to a program with the most amusing acronym in government, the Leaking Underground Storage Tank (LUST) fund*. Meanwhile, Congress has changed the gas tax rate numerous times, including different rates

---

*The LUST fund was created in 1986 to provide funds for the Environmental Protection Agency in the administration of storage tank cleanups, or to actually perform the cleanup if the owner is unknown or unwilling. These tanks typically contain gasoline or other hazardous materials that can contaminate groundwater.

and rules for diesel and ethanol taxes. The federal gas tax currently stands at 18.4 cents per gallon. Nonetheless, the basic structure of the Highway Trust Fund remains the same—gas taxes are collected nationwide, and that money is divided up among the states for use on surface transportation infrastructure.

Other Aspects of the Legislation

Congress rarely passes a bill that calls for something to endure in perpetuity. For a variety of reasons, members tend to force themselves to reconsider authorizing legislation on a regular basis. Needs change over the years, political circumstances turn about, and in the event a bill is very popular, members want a chance to take credit for it again and again. In this vein, the surface transportation bill comes up for reauthorization every six years. Six years is about as long as an authorization bill can be. If it were any longer, the bill term would exceed the terms of all members of the Congress that passed it. If it were shorter, it would be hard to do all the planning and engineering necessary to build the roads before Congress had a chance to rewrite the bill again. So the six-year term has been adopted as convenient to both politicians and road-builders. (See Table 1.1.)

Moreover, the six-year term provides a deadline mentality that forces competing political forces to resolve their differences. If Congress fails to reauthorize the bill, or at least extend current transportation spending authority temporarily, the federal highway department and all funding for surface transportation in the United States shuts down.

TABLE 1.1	Major Federal Highway Statutes in the United States

- National Interstate and Defense Highways Act (1956)

- Surface Transportation and Uniform Relocation Assistance Act (1987)

- Intermodal Surface Transportation Efficiency Act (1991)

- National Highway Designation Act (1995)

- Transportation Equity Act for the 21st Century (1998)

- Safe, Accountable, Flexible, Efficient Transportation Equity Act: A Legacy for Users (2005)

Another development has been the role of transit. Beginning in the 1970s, funds from the highway fund were permitted for use on transit, and the role of transit and flexibility in the use of highway funds continued to grow marginally over the years. However, not until 1991, with the passage of the Intermodal Surface Transportation Efficiency Act, known as ISTEA (pronounced like "iced tea"), were states allowed substantial flexibility in how much funding they devoted to highways versus transit. ISTEA, which was signed by President George H. W. Bush, was considered landmark legislation in that it was the first highway bill Congress passed after the completion of the interstate system, and thus set the direction of transportation policy in a nation that had been almost singularly focused in that area on building a national highway network since 1956.[26] The basic structure set forth by ISTEA is still in use today.

The Transportation Equity Act for the 21st Century, signed by President Bill Clinton in 1998, was the follow-up bill to ISTEA, and it set a precedent by largely maintaining the major structural elements of its predecessor and making only incremental policy changes. TEA-21 was set to expire at the end of 2003, thus setting the stage for the next reauthorization, which is the subject of this book. The new bill was expected from the start to be similar in structure to TEA-21, as indicated by both Congress and industry groups during congressional hearings held in 2002 prior to reauthorization.[27] A detailed description of TEA-21 is presented in Box 1.2.

The programs outlined in Box 1.2 form the backbone of the surface transportation bill. As mentioned above, only marginal changes were even expected to be part of any successful piece of legislation, so any changes to the bill were likely to occur in other areas of the bill. The most fertile area for changes was in regulation.

The federal government cannot legally dictate state law directly. In other words, the federal government cannot tell the states that they must set their drinking age to 21. And yet we happen to know that the federal government has done exactly that by withholding highway funds from states that did not increase their drinking age to 21.[28] A similar effort occurred in forcing states to set their speed limits at fifty-five miles per hour (this has since been repealed). In both cases Congress would most likely have seen its laws overturned by the Supreme Court had they not used

---

BOX 1.2   **Funding for Federal Transportation Programs**

There were five major funding mechanisms for U.S. highways created in the 1991 Intermodal Sur-face Transportation Equity Act (ISTEA) and subsequently reauthorized in the 1998 Transportation Equity Act for the 21st Century (TEA-21). They are the National Highway System (NHS), Interstate Maintenance (IM), the Surface Transportation Program (STP), Congestion Mitigation and Air Quality (CMAQ), and Bridge Replacement and Rehabilitation (BRR). Of these, NHS, IM, and STP are by far the largest, and STP and CMAQ provide funds that may also be used for transit. Each of these programs is described below.

The **National Highway System** program provides funding authorization for virtually all major highways in the United States, including the interstate system, principal arterial roads, and connectors to federal highways. The program was authorized at $28.5 billion, accounting for about 13 percent of TEA-21 funds. It is distributed to the states according the following formula:

25%	State percentage of principal arterial non-interstate lane-miles
35%	State percentage of principal arterial non-interstate vehicle-miles-traveled (VMT)
30%	State percentage of diesel fuel used (on all roads)
10%	State percentage of principal arterial non-interstate lane-miles, divided by population

The **Interstate Maintenance** program authorizes funds that can only be used for mainte-nance of the interstate system. The program was authorized at $23.8 billion, accounting for about 11 percent of TEA-21 funds. It is distributed according to the following formula:

33%	State percentage of interstate lane-miles
33%	State percentage of interstate vehicle-miles-traveled (VMT)
33%	State percentage of commercial vehicle contributions to trust fund

The **Surface Transportation Program** authorizes flexible funds that may be used for any federal-aid highway, a bridge on any kind of road, and transit capital projects including public bus terminals. However, there are some restrictions, as 10 percent of the funds must be used for safety-related construction, and 10 percent must be used for transportation enhancements. The program was authorized at $33.3 billion accounting for about 15 percent of TEA-21 funds. It is distributed according to the following formula:

25%	State percentage of total lane-miles on federal-aid highways
40%	State percentage of total vehicle-miles-traveled on federal-aid high-ways
35%	State percentage of contribution to trust fund

The **Congestion Mitigation and Air Quality Improvement** (CMAQ) program au-thorized $8.1 billion for any transportation project that could potentially help a state meet the requirements of the Clean Air Act. Funding is distributed based on a state's percentage of people living in non-attainment areas, weighted by the severity and quantity of pollutants.

The **Bridge Replacement and Rehabilitation** program authorized $20.4 billion for bridges on any public road. It is distributed based on each state's percentage of the national total cost of repairing bridges.

Most mass transit funding ($18 billion) is distributed through the **Urbanized Area Formula Grant** (UAF) program, which is available for cities with greater than 50,000 population. However, cities with between 50,000 and 200,000 people may use this funding for capital or operating expenses, while cities with greater than 200,000 people can use this funding only for capital costs. Cities with populations under 50,000 are eligible under rural formula grants totaling $1.18 billion.

Most of the UAF (91 percent) is distributed to cities with greater than 200,000 people. About 32 percent of this is distributed based on fixed guideway (typically, rail) miles according to the following formula:

60%	Urbanized area percentage of guideway revenue vehicle-miles
40%	Urbanized area percentage of guideway route-miles

Most of the rest (61 percent) of this portion of the UAF is based on bus service and is distributed according to the following formula:

50%	Urbanized area bus revenue vehicle-miles operated
25%	Urbanized area population
25%	Urbanized area density weighted by population

In addition to the UAF there are three types of **Capital Investment** grants. First, the **Fixed Guideway Modernization** program authorizes $6.59 billion specifically for fixed-guideway systems that are at least seven years old. Most of where this money goes is specifically written into the TEA-21 bill. Some of it is distributed on a formula basis similar to those in the fixed-guideway section of the UAF.

The **New Starts** program accounts for $8.18 billion. That program provides funds for new transit projects, mostly for final design and construction, on the basis of applications to the Department of Transportation (DOT). DOT submits its recommendations to Congress, where final authorizations are made each year. Any major rail transit capital project in the United States usually applies for assistance under this program.

There are also special **Bus** grants distributed on a discretionary basis that provide $3.55 billion to aid transit agencies in the purchase of buses and bus-related facilities. The funding is distributed in a similar manner to the New Starts program.

this fund-withholding tactic, which essentially extorts the states' compliance. Because states are so dependent on the federal government's ability to raise revenues through gas taxes, the money Washington then distributes back to the states is a very effective means for imposing federal mandates.

The surface transportation bill is full of such mandates. In fact, the bulk of the bill consists of what procedures states must follow in order to receive their highway funding. This can range from procedures for state and regional planning to safety regulations and environmental requirements. In fact, some of these environmental regulations were so contentious that, as we will see, they played a big role in holding up the bill's progress.

THE ROLE OF THE WHITE HOUSE

As mentioned above, the White House is often the impetus behind a legislative initiative, and presidents will frequently have strong preferences about the content of congressional legislation. In the case of the surface transportation reauthorization, the relevant committees—the Committee on Transportation and Infrastructure in the House, and the Environment and Public Works Committee in the Senate—could have written their own versions of the transportation reauthorization bill for introduction. But since the White House and Congress were both controlled by the Republican Party at the time, there was value for all players in working from a similar starting point. Having more than one bill as a template would have slowed down what was bound to be a laborious process anyway. So the White House, along with the Department of Transportation, played a leading role in getting the ball rolling on the transportation reauthorization legislation.

The Transportation Department, the agency of the federal government most deeply affected by the proposed legislation, was run by people appointed by, and loyal to, the president. At the time this bill was initially released it was early 2003, less than two years after the September 11 terrorist attacks on Washington and New York, and the Bush White House was determined to make this bill coincide with its mission of keeping the country safe from another terrorist attack. The other main objectives were to demonstrate that the administration was promoting the economy by creating jobs while, at the same time, keeping federal spending in check. It was a delicate political balancing act for President Bush, who had found himself in the middle of a mild recession and thus could not appear to be opposed to building infrastructure, which is perceived as a catalyst for economic growth. At the same time, his most conservative constituency was counting on him to keep spending on domestic programs down through both tax and spending cuts.

The White House melded these twin objectives—homeland security and fiscal stimulus/responsibility—in its initial framing of the highway bill. For openers, administration strategists gave the bill a new name to convey the anti-terrorist theme. Up until this time most people in the transportation policy world had been referring to the bill as "T-3"—the successor to "Iced Tea" of 1992 and "Tea 21" of 1998—but the T-3 moniker had too close an association with then–movie star Arnold Schwarzenegger's third turn as the "Terminator." So the White House came up with this mouthful of a title: the Safe, Accountable, Flexible, and Efficient Surface Transportation Equity Act—or (you guessed it) SAFETEA.

Obviously the highway bill had very little to do with the kind of safety that most people were worried about at that time, so administration spinners came up with a new program to justify their clever name. Their idea: additional incentives for safety standards such as getting people to wear seatbelts. But existing law already contained numerous safety incentives, and the changes the White House could reasonably suggest were incremental at best. So the administration proposed moving funding for safety-related programs from one section to a new one, where it would have more prominence, and then sought to slightly increase the funding levels. The net result was that states would be forced to spend slightly more on safety than they had previously.

The second objective—improving the economy while keeping spending low—would prove more challenging. (In fact, as we'll describe later, the administration would wind up fighting this battle until the bitter end.) The White House took an early, hard-line position on the total cost to the Treasury that the president could accept. Bush put forward a bill that was estimated to cost $256 billion over the six-year life of the bill, and he made it pretty clear that he was not inclined to go any higher than that. His figure represented a 17 percent increase over the total price tag of TEA-21, discounting inflation. Members of Congress, who remembered that the 1998 reauthorization bill had increased nominal spending over its predecessor by 41 percent, had similar notions of what they wanted from SAFETEA.* (See Figure 1.3.)

For Republicans in the White House and Congress, two fundamental political issues were overlapping here. First, there was the issue of fiscal responsibility, a cornerstone issue for most Republicans. If the price tag for SAFETEA was substantially higher than the previous bill, it could easily be criticized as an example of congressional—that is, Republican—excess. Second, and perhaps more gut wrenching, was the issue of how to actually pay for such a bill. The spending could only be as high as the projected available funds in the Highway Trust Fund. As explained above, those funds could only be as high as provided by the federal gas tax. President Bush had run for office on a platform of cutting taxes, and had spent most of his first term pushing through major tax-cut legislation. The last thing he could do in the highway bill was to be perceived as responsible for allowing an increase in the gas tax.

The Price Tag Battle

But while the administration and the GOP at large could afford to take the conservative position of putting a spending cap on the highway bill, individual members of Congress were under a different kind of pressure. The president did not need to bring home any bacon to ensure his reelection. An incumbent seeking reelection in his district or state could never be so sanguine.

Enter Don Young, Alaska's sole representative in the House and the chairman of that chamber's Transportation and Infrastructure Committee, which had jurisdiction over the highway bill reauthorization. Even before the White House released its $256 billion bill, Young was suggesting funding levels for the bill that reached $350 billion. But even that

---

*Calculated with the following spending levels: $155 billion for ISTEA ($181 billion in 1998 dollars), $218 billion for TEA-21 ($240 billion in 2003 dollars), $256 billion for the Bush proposal, and $375 billion for the Young proposal.

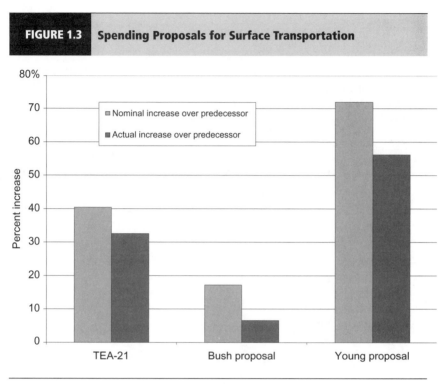

FIGURE 1.3   **Spending Proposals for Surface Transportation**

Note: TEA-21 = Transportation Equity Act for the 21st Century.

figure was not the height of his ambitions for "T-3." When Young finally introduced his surface transportation rewrite, his proposals totaled $375 billion, a 72 percent increase over TEA-21.

Of course, neither side realistically expected that their proposed number would be ultimately prevail, but like any good negotiator they knew they had to start at the far end of the spectrum before working back to the middle.

The political calculus for Bush was now fairly self-evident; he had to force Congress to bend to his will as a fiscal disciplinarian while also showing that his highway bill furthered his homeland security agenda. Don Young (see Box 1.3), on the other hand, had no such lofty concerns. He was the chairman of the House Transportation and Infrastructure Committee, which meant his state was positioned to benefit the most from any spending on this bill. He could give himself and his home state

---

BOX 1.3   **Rep. Donald E. "Don" Young, R-Alaska**

Current Office: U.S. Representative
Current District: At-Large
First Elected: 1973
Party: Republican

Committees:
Homeland Security [House]
Resources [House]
Transportation & Infrastructure [House],
   Chair

Don Young

BACKGROUND INFORMATION

Gender: Male
Family: Wife: Lu; children: Joni, Dawn
Birth date: June 9, 1933
Birthplace: Meridian, Calif.
Home City: Fort Yukon, Alaska
Religion: Episcopalian

---

of Alaska a large amount of money to spend on "high-priority" projects, and he could tinker with other formulas to maximize his state's rate of return from the gas tax. The people of his home state would barely notice that spending was high nationally. They would notice new bridges and highways that his extra funding brought in. With no desire for higher office, Chairman Young would likely be reelected by incredibly wide margins in Alaska even if the nation as whole was put off by the extravagant spending initiatives he was proposing.

Indeed, Young had been waiting for this opportunity for quite some time. He was first elected to Congress in 1972, giving him thirty years of experience in the House. His predecessor as chairman, Bud Shuster, was notorious for his ability to deliver the goods to his south central district in Pennsylvania. For example, you'll know when you arrive in his former congressional district, because you'll likely be driving on either the "Bud Shuster Highway" (Route 220) or the "Bud Shuster Byway" (Route 30/26). Young had been lying in wait, observing what Shuster accomplished,

Education:
Honorary Doctorate of Law, University of Alaska, Fairbanks, 1985
BA, Teaching, Chico State University, 1958
AA, Yuba Junior College, 1952

Professional Experience:
Riverboat Captain, 1966–1972
Elementary School Teacher, 1966–1970
Trapper, 1960–1967
41st Tank Battalion, United States Army, 1955–1957
Construction

Political Experience:
Representative, U.S. House of Representatives, 1973–present
Senator, Alaska State Senate, 1970–1973
Republican Nominee, U.S. House of Representatives, 1972
Representative, Alaska State House of Representatives, 1966–1970
Mayor, Fort Yukon, 1964–1966
City Councilmember, Fort Yukon, 1960–1964

knowing that this was his opportunity to capitalize on his status and seniority in Congress.

Young did not shy away from his moment. Moving quickly in 2003,
he came forward with a bold—some said politically reckless—proposal
to pay for his big-ticket highway bill by increasing the gas tax by 2 cents
a year, raising it from 18.4 cents to 30.4 cents over the life of the six-year
reauthorization bill. It was a brazen disregard for the tax-cut zeitgeist.
At that time, anyone proposing a tax hike—a Republican, no less—was
considered to be a political heretic. If a Democrat had dared propose
such a scheme he would immediately be tarred as a "tax and spend liberal" who had no concern for bloating the federal budget beyond its
means. Any Republican who put forward such a notion would raise the
ire of the president, who at the time was riding a wave of popularity
from his responses to September 11 and his aggressive run-up to the
Iraq war. Yet Chairman Young remained unbowed. He had his own political agenda.

In one sense, Young was one of the few people in Washington who could get away with such a no-holds-barred proposal. He clearly had few qualms about reelection chances. The only peril was angering the president, the titular leader of his party and the man who had brought the GOP out of the wilderness of the Clinton-Gore years. But Young's power as committee chairman enabled him to take that risk, and his doing so actually worked out well for both sides. Young could appear to be doing all he could to increase spending on highways in his state and others. The White House, meanwhile, using Young as its foil, could take a principled stand against higher taxes and increased spending.

Given such formidable opposition, Young's strategy depended on finding a middle ground and finding it quickly. His original proposal tested the waters and found them quite cold. He garnered little support among fellow congressmen, especially in the Senate, where not one senator would publicly endorse a tax increase. Young soon agreed to a slightly different tack, a concept known as "indexing" the gas tax to keep track with the rate of inflation. Set at 18.4 cents per gallon since 1994, the gas tax had actually been decreasing in inflation-adjusted terms over the years.[29] By simply writing bill language requiring the government to adjust the tax each year to match the inflation rate, Young could avoid having to insert an explicit (and politically unpalatable) tax increase, yet the gas tax would still rise to 23.8 cents per gallon in the first year, and then would continue to go up in each succeeding year in accordance with the government's official inflation index.

Young's gas tax proposal represented an opening bid in an expected negotiation between all parties involved. But the tax was just the funding mechanism; the need for the tax hike was driven by the actual spending proposed in the bill. This is where the real negotiation would take place. The funding mechanism would ultimately be determined by the total amount Congress authorized in the bill.

All of these machinations about the size and cost of the bill and how to fund it were happening publicly, as described above.* But the same kind of debates were also occurring behind the closed doors of the Senate and

---

*Including the House Ways and Means Committee, which must approve all tax increases.

House office buildings, where staff aides, anticipating the ultimate show-down with the Bush White House, were desperately trying to position their respective bosses for a political victory they could trumpet back home.

RUSTLINGS ON THE HILL

People outside of Capitol Hill are generally unfamiliar with the concept of "constituent" or "surrogate" meetings, but they are a substantial part of a legislative staffer's day. These sorts of euphemisms are employed because they sound much better than "meeting with a lobbyist," which is what they usually are. The meetings originate with petitioners, typically professional lobbyists but not always, calling or faxing an office requesting a meeting with a congressman or a senator. Every office has a scheduling department that fields these requests. That department has to make an initial determination—is the person someone who gets to meet with the boss or not? Perhaps that person might be important enough for a photo opportunity, but not a full-on meeting. Or perhaps they might be worth a drop-by, wherein a staffer meets with them but the boss attempts to make a brief appearance at the meeting. Regardless of which option is chosen, the scheduling department will take a guess as to which staffer should take the meeting, with or without the boss.

These meetings tend to be rather tedious and rapidly foster cynicism among staffers. A lobbyist brings to the meeting the "constituent" he or she is representing, and both talk briefly about their issue and why it is important. At some point they reveal their goal—what it is that they need from the member of Congress. Most of the time in transportation they want money—either in the annual appropriations bill for transportation, or as a "high-priority" project in the surface transportation reauthorization bill. Sometimes they have legislative language or a specific amendment that they are pushing for and want support.

As a staffer it is hard not to become jaded about human nature while going through these meetings. Because of what you see in those coming to meet with you—mostly they are corporations or other high-powered groups with enough money to hire lobbyists—you know they have simply come to get more money from the federal government for their own business interests. In other words, it is those with money trying to get more money because they have the money to do it. Everyone has a problem and they all need help, yet there is a finite amount of resources to help them. At your first constituent meeting, you might really care about their cause. By the last one, all the causes sound the same.

The Battle among the States

Nonetheless, these constituent meetings began to set the tone for the transportation bill. With this bill almost all of the constituents were going to be from a congressman's home district or a senator's home state. Unlike most legislation, the surface transportation bill tends to divide Congress along regional, rather than party lines. Certainly there are party issues—some Republicans will make noise about keeping spending down while Democrats will insist on more spending to stimulate the economy—but the most animated disputes are advanced along regional lines.

The transportation bill is regional because it is a bill that essentially divvies up money among the states based on a formula. It is an enormous pot of money and every state wants to grab as much of as it possibly can. Any formula that determines distribution is going to depend, at least to some extent, on the characteristics of each state, and state characteristics typically do not align with political parties. More often, they align with other states in their region.

As an easy example, imagine you are writing the funding formulas for public transportation. They would have to be based to some extent on need—how much public transportation actually exists in a state. Right away, you will create a political battle that would divide states along regional lines, since states with more public transportation tend to cluster in the northeast. These states would get a greater proportion of the public transportation funding by any such formula, leaving other states with less existing public transportation systems crying foul. Consider New York, which, if funds were allocated on the basis of utilization (passenger miles), would receive almost 40 percent of all federal funding for public transportation. Together eight metropolitan areas account for over 70 percent of all transit ridership.[30] Looked at this way, it doesn't take long to figure out that allocating funds on this basis could never work politically.

The fact is, every member of Congress in every region of the nation wants to show success in bringing home federal dollars for transportation. The hard part is defining what you mean by success. A member could issue a press release trumpeting how much he or she has secured, but that number is meaningless until it is compared to what others states have gotten. But that's not a fair comparison, either, since a small population state like Wyoming could not possibly expect to take home as much as an enormous state like California.

So instead, members of Congress have latched on to an easy measure of comparison that clearly and objectively identifies how well each of the states would fare under various funding proposals. Indeed, this measure is so good at telling you how much your state will receive compared to other states that it inevitably produces the greatest amount of political infighting whenever a highway bill comes before Congress. It is the source of everyone's grief and glory.

Donors versus Donees

Here's the gist of it: How much of your state's contribution to the federal gas tax comes back to your state in the form of transportation spending? Every state contributes a certain amount in federal gasoline taxes, but by the very nature of highway and mass transit needs, some states receive more than their state's gas tax contribution, and others receive less. There is even a special name for each: states receiving less than 100 percent of their gas tax contribution are called "donor" states; those that receive more than 100 percent are called "donee" states.

This whole concept may seem baffling to those on the outside. The overall point of a federalist system, one might argue, is that different states have different needs, so while one state might need water desperately, another state has more need for farm subsidies. The tax revenue of the federal government is not just distributed equally among the states for everything, or else there would be little point in having a federal government. This also holds true on a micro-level; it would be rather pointless to collect all of the federal gas tax revenue and then give it back in absolutely proportionate shares based on contribution.

But for political rather than policy reasons, the popularity of the donor-donee measure can be explained by the fact that it is a simple and effective way for the press, the public, and congressional members themselves to evaluate how well their states are fairing in the battle for transportation dollars. It can easily become a hot-button campaign issue at election time, allowing an opponent to rant and rave about how the incumbent has stood by while Congress was raiding the state of its precious gas taxes. Indeed, this measure is so powerful that it can defy the bigger picture. States that are "donor" states for highways may be "donee" states in every other spending bill that comes before Congress, but this does not keep representatives from those states from arguing that they should be "donee" states in the highway bill, too. Framing the issue in this way allows states receiving less than 100 percent of their gas tax contributions to argue their case for more funding on the basis of simple fairness and equity.

This fight is as old as the highway bill itself. Long before the ISTEA debate in 1987, the "donor" states had won a provision in the law guaranteeing that 85 percent of their contributions to the highway trust fund would be returned to each of them.[31] In 1991, this was codified in a separate funding formula called the Minimum Guarantee, which distributed additional funding to all states in order to ensure that every state received at least 90 percent of its original contributions. In TEA-21, that minimum was raised to 90.5 percent, which became the starting point for debate in the next go-round. Donor and donee states under TEA-21 are indicated on the map on page xx.

REGIONAL ALLIANCES

The Minimum Guarantee, then, is what foments regional, rather than party, alliances when the transportation bill comes up for debate. To figure out what these alliances are, first consider which states are likely to contribute the most to the Highway Trust Fund. These would be the states with the greatest population, such as California, Texas, Florida, and New York. States with sparse and rural populations, on the other hand— Wyoming, Alaska, Montana—contribute the least to the fund.

The sparsely populated states receive far more than 100 percent of their contribution, as one might expect. Their small populations are overrepresented in the Senate, and this helps a great deal, but what really matters is that their transportation slices are so small relative to the entire pie. In other words, even though these states may get more than 100 percent of their contributions, it doesn't really impact anyone substantially because even then they are receiving so little compared to mammoth states like Texas. The complaints by the "donor" states are not against these low-population states.

Then with whom are they fighting? Well, not all large states are created equal. Among the biggest states, a few outliers contribute less to the highway fund than one might suppose based on pure population. The reason: public transportation.

Public transportation causes two problems for these states. First, having many constituents who ride public transportation means having fewer constituents buying gasoline. Second, having many constituents who ride public transportation means more demand for public transportation funding. It is this extra need, not borne out of gas tax consumption, which separates some large states from others.

The result creates unusual divisions along regional lines. States such as New York, Pennsylvania, Massachusetts, and Connecticut all have substantial public transportation needs, large populations, and lower than expected contributions to the highway fund. States such as California, Texas, and Arizona all have relatively low public transportation needs, large populations, and high gas tax contributions. So, in general, northeast donee states line up together against Sunbelt donor states. The mountain states are donees too, and so are aligned with the northeast. Then again, these regional lines are not concrete; exceptions include New Jersey and Ohio, which are both donor states. Such exceptions to the rule show that unseen powers are also at work in the netherworld of highway funding allocations.

The analysis so far shows why alliances form in Congress based on state demographic characteristics and not just ideology or party identity. Yet, not everything can be explained even by these regional, formulaic differences; some states get their determined share of funding at least in part due to their power status within Congress.

For example, Pennsylvania was one of the biggest donee states coming out of TEA-21 in 1998. While some of this can be explained by the state's high transit use in Philadelphia and Pittsburgh, its positive cash flow can also be attributed to the fact that Rep. Bud Shuster, who represented the south central 9th District of Pennsylvania, was the chairman of the House Transportation and Infrastructure Committee from 1995 to 2001. Massachusetts benefited from the presence of Tip O'Neill as the Speaker of the House during the 1980s. His push for the "Big Dig" (a $20+ billion dollar project in Boston) helped divert more funding to that state under ISTEA. In other words, which states are donors and which are donees, and by how much, is to a certain extent determined by sheer political power.

By the time SAFETEA came to the fore in 2003, the power had shifted yet again. Although the new chairman of the House Transportation and Infrastructure Committee, Don Young, was from a donee state (Alaska), he was from a low-population and non-transit state. This suggested that he would gladly give ground on transit funding to satisfy his opponents. It also meant that raising the level of Minimum Guarantee beyond 90.5 percent was substantially less disconcerting to him than, say, to donee state Connecticut. If the Minimum Guarantee were increased at all for the donor states, it would have to come out of the pockets of the donee states. Connecticut would lose billions, while Alaska would lose nothing because it receives so much less funding to begin with. Taking an extra slice from Alaska would barely make a dent in California's donor status, so California and other donor states would never be interested in Alaska's take. The large donee states were the ones in trouble, especially because the House Majority Leader, Tom DeLay, was from one of the biggest donor states of all—Texas—and he had no hesitation about leading a fight to increase the Minimum Guarantee.

The Senate Side

The power had shifted even more dramatically on the Senate side. Under ISTEA, the chairman of the Environment and Public Works Committee was Daniel Patrick Moynihan, who wrote the legislation to favor New York and other northeastern states. In fact, the entire Congestion Mitigation and Air Quality (CMAQ) program was created for that purpose. Although the program ostensibly provides funding to build transportation projects that reduce congestion and improve air quality, it was no accident that the states suffering most from these problems were those in the northeast. It was also no accident that states could use funding from the CMAQ program to build mass transit systems, even though there is little evidence that building mass transit works to substantially reduce congestion or improve air quality.[32]

When Republicans took control of the Senate in 1995, John Chaffee of Rhode Island became chairman of the Environment and Public Works

Committee, thus keeping the northeast at the forefront during TEA-21. By 2003, however, the committee's gavel was held by James Inhofe of Oklahoma, which was a strong donor state. Even more important, as we will see, the chairman of the Environment Subcommittee on Transportation, Christopher "Kit" Bond, was from neighboring Missouri, a donor state as well.

The stars were aligned for a major push by the donor states, a power play they could not have attempted in the past.

FOLLOW THE MONEY

The slight problem facing this new power structure, at least in the Senate, was that simply having control of the levers of committee power did not mean that donor states could raise the Minimum Guarantee as high as they wanted. They would need the votes to do it. The fact is, Inhofe and Bond could have chosen to avoid the entire conflict by merely inserting some extra earmarks for their respective states, tweaking the formulas a little, and thus improving their states' bounty from the transportation bill quite substantially without messing with the Minimum Guarantee. They might have avoided a fight and still done very well for their states.

Inhofe and Bond did not choose this route. Instead, Inhofe made the early public announcement that his goal was to increase the minimum rate of return for all states to 95 percent. There are two likely explanations for this strategy. One is that Inhofe and his staff were guessing that the strength of the donor state coalition, combined with their power at the top of the committee, was enough to reach this goal. They may have figured that such an accomplishment would not only bring them accolades from their home states, but also make them some good friends in the Senate among other donor states. These friends might come in handy when Oklahoma or Missouri needed some favors.

Another explanation is that they thought their strategy would play well among the news media and the public at large—that it would be perceived as a simple effort to achieve equity in transportation funding. A brazen effort to boost home-state revenues might fly on the House side, where national politics is always secondary, but on the Senate side it was considered uncouth. Even if it was a naked power grab, it could not be stated openly as such. But the equity argument helped them paper over their more parochial interests.

There remained one problem, however. Increasing the Minimum Guarantee to 95 percent meant that several donee states would have to take a hit on their rate of return. More than just a percentage hit, too; the donee states stood to receive less in actual funding than they had in the previous bill. There was no way any bill could pass under these circumstances, especially in the Senate, where as few as forty of the one hundred senators have the power to block legislation through the right of unlimited debate, also known as the filibuster. Senate rules allow individual senators to continue debating a bill on the floor ad infinitum unless a three-fifths majority, or sixty senators, vote to invoke cloture, which puts a time limit on debate and prohibits non-germane amendments.

The only way to avoid an actual cut in funding for these states and eliminate the threat of the filibuster was to increase the total amount of funding in the bill beyond what President Bush had already indicated he would accept. Certainly Inhofe and Bond knew that this would cause problems with the White House, but before they could deal with that problem they had to solve the first problem: where would the extra funding come from? Raise the gas tax? Not likely. Even if they could get the president and all of Congress on board with the concept of greater spending, they would have virtually no chance in getting GOP leaders in either chamber to put a tax increase before their members. They would have to devise a more creative solution.

Transit Debate

To make things even more complicated, Inhofe and Bond had some institutional hurdles to overcome. Unlike the House, where the lion's share—although not all—work related to the surface transportation bill comes under the purview of the Transportation and Infrastructure Committee, there are four separate Senate committees with jurisdiction over various aspects of the bill.* Each committee chairman spends considerable time jousting with other chairman for control of the areas of the bill that intersect.

---

*Several specific provisions in the transportation bill fall within the jurisdiction of other House committees, such as the House Ways and Means Committee, whose jurisdiction includes all tax-related provisions.

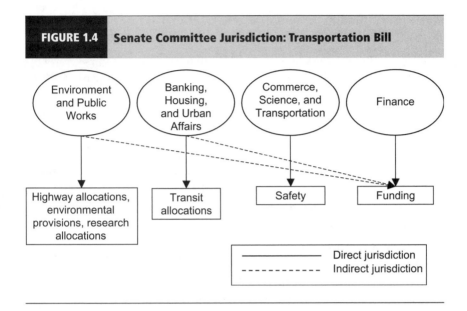

FIGURE 1.4   Senate Committee Jurisdiction: Transportation Bill

The chart in Figure 1.4 shows how Senate committees and their responsibilities play out in transportation policy. Inhofe's Environment and Public Works Committee had jurisdiction over the largest portion of the bill and so he was likely to guide the process. But the Finance Committee actually controls the most important part of the bill—the revenue side. Yet even Finance could not simply announce what the funding level would be and how to pay for it and then turn it over to the other committees. The Environment and Public Works Committee and the Banking, Housing, and Urban Affairs Committee, which has jurisdiction over mass transit, had indirect control over funding because they had to agree on whatever Finance suggests before the bill could move forward to the Senate floor. If Finance suggested a plan for paying for the bill that completely ignored the needs of the Environment or Banking chairmen, either of those committees could shut down its portion of the bill. (The fourth committee of jurisdiction, Commerce and Science, handled certain safety sections of the bill but little of the funding sections, and thus had far less clout over its salient provisions.)

The Finance Committee had the most clout, at least at the outset, because the process of writing a bill in the Senate had to begin with that committee's funding proposal. It was clear that no one on that panel, least of all Chairman Charles E. Grassley, a Republican from Iowa, or ranking Democrat Max Baucus of Montana, wanted to propose a gas tax increase. Yet the entire Senate just as clearly wanted to increase highway funding, and so all eyes were on Grassley and Baucus to come up with something. The tricky part was to propose an increase in funding without proposing an increase in revenues. Some might say this is fairly simple, given that the government is constantly running up deficits that reach hundreds of billions of dollars every year. But deficit spending is not as easy as that. It's one thing to put the government into debt when you are using the money to fight a War on Terror or give tax breaks back to constituents. But running up the nation's debt to build and maintain its roadways is not as popular.

The Finance Committee had to come up with something that increased spending without increasing revenues, but also did not increase deficit spending. This seems logically impossible, but it did not prevent the panel's most imaginative minds from devising a plan.

Enter the staff, and the master staff member, Dawn Levy.

NOTES

1. David Mayhew, *Congress: The Electoral Connection* (New Haven: Yale University Press, 1974).
2. Richard Fenno, *Congressmen in Committees* (Boston: Little Brown, 1974).
3. Mayhew, *Congress*.
4. Bruce Cain, John Ferejohn, and Morris Fiorina, *The Personal Vote* (Cambridge: Harvard University Press, 1987).
5. Gary C. Jacobson, *The Politics of Congressional Elections*, 6th ed. (New York: Pearson Longman, 2004).
6. Robert Stein and Kenneth Bickers, "Congressional Elections and the Pork Barrel," *Journal of Politics* 56, no. 2 (1994): 377–399.
7. Mayhew, *Congress*, 57.
8. Ibid., 54.
9. Ibid., 55.
10. Ibid., 55.
11. Keith Krehbiel, *Information and Legislative Organization* (Ann Arbor: University of Michigan Press, 1992).
12. Kenneth Shepsle, "Institutional Equilibrium and Equilibrium Institutions," in *Political Science: The Science of Politics*, ed. Herbert Weisberg (New York: Agathon, 1986), 69.

13. Nolan McCarty, Keith Poole, and Howard Rosenthal, *Polarized America: The Dance of Ideology and Unequal Riches* (Cambridge: MIT Press, 2006), 1.
14. Ibid.
15. Ibid.
16. Mayhew, *Congress*.
17. Steven Balla, Eric Lawrence, Forrest Maltzman, and Lee Sigelman, "Partisanship, Blame Avoidance, and the Distribution of Pork," *American Journal of Political Science* 46, no. 3 (2002): 515–525.
18. Barry Weingast, "Reflections on Distributive Politics and Universalism," *Political Research Quarterly* 47 (1994): 319–327.
19. Melissa Collie, "The Legislative and Distributive Policy Making in Formal Perspective," *Legislative Studies Quarterly* 13 (1988): 427–458.
20. Balla et al., "Partisanship."
21. Michael Grunwald, "Pork by Any Other Name," *Washington Post*, April 30, 2006.
22. John W. Fischer, "Past as Prologue: A Brief Legislative History of the Modern Federal-Aid Highway Program" (presentation to the National Surface Transportation Policy and Revenue Study Commission, July 25, 2006).
23. Kenneth T. Jackson, *Crabgrass Frontier: The Suburbanization of America* (New York: Oxford University Press, 1985).
24. Robert Puentes and Ryan Prince, "Fueling Transportation Finance: A Primer on the Gas Tax," Report issued by the Center on Urban and Metropolitan Policy (Washington, D.C.: The Brookings Institution, March 2003).
25. Ibid., 3.
26. Ellen Schweppe, "Legacy of a Landmark: ISTEA after 10 Years," *Public Roads* 65, no. 3 (November/December 2001): 1; Robert J. Dilger, "ISTEA: A New Direction for Transportation Policy," *Publius: The Journal of Federalism* 22, no. 3 (1992): 67–78.
27. Senate Committee on Environment and Public Works, *Review of Proposals to Reauthorize Public Law 105–178, the Transportation Equity Act for the Twenty-first Century*, 107th Cong., 2nd sess., 2003.
28. Douglas B. Feaver, "House Bill Ties Highway Aid, Drinking Age," *Washington Post*, June 8, 1984.
29. Puentes and Prince, "Fueling Transportation Finance," 6.
30. National Transit Database, Federal Transit Administration, U.S. Department of Transportation (2005).
31. Fischer, "Past as Prologue," 10.
32. Alan Altshuler, *The Urban Transportation System: Politics and Policy Innovation* (Cambridge: MIT Press, 1979).

CHAPTER 2

BILL INTRODUCTION AND MARKUP

THE SURROGATE STAFF SYSTEM

Every member of Congress employs staff, as does every House and Senate committee. They are often described as the glue that holds the legislative process together, making it possible for 535 elected officials to conduct the important business of a nation of 300 million people. They schedule appointments, they answer letters and e-mails from constituents, they conduct research on complex public policy issues, and they bring a level of subject expertise that few politicians can hope to practice by themselves. But even more than that, congressional staff aides play a significant role in writing and formulating policy. They make suggestions to their bosses that often, due to constraints on time and inclination, become a member's policy. Members have so many conflicting demands on their time that they often have to trust their staff to do their political thinking for them—especially on less contentious issues such as transportation policy.

The rapid growth of the federal government's executive branch since World War II has been well chronicled.[1] Receiving less attention has been the equally outsized enlargement of the legislative machine on Capitol Hill. As reflected in Figure 2.1, that growth has been largely a function of the increased number of staff aides. In 1947, the average House member had access to three staff members; the average Senate office housed six staffers. By 1972, the staff size of the average member of the House had quadrupled (to twelve staffers) and the average Senate office employed

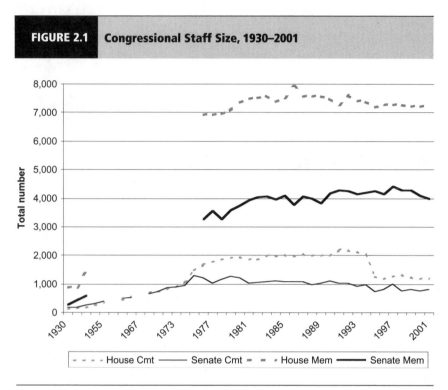

FIGURE 2.1 Congressional Staff Size, 1930–2001

Source: Harold W. Stanley and Richard G. Niemi, *Vital Statistics on American Politics, 2007–2008* (Washington, D.C.: CQ Press, 2008), 211.

two dozen staffers. That number has since risen to an average of seventeen staffers employed by each House member and forty aides employed in each Senate office. Similar patterns of explosive growth occurred in members' district offices over the postwar period.[2]

Larger staffs permit members to perform more constituent services, but they also help to manage a largely expanded legislative agenda. Figure 2.2 indicates the pattern of growth in the overall number of bill introductions since 1789. It is not uncommon for close to ten thousand measures to be introduced in contemporary Congresses, of which about 5 percent will be enacted. Many measures introduced signal token support to satisfy special interest groups or local constituencies, but they rarely go very far. Bill introduction is a relatively easy process in Congress. "Dropping" a bill, as it is called, consists of writing as little as a few sentences on a piece of

FIGURE 2.2	Total Number of Measures Introduced and Passed, 1789–2004

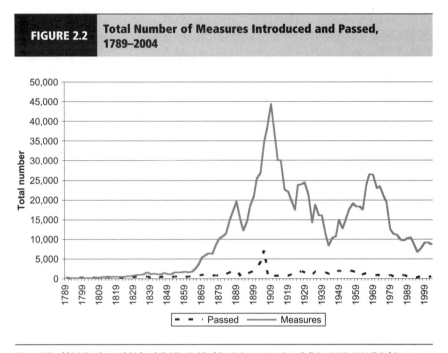

Source: Harold W. Stanley and Richard G. Niemi, *Vital Statistics on American Politics, 2007–2008* (Washington, D.C.: CQ Press, 2008), 215.

paper and sending it to the floor for consideration. Technically, only members of Congress can introduce bills, but this does not even require the member to be anywhere near Washington, D.C., at the time. A bill can be written by a staffer, signed by a member, and sent to the floor for consideration often with little action or consultation with the actual elected official. Here is how the process works: the staffer writes the bill and submits it to his or her immediate supervisor, typically the chief of staff or the legislative director (the two top posts in a member's Washington office). They will run it by the press shop before approving it, at which point it is signed—by an automatic pen machine—in the member's office. An intern runs the bill down over to the Capitol Building, where the member's party leader will ensure its introduction on the floor. The staffer may even choose to include a statement about the bill by the member—a statement that will never be read aloud by any human being, but along with the bill itself, will become part of the *Congressional Record.*

In other words, members of Congress place great confidence in their staff aides, and for the most loyal and trusted staffers among them, the members place a high degree of political and legislative discretion. Dawn Levy had such confidence and authority from her boss, Sen. Max Baucus of Montana, on matters pertaining to transportation. She had worked in transportation for years and knew the landscape well. She also kept her boss's interests at heart at all times.

As a top aide to the ranking Democrat on the Senate Finance Committee, Levy took it upon herself to solve the central riddle of the highway bill—how to make room for increased spending beyond President George W. Bush's stated target without raising the gas tax. She and her team came up with a proposal that was quite radical in the hopes that being the only proposal out there, it might have a shot at success. The initiative aimed to use all of the monies in the Highway Trust Fund currently devoted to transit—known as the Mass Transit Account—for spending on highways. This would provide sufficient funds for highway investment so as to allow broad enough support for the bill. At the same time, Levy knew she had to satisfy transit supporters, and so here she came up with a brand new financing scheme to pay for the transit portion of the bill. Her solution: bonds.

"Bonding" is one of those words that are thrown around Congress to describe deficit spending without the words "deficit" or "spending." It means selling bonds and paying them back, with interest. It is the way local governments finance the building of roads, sewers, schools, and baseball stadiums, but at bottom it is essentially a euphemism for borrowing money. Yet to hear Dawn Levy tell it, bonding was the solution to all of the Senate's problems. There would be sufficient funds to pay for everything, and everyone would be happy.

This proposal made staffers from states with large mass transit systems apoplectic. The proposal would mean cutting off the dedicated funding stream for mass transit that had been keeping transit alive for the past 30 years. Although bonding sounded better than "deficit spending," it was under no circumstances the same as having a dedicated funding source. Amtrak, the interstate passenger rail service, has not had a dedicated funding source since its inception in 1971, and every year Amtrak officials must come before Congress to beg for money. Every year Congress gives Amtrak a little less than they need to reach a state of good repair, but just enough to keep them from being killed off, thus ensuring that they return the next year hat in hand. If Levy's proposal were to go through, the entire mass transit system could have been thrown into a loop similar to Amtrak's.

Upon hearing of Levy's bonding proposal, staff aides from the transit states immediately mobilized a coalition. This is what you do when you have no power in Congress; you get together with other people who have no power to complain about the people with power. The coalition started to meet every week. The interesting thing about these meetings is that the coalition never really acknowledged its actual goal—obstruction. They all wanted to preserve mass transit funding, but they knew that no senator could possibly risk getting behind an alternate funding proposal. Thus they had no alternative but to do everything they could to derail Levy's proposal.

The first thing the coalition of staffers did was to take the issue to the entire Democratic caucus and try to get the senators themselves riled up about it. They organized several "members meetings"—fun events where senators got together and grumbled about mass transit for a few minutes until they all had to go somewhere else. The meetings took on the air of a gripe session with little or no action items, and it would be easy to be cynical about their value were it not for the fact that they produced the desired result. Here's how: Senators most knowledgeable about the topic would join their colleagues to explain some details. These members' explanations were not always clear, sometimes confusing the situation further. Senators would take turns saying something about the issue at hand, but most would just leave quietly without much real progress, only promising to meet again for a similar session.

Somehow, strangely, this meeting strategy worked because the senators now knew that this issue was important, and word spread that they were grumbling about it.

Dawn Levy had to respond accordingly. She was a master at the other side of this game and she tried several of her own strategies to keep her proposal alive. The transit caucus, composed mostly of Democrats, tried to arrange a "members meeting" with her boss (who, recall, was also a Democrat despite being a rural conservative) so that they could ask him to call Levy off of her bonding scheme. Levy's office kept dodging the coalition's phone calls. At one point Baucus's office accepted a meeting, but then cancelled at the last minute. Levy was also sure to never put her proposal on paper. No one ever saw a copy of it, so no one could be sure what she actually proposed. She did invite staffers to a briefing on the proposal, but when the turnout was incredibly large due to the mounting backlash against it, she abruptly changed the agenda of the meeting.

Levy tried to convince everyone that her bonding initiative would not hurt transit. It would probably provide more money for transit, she said. Bonding was great, bonding was the answer, was her constant message. Of course, few believed her, especially since she had argued vigorously against bonding just the year before, when a proposal was circulated to support Amtrak. It was sarcastically noted that if bonding was so great then there should be no problem in using it to support highways.

Months dragged on and there was still no proposal on the table except for Levy's, but there was little support for her proposal either. Her bonding scheme wasn't moving, and it wasn't helping to move the rest of the bill. Dawn Levy was down, but she was far from out. If the legislative process was a baseball game, this was just the first inning.

THE SENATE ENVIRONMENT AND PUBLIC WORKS COMMITTEE

The committee with jurisdiction over any bill has the most power to craft the starting point for the legislation. In the case of the transportation reauthorization bill, the measure falls under four separate Senate committees but only one House committee. While tracking progress in both chambers of Congress, this chapter will now focus on the Senate panel, the Environment and Public Works Committee, which would write the most controversial and largest portion of the bill. We will track the bill as was it released by the committee staff, analyzed by the staff of the senators on the committee, and amended in committee meetings. A key theme here will be how the committee staff and the staff of the senators on the committee vie for power over the bill while senators themselves play a minor role. For example, one veteran staffer organized a revolt against the committee staff because she personally felt left out of the process—she later sold out her fellow revolutionaries for her own state's gain. Another key personality is the committee chairman himself, who sets unrealistic goals, consistently fails to meet them, and then must do his best to save face.

Behind the Scenes

The chairman of the Senate Environment and Public Works Committee was getting restless. James M. Inhofe of Oklahoma, who had just assumed the gavel at the beginning of 2003, had announced at the beginning of the year that the transportation bill was his No. 1 priority and that he intended to put it on the fast track for a markup by Memorial Day at the end of May. His schedule was quite ambitious because it would mean writing an enormous bill that satisfied all parties concerned and resolved the looming funding issue within just a few weeks. His timeline had been met with snickers from incredulous Senate staff members, and as it turns out their skepticism was justified—there was no way this fast-track schedule could be met. When Memorial Day came and went, Inhofe then announced that July 4 would be the new deadline (Congress likes to use its holiday recesses as legislative benchmarks). The Fourth of July recess came and went and there was still no bill. Finally, the committee announced that there would be a bill by the end of the month long August recess so that it could be brought before the members in September. And this time, they really meant it.

It got to the point of a joke, but for the staffers, which state you were representing determined how hard you were laughing. Staffers from big winners under TEA-21, such as New York, Pennsylvania, and Connecticut, were thrilled to see the process drag on. If a bill wasn't passed in this session of Congress, TEA-21 would have to be extended by a few months or even a year in order to continue providing highway funding for previously authorized projects.

Staffers of individual senators would have a meeting every week with the committee staff, and every week the committee aides would inform them that the bill would be out very soon. Committee staff continued to extend the delays in subsequent meetings with members' staffers. The current law was set to expire on September 30. The committee would have to move a short-term extension by that date in order to keep highway funding flowing, and that would mean an admission of failure on the larger bill.

Still, the delays continued. The September deadline came and went; Congress passed a five-month extension, and promises of a bill continued. At this point those promises were falling on deaf ears. What was going to change? How were they going to resolve the funding issue that had been stalling them thus far? The only thing that could change was the people in charge and the electoral circumstances. An election was more than a year away, but it would include choosing a new president. If Bush were to be re-elected, some thought, it is possible he might support a gas tax increase at that point. If a Democrat came on board, he would be more likely to support a gas tax increase as well. There were several scenarios that would allow for passage of the bill in two years. But nothing could change this year—that seemed clear. Staff began to prepare for the likely scenario that nothing was going to happen until the next Congress convened in January 2005.

Then, one day, just when there really wasn't any time left, it finally happened. Committee staff announced that a compromise had been reached and the bill was now ready. The bill would be based on the president's SAFETEA directive, but obviously it contained numerous adjustments that had been created through discussions and compromises in the past several months. Staff was invited to come and look at the bill, and informed that the Senate Environment and Public Works Committee would convene in two weeks—the minimum amount of time allowed between the release of new legislation and when it can be "marked up" in the full committee.

Finally, the game was afoot.

GETTING TO MARKUP

Legislative proposals that have been referred to standing committees in either the House or the Senate are evaluated by the committee leaders and staff. In certain cases, committees or subcommittees may decide to hold initial public hearings on a bill in order to consider testimony from expert witnesses, advocates, and/or opponents. If the committee decides to proceed with moving the proposal along for further legislative action, a series of so-called markup meetings are held to give committee members an opportunity to consider amendments to the bill.

As we will see clearly below, committee chairs play major roles in the markup process. Chairs generally set the agenda for the committee and direct the committee proceedings. The chair also has the authority to permit or restrict opening statements on a bill. Once opening remarks have been completed or dispensed with, the chair calls up the bill for consideration, which constitutes the formal start of the markup process. Throughout the markup, members offer, debate, and vote on amendments to the bill. It is important to note that the committee does not actually amend the bill itself in the markup process. Only the chamber as a whole has the authority to alter the text of measures introduced by a member. During markup, members vote on amendments that the committee may then recommend to the entire chamber, which can adopt or reject them when the bill is considered on the floor. (They are almost always adopted.)

The process of offering and debating amendments during a committee markup closely resembles the amending process on the floor. The chair directs the committee clerk to read sections of a bill, and then members have an opportunity to offer amendments to that section. Once action on all amendments to the section is completed, the clerk proceeds to the next section and the process repeats itself until all sections have been read and decisions to any and all amendments to each section are rendered. Committee decisions can be decided by voice votes, which usually means they are non-controversial, or by a call of the roll, when each member must publicly state a "yea," "nay," or "present." The chair typically asks for a voice vote and then announces the result based on what he or she hears. Members can demand a "division" vote (show of hands) if they disagree with the chair's assessment. At any point before the voice or division vote is completed, any member may call for a roll call vote, which must be approved generally by at least one-fifth of members present. "Proxy" voting—giving your vote to another member who announces it to the chair or clerk in your absence—is allowed in the Senate but has been prohibited in the House since 1995. So senators often miss key portions of the markup while members of the House, who fear getting a reputation for a poor voting participation record, make valiant efforts to be recorded on roll call votes.

Markup is perhaps the seminal event in the life of a bill. It is the chance for members of the committee to amend a bill and vote on it to determine whether it will be sent to the floor for consideration. Once a bill passes through markup, it is substantially more likely to actually become a law. The reason for this is that the same party controls the chairmanship of committees and the floor of the House or Senate, so the chair of any given committee is unlikely to bring a bill to markup unless he or she knows that it will be put on the floor schedule by the majority leader. In the closely divided Senate in 2003, the best chance for the minority party to exercise influence would be during markup.

The Big Four

On the Senate side, the long road to markup had been paved with compromise, but the compromises had been made within a very small group of people. The Environment and Public Works Committee leaders had decided that their best chance of running this bill through the committee gauntlet lay with coalescing into a solid voting bloc. There were four such leaders: Chairman Inhofe; Christopher "Kit" Bond, a Republican of Missouri and chairman of the Subcommittee on Transportation; Jim Jeffords, a Vermont Independent who served as ranking minority member of the full committee; and Harry Reid, a Democrat from Nevada who was the ranking member on the Transportation Subcommittee as well as the Democratic minority whip in the full Senate.

Seniority remains a potent characteristic in the Senate. This status, afforded to members based on length of service in the chamber, entitles them to preferential treatment in a variety of matters including committee assignments. Committee chairs are drawn from the majority party in the chamber and generally are appointed by seniority, especially so in the Senate. Ranking members are the highest ranking (and usually longest serving) members of the minority party on the committee or subcommittee. Senators may not serve as chair or ranking minority member on more than one standing committee.

These four leaders knew that if they banded together, they would likely be able to move any bill they agreed on through the nineteen-member committee. Four against fifteen might seem like a mismatch, but the leaders could count on the fact that of the remaining fifteen members,

The "big four": James Inhofe, Christopher "Kit" Bond, Jim Jeffords, and Harry Reid.

eight were Republicans. The Republican senators on the committee were unlikely to vote against the bill brought forth by their chairman, a very senior individual in their own party, without very good reason. In turn, their chairman was likely to make sure that their interests were protected in the bill. He would not allow a bill to come before the committee that hit one of the Republican senators too hard.

The Democratic leaders were in a much different position. First, they had more conflicting interests to begin with. Recall that some donee states were targets, while others had little to worry about. Donee states with small populations and small amounts of funding did not have to concern themselves with the Minimum Guarantee because the amount needed to maintain their rate of return was very small. While Republican senators on the committee represented only donor states or very sparsely populated donee states, the Democrats had senators from two large donee states—Connecticut and New York. These two states, despite their size (and celebrity senators, Joseph I. Lieberman and Hillary Rodham Clinton), were a very small minority on the committee. Even so, the Democratic committee leadership could not ignore their interests completely without risking damage to their relationships. Therefore, Jeffords (who voted with the Democratic caucus) and Reid could not simply forge ahead to meet Inhofe's Minimum Guarantee goal at all costs.

Also, Jeffords and Reid differed strongly with the Republican leadership on certain environmental provisions, in particular, plans to expedite the environment review process required by the National Environmental Policy Act of 1969. NEPA was borne out of a reaction to the centralized, technocratic style of transportation planning that dominated the postwar era in the United States. Although the style helped to successfully prevent states from leveling communities to make way for expressways, it also brought a new level of time and cost to transportation projects. Whereas governments used to just draw up the plans, seize the property by eminent domain, and build the project, now they were forced to hold community meetings, make their plans accessible to the public, and show that they were not going to create any negative environmental impact. These additional regulations not only slowed projects considerably, but also made it likely that many projects would never get built at all. The Republicans wanted to "streamline" the environmental provisions to make it easier to build things faster and at a lower cost.

The word "streamlining" was adopted for a reason. If the Republicans had proposed, instead, to "eliminate" the environmental provisions, they would have created more of a stir. Which word was more accurate was a matter of debate. For example, Republicans wanted to let the states assume responsibility for federal environmental roles in certain cases. This might streamline the process, but it also would almost certainly reduce the amount of environmental oversight.

Republicans saw an opportunity to play to two elements of their base constituency on this issue. Business interests would approve because streamlining purported to help state and local governments build infrastructure faster with less environmental oversight. Tax watchdog groups would also get behind it because it purported to save taxpayers' money. A fiscally conservative move that promotes business and economic growth is about as appealing as it gets for Republicans on the Environment and Public Works Committee.

The Democratic leadership, however, had to contend with their own political interests. Environmental groups had begun lobbying committee and other Senate staff on this issue many months before. They knew Republicans were likely to make a push to streamline, and they were prepared to fight back. Furthermore, there were Democrats with strong environmental records on the committee, particularly Barbara Boxer of California and ranking member Jeffords. So Reid and Jeffords had to stand up to the Republican leadership on this issue as well.

The compromise solution found a way for the big four to agree on these points of contention. As part of their agreement, they decided they would vote together in a bloc on all committee amendments. Therefore, even if a Democratic senator attempted to repeal one of the environmental provisions with an amendment in committee, Jeffords and Reid would be obligated to oppose it. This would guarantee passage of a bill in line with the compromises these four had struck.

THE BILL ARRIVES

Ann Loomis was a staffer for John W. Warner, a Republican senator of Virginia. Typically there is not much interaction between staffers from opposing political parties. They will look for opportunities to cosponsor amendments together, since that always looks good and helps to show bipartisanship. But otherwise there isn't much cross-party discussion at the staff level, and it certainly isn't much more than superficial. So when Ann Loomis decided to call Democratic staffers of senators on the Environment and Public Works Committee, that meant something big was happening.

Loomis told the staffers that the committee was about to release a copy of the new transportation bill (numbered S 1072) and that the panel would proceed to a markup in less than two weeks. But she never would have called just to tell them that—they would have found out eventually and it made no difference to her if they knew. But there was a kicker: She knew that the bill was going to be released without any funding tables. There would be a bill, she told them, but it would not reveal how much money each state would get. The committee staff had decided that they would provide staff and senators with one number—their own state's six-year average take for the bill—and that would be all. Senators on the committee would not learn the Minimum Guarantee percentage, would not learn the formulas for distributing the funding, and would not learn how much other states would get.

Loomis was beside herself. She had worked in the Senate a long time. Ordinarily this kind of longevity is something that staff aides like to avoid, as working on the Hill is very draining and pays comparatively little. But Loomis was quite content with her job, and she was good at it. She had worked on the last reauthorization bill and knew the process quite well. She could not believe that the committee was actually releasing a bill without funding formulas. Moreover, she told her Democratic counterparts, they would not be allowed to see the bill just yet. They could go over to the committee offices and view the one copy of the bill, but they could not take notes or make copies.

The Democratic staffers rushed over to the committee offices and perused the bill, illicitly taking notes. Meanwhile, Loomis berated one of the Republican committee staffers. "How can you do this?" she yelled. "This is totally unheard of. You've left out the most important part of the bill! How can you expect members to vote on a bill that is missing its most important component?"

The woman Loomis was yelling at was Ruth Van Mark, the top staffer on the committee responsible for the transportation bill. Loomis came back into the room after yelling at Van Mark for a while, and sat down with the rest of the staffers to review the bill. Another staffer from a Republican senator's office came into the room. When told there were no funding tables in the bill, he gave a look of incredulity and left.

Two things were exceptional about this turn of events. First was the sheer confidence being displayed by the chairman and his staff to think that they could pass an enormous multi-billion dollar bill without any kind of funding distribution in it, and with no explanation as to why they left that part of it out. Second, it was a little odd how incredulous everyone was. They were not upset about policy, or even the total funding level of the bill. Mostly the staffers were upset because they would not be able to issue a press release trumpeting how much money they were going to get for their state from this bill. The central benefit of being a senator on this committee had been taken away from them. All of the political value inherent in the rate-of-return issue had been snatched from staff and their bosses alike.

In retrospect, it seems obvious that *of course* the committee had withheld formulas for the bill. The formulas had been written; they just weren't showing them to the staff or the lower-ranking senators on the committee. They let everyone read the bill a few days later, but still withheld the formulas because they saw that as their best chance to exert power over a large pile of cash. The four most powerful senators had joined together to form a bloc. This bloc had made a deal with compromises on both sides on several issues, and that deal included a funding formula. The bloc figured that with their positions and authority, they could pass a bill if they acted as a unit, even without funding formulas and—this is the most brazen part—even without a method of paying for the bill. Then they could introduce their secretly agreed-upon funding mechanism on the floor of the Senate as part the "manager's amendment," which is automatically accepted when a bill comes to the floor for debate.

Chairman Inhofe had grown tired of waiting for a method of funding. He was sick of people laughing at him for not getting this bill done. So he decided to form a bloc, ram the bill through committee, and let someone else figure out how to pay for it. The only people who could stop him would be the remaining senators on the committee. The question was, could they and would they?

THE REVOLT

It was not necessarily apparent at the time, but the revolt was just an example of a time-honored Washington institution—a pissing match. Such a battle has been defined as an argument where each contestant is trying to outmaneuver the other one, not for the sake of reaching a substantive result, but simply to win. And it has been used by no less a practitioner than President (and former senate majority leader) Lyndon Baines Johnson. Not every pissing match in Congress was like this one; in this case, the senators were almost totally uninvolved. No doubt the senators had played some role in brokering the compromises that eventually created the bill and the strategy of withholding information regarding the bill. But the contest that followed was all about the staff.

The battle was between the staff of the committee, meaning staffers from the big four who had formed the bloc, and staffers for the other fifteen senators on the committee. The committee staff was, through the tactic of releasing a bill less than two weeks before markup and without funding tables, shutting the staff of the senators out of the process. The latter, ostensibly on behalf of their bosses but also for their own egos, were none too pleased. It was their job to stop the committee staff from exerting this kind of power, and the only way to do that was to join together, Democrats with Republicans. As soon as the bill was released, the rebellious staffers began meeting regularly to discuss strategy. Democrats and Republicans both got together to figure out how they were going to take this bill back into their own hands. The group of angry staffers lacked organization, however, and soon, a leader emerged—Dawn Levy had arrived.

Although Levy was really on the Finance Committee staff, she still worked for her senator (Baucus) on transportation issues and he was a member of the Environment and Public Works Committee, too. If there was anything Levy did not like it was being disrespected, and she was already sharpening her horns when she heard the news about the Inhofe bill. She was in a perfect position to organize everyone because her boss was so right-leaning that he typically worked exclusively with Republicans. She knew all the Republican staffers, and even though she did not know the Democratic staffers on this committee, her credentials as a Democrat gave her easier access to them.

Levy seized control of the revolt in part by controlling room space. That's right—room space can mean a lot in the Senate. Senators are assigned offices on the basis of seniority, so the more senior senators have bigger offices. If a senator is a relative newcomer, he or she can get virtually no meeting space—sometimes just one small conference room that can get very uncomfortable with more than eight people in it. Levy's boss, on the other hand, was a ranking member on one of the most powerful committees in the Senate, and she had access to all the committee staff space. She immediately compiled an e-mail list of all the relevant staffers, and began organizing meetings in her large conference rooms.

Now one might think, given that there were nineteen senators on the committee and only four of them in the leadership bloc, that it would be relatively easy for the rebels to block anything. The rebellious staffers' bosses vastly outnumbered the committee staffers' bosses, so it would seem that they could do anything they wanted. In fact, in the initial meetings, it looked that simple. Levy was filled with rage and suggested a boycott of the markup. Ann Loomis, despite working for Virginia Republican John Warner, was almost equally angry (in a southern kind of way) and said her boss might not show up at the markup either.

Most staffers knew that it would be difficult for their bosses to risk missing the markup unless everyone else was absent, too. Some senators with little to lose could potentially be mavericks, but others, namely those from major donee states New York and Connecticut, had way too much on the line to risk such a tactic. Those states were counting on their minority leadership to keep them from getting completely hammered in this bill. They were clinging to whatever help they could get from that leadership, never forgetting the fact that the Republicans had no interest in helping them. On the other hand, if everyone else was going to boycott, those senators could take the chance as well.

Once everyone had calmed down a little, however, it became increasingly clear that a boycott was not going to happen. Ann Loomis talked to her boss and realized that a boycott would ruin Warner's relationship with Chairman Inhofe. Other Republican staffers also made it clear that their bosses would have to show up. Levy was still ready to boycott because of her boss's position on Finance (thus he could retaliate against Inhofe if Inhofe tried to punish him), but she recognized that this strategy was dead and moved on to a new one.

What was interesting about the boycott strategy was that it was a perfect example of congressional staffers getting ahead of themselves and caught up in their own battle. It's likely that when Ann Loomis originally talked to her boss, he expressed anger at the process. She probably interpreted that anger to mean that he was not going to stand for it, given his high ranking and respect within the Senate. However, even the highest-ranking politician must pick his battles, and it's clear that he and the other senators realized that there was no reason to pick this one. Sure, they had been shut out of the process, but senators typically don't get that involved in the process anyway—that's the staff's job. A senator's concern is whether he will look good when this bill passes. Given that Loomis's boss was from a donor state, it was very likely that he would do very well under any bill proposed by Chairman Inhofe. The chairman probably assured him as much, and he realized that attending the markup was the wise thing to do. Other lower-ranking senators were much more likely to follow suit.

The Walk-through

Needing a new strategy, Levy proposed that the staff rebels try to disrupt the process in other ways. If they could delay the proceedings at all, they would buy themselves a lot more time to scrutinize the bill and wrestle the formulas out of the committee staff. The Senate was due to adjourn in just a few weeks and not return until January. That would give them plenty of time. And time was something they desperately needed, not only from a strategic point of view, but also from a personal stand-point. In all likelihood, one of the reasons they were all so panicked about this markup was that they were staring at the amount of work they would all have to do to get ready for it, and it was not a pretty prospect. They would each have to read a bill of 600-plus pages, draft amendments, and prepare their boss's statements and votes, all within just ten days.

The life of a Senate staffer is, as a rule, brutal. You are expected to work long hours, often weekends, for a salary that is half of what you could get in the private sector. You are typically on call for your boss twenty-four hours a day, as being a senator is a full-time job. You spend most of your day in constituent meetings or briefings, and so you have to actually do the work of drafting memos, letters, and amendments in the evenings and on weekends. When Congress is out of session, things lighten up a great deal, but if you waste that time you will be pummeled again when members come back from recess. This bill came out in October in a non-election year, which is about the busiest time in the calendar. There are no election distractions, and Congress is hastily trying to finish things up before the Thanksgiving recess. This is the time when things actually get done. A bill of this magnitude with so little lead time meant two weeks with little rest for these staffers. If they weren't fighting for their bosses, or their right to have a say in the process, they were fighting to get some rest.

Delay was crucial. The rebels' first dilatory tactic was to take place at the walk-through. A walk-through is when the committee staff goes over the main points of a draft bill for the other staff members. For a large bill like this, a walk-through would be likely to take several hours. The rebels' plan was to make it last several days. They showed up prepared with questions on every piece of the bill. They were not shy about arguing why they thought some minute, essentially irrelevant language was wrong. And if the committee staff gave their explanation and moved on, the rebel staffers made it clear that one of their bosses would be offering an amendment on that issue. They succeeded in making the walk-through last two days, and by the time they were done, the committee staff knew they were in trouble. They broke down and came clean.

The head of the committee staff was Andy Wheeler, a short, stocky man in his forties with a big round head and glasses, who looked like he might have just ambled out of a Far Side cartoon. As the committee staff neared the end of the marathon walk-through, Wheeler made a rare appearance and headed to the front of the room. He looked somewhat disheveled, which is unusual for a Republican staffer, as he announced that markup would be pushed back one day. One day was not much of a delay. When probed about why the committee staff seemed to be in such a hurry, he explained that they needed to mark up the bill before the session ended so it could be the first bill on the floor in January and have a chance to pass it before the short-term extension expired at the end of February. Never mind that none of the other committees working on this bill were even close to marking up their portions. Never mind that no one had come up with a proposal as to how to actually pay for the bill. The chairman wanted to show that he had done his part, and any delay was someone else's fault. Wheeler was asked why they would not release the funding tables. He said they did not want the tables "out there" while the Senate was out of session because then there would be too much opportunity to contest them. In other words, they were trying to protect their power by limiting input.

Once Wheeler announced the one-day delay, the cat was out of the bag and he had to delay markup further because it was clear that a delay was at least in the realm of the possible and reasonable. If their goal was to get the bill marked up before the session ended, they had at least one additional week to play with and everyone knew it. They were facing a large-scale revolt and they knew it. So the committee staff threw the rebels a bone. They still weren't going to release the funding tables before the next session, but when the rebel staffers returned to their desks, they found an e-mail letting them know that markup had been postponed one week.

THE EMPIRE STRIKES BACK

The rebellion had come charging out of the gate and won its first battle. The rebels had bought themselves an extra week to work with, a week during which they could find ways to derail the bill. But the committee staff was not stupid—they were going to use that extra time wisely as well. The first thing they did was to get their side in line.

Republican staffers had been joining the rebel meetings from the beginning. This was mostly due to Ann Loomis, who brought with her some folks from other offices, but also due to Dawn Levy, who probably called them every few hours to make sure they showed up at the meetings. Within days there were noticeable changes in the Republican attitudes. Loomis said there was no way her boss could avoid the markup or even vote against the bill. The other Republicans agreed and that was the end of that possibility.

The concept of attending the markup but voting against the bill was an interesting one. One might think it would have been perfectly acceptable for the Republican senators to attend a markup and vote against the bill on the basis of the fact that they had no way of knowing whether their state would stand to benefit. However, there were two factors that made this impossible. The first was the zeitgeist; this was a period of Republican unity. This was November 2003. The 2004 presidential election was approaching, and Republicans were rallying behind their party leader in an effort to secure their power in the next Congress. To cross the chairman of the committee at this point would have not only displayed disunity, but also would have raised the ire of the majority leader and possibly the White House. Second, there was that little piece of paper. That piece of paper was one sheet, handed to each Senate office on the committee, indicating the amount of funding that state would receive over six years in the bill. It was like a secret game of "Clue." The paper had one number on it in the center of an otherwise blank page. It was typically referred to on the Democratic side as "not worth the paper it was written on." But to Republicans, it was actually worth something. Democratic staffers knew that the Republicans would not hesitate to pillage the funding of Democratic states in order to get the bill passed as it moved through Congress. On the floor or in conference, that funding could be taken away to satisfy the demands of other members. Republicans were likely to see their numbers remain the same because the party in power would be less likely to turn on their own. In short, Republican Party unity was strong enough to hold trust on both sides. If both sides just moved forward, each would stand to benefit.

Just because their bosses had to show up at the meeting and vote for the bill, this did not mean that Republican staffers had to stop their rebellion. Their interest lay in disrupting what they saw as an unfair process—this was not necessarily the same interest as their bosses'. Depending on how removed their bosses were from the process—and judging by what happened, some were almost completely uninvolved—a staffer could potentially decide unilaterally how his or her boss would act at the markup.

Levy was forced to come up with a new strategy, and here is where her smarts and imagination as a staffer showed. Part of what makes for a good Hill staffer is the ability to be completely flexible and adapt to ever-changing situations. Politics can change on a dime, and the same staffer that argued for hanging the bastard one day may argue just as vociferously for letting him free the next. In this case, Levy came up with a strategy that aligned with those staffers who believed there were serious problems with the policy implications of the bill.

Remember policy? That was why many staffers got involved in the congressional staff work in the first place—to have a direct impact on policy. These staffers were poised to affect transportation policy dramatically, but that was true only because it happened to work well for them in their grudge match against the committee staff. Levy's strategy was for each rebel staffer to submit as many amendments to the bill as he or she could write up. She wanted amendments of any kind—even just to change the name of the bill or add unnecessary words, along with amendments that involved good policy for their states, of course. Given that there were fifteen senators outside the leadership bloc, if each submitted a multitude of amendments, the committee would have no choice but to postpone the markup. If they held the markup as planned, they would risk the embarrassment of having a never-ending markup that could not maintain the quorum necessary to move the bill on to the floor. The rebels all immediately got to work drafting amendments.

There was a serious demarcation among staff members, between those who really understood and sometimes cared about policy, and those who were completely focused on their own state's needs and little else. Some staffers, like Ann Loomis, had been through this process before and understood the policy implications of the bill very rapidly. They might have some pet policy concerns, like seatbelt safety or environmental regulations, which they or their bosses actually cared about. Typically these were motivated by strong lobbying within their state, or by the needs expressed by the state departments of transportation. In some cases, policies were motivated by staff preferences. In addition, individual members often pursued their personal policy priorities vigorously.

Elaborate discussions about potential amendments ensued. Still, not all ideas were necessarily embraced. Consider, for example, a series of amendments proposed by Sen. Hillary Rodham Clinton of New York. The staff devised amendments whose ultimate policy goal was to assist the economically disadvantaged. One amendment would provide for preferential hiring on transportation projects for low-income citizens; another accounted specifically for their needs in a transportation study. And a third proposal would create a research program to examine how transportation infrastructure investments affect poor Americans. When these amendments, initially perceived by the Clinton staff as rather benign and noncontroversial, were brought up for consideration at one of the staff meetings, however, they were dismissed summarily. Few volunteered to cosponsor them. "Where did these come from?" Levy asked. The general reaction seemed to reflect astonishment that members would use the transportation bill as an opportunity to affect the nation's social policies.

By this time Levy was calling for meetings at least once a day, usually twice. The staffers were all working long hours and bunkered down in their own little world of transportation legislation. A staffer would be at his or her desk plugging along as late as 11 p.m. and have a question, and he or she could call anyone else involved in the rebellion knowing that they, too, would be at their desks to answer the phone. The staff grew into a tight-knit group with a well-planned strategy. First, they would draft their amendments. Then they would share the amendments with one another and try to get cosponsors, thus increasing the likelihood of passage. Levy's credo was "if it doesn't hurt your state—you should get on it!" She wanted to totally usurp the process by submitting dozens of amendments with enough cosponsors to pass. And she showed she was willing by signing on to almost every amendment put forward.

This process, however, did not go unnoticed by the committee staff. The committee staff knew they would be in trouble if they did not fight back, so they quickly counterattacked. The staff started by threatening the Republicans again, having gotten word that the rebels were thinking of submitting an amendment that would put a formula into the bill. The rebels were planning to devise a funding formula that benefited all of their states, and all fifteen senators would cosponsor it. This would have been real trouble for the committee staff, so in the name of GOP unity, they strong-armed every Republican, urging them against adding their names to any formula amendments. Sure enough, the Republicans fell in line and refused to play along with any such amendment.

A formula amendment would have put an end to the committee staff tactics. The formula was the most important component of this immense piece of legislation, and the rebels outnumbered the big four. If the rebellion had been able to stick together and agree on a formula, they would have easily wrestled control of the bill from Chairman Inhofe. The chairman would have had little choice but to play ball and at least compromise instead of forcing through his own agenda. But the committee staff effectively nipped this rebellion in the bud by breaking off the Republicans from the group yet again.

However, this strategy had its limits. The staff still knew that they were facing too many amendments to handle, and they could not easily pressure senators to withhold amendments to a bill. Their chosen tactic was to invite each senator's staff members individually to meet with them to go over the rebel group's amendments. The rebels looked forward to these meetings as opportunities to scare the committee staff with the sheer number of amendments they were preparing. The committee staff, in turn, looked forward to deviously dismantling the rebels' strategy.

Some staffers arrived at these meetings with over seventy amendment ideas written down. The meetings were held at all hours of the day, in part to show everyone how many long and hard hours the committee staff was working. Each senator's staff aide would slog through his or her policy amendments, and the committee staff would usually offer no reaction as each one was described. At some point the staffer would get around to the amendments regarding IPAM.

IPAM stood for Interstate Performance and Maintenance, and it was the largest brand-new funding program present in Inhofe's draft legislation. Typically, a new program was tough to get passed because everyone wanted to have some sort of say in it. It was even tougher when the program would allocate lots of money. IPAM was supposed to distribute approximately $2 billion a year over six years. What was odd about the proposal was that the bill provided very few details about it. IPAM was supposed to provide quick and accessible funding for states that had "ready to go" transportation projects. Yet there was no language in the bill that explained how states could obtain this money.

For that reason, the proposed program was generally unpalatable and presented itself as a target for amendments. Most staffers had close to ten amendments each to the IPAM section. However, when staff members began going over their amendments to IPAM with committee staff, the committee staff informed them that they messed with IPAM at their own peril. IPAM, they explained, was a pot of money they were reserving to help assuage senators from the states that would be hurt by the bill when formulas were actually released. IPAM was holding the surplus funds that would be necessary to get the bill passed, and was the only thing protecting the donee state's takes from an all-out pillaging.

The committee staff used these private meetings not just to threaten individual staffers on the dangers of putting forth various amendments, but also to learn what the rebels were going to submit so that they could accept certain amendments in advance. Two days later committee staff unveiled a "manager's package," a package of amendments submitted by the chairman and almost automatically accepted by the committee at the outset of the markup. Several of the rebel amendments were included. Although staffers were happy to see their changes incorporated into the bill, it also meant that their overall delaying strategy was faltering. The committee staff had successfully knocked out over one hundred amendments from the rebels' original list.

LAST-MINUTE DEALMAKING

As markup neared, the rebels were working at a feverish pace to get their amendments in order and figure out which of the other senators' amendments they wanted to cosponsor. They were meeting with the other staff members virtually every day, throughout the day, and then writing amendments at night.

However, there was a noticeable difference emerging at these meetings. First, Dawn Levy decided to join with two Republicans from rural states to offer their amendments as a group. This was a fact mentioned casually by Levy as if it was insignificant. Given that the overall goal—her original goal—was disruption of the process, this seemed an odd shift. By joining together, the three staffs had combined amendments, thus *reducing* the overall number they would file. This was despite the fact that the rebels had previously agreed to file duplicate amendments in order to increase paperwork and time consumption for committee staff. Levy seemed to be shifting away from her own strategy.

There was another difference at these meetings: Attendance was poor. Republicans were less interested in showing up and less likely to cosponsor amendments. Staffers from a couple of offices had never joined the coalition, and they moved further away from the rebellion. One of them, for example, was told by committee staff that he would get an amendment that was very important to him if he did not join the rebellion. Others were just uninterested, or had no power to do anything without their bosses' consent.

The game was changing. Although the rebellion would be proved wrong in the end, at the time it seemed like the original plan to disrupt the markup was still in place. Levy certainly wanted the rebels to think that was the case. Meanwhile, she was not only the ringleader, but also the best at organizing people to get behind her amendments. Mostly she resorted to intimidation. If someone said he didn't want get behind one of her amendments, she bellowed at him in front of the group. Then later she would call and try to assure him that this amendment was not going to hurt his state, cajoling some more. Eventually she had amassed a wealth of amendments with enough cosponsors to ensure passage even before markup began.

Amendments had to be filed twenty-four hours before markup—this is a Senate-wide rule. That meant they were due at 9:30 a.m. on Tuesday, November 11, in advance of the Wednesday morning markup. The fact that this was Veterans Day—a federal holiday when the rest of the government shut down—held almost no relevance to the Senate this particular year. The Republicans were desperate to show that they could get legislation through faster than the Democrats had when they controlled Congress, and they would demonstrate that even if it meant working on Veterans Day. The timing did mean that waiting until the last possible moment to file amendments, which the rebels wanted to do as a tactic, would also be the inevitable result of trying to do so much in so little time. This would necessitate working all night on Monday, November 10.

Amendment filing is a strange procedure. First, you draft your amendments and e-mail them to the Office of the Legislative Counsel. This group of lawyers working for the Senate understands how to actually write legislative language so that it passes muster in affected agencies and the courts. The Legislative Counsel e-mails back your amendments in very serious-looking amendment form, with lots of extra, even unnecessary official-looking words like "A BILL" in big bold letters and "be it enacted" and always mentioning something about the bill being read twice, etc., which is somehow essential to democracy. There are often some mistakes in their amendments, which is understandable in this case because the folks working on transportation amendments had hundreds of them going in and out of their office in just a few days. Staffers had to send many amendments back and forth sometimes more than once.

A staffer might write up an amendment such as the following:

Amend Section 1203 page 2–14 line 25 insert after "congestion" "system reliability."

The amendment would return from legislative counsel as shown in Figure 2.3. This particular amendment proposed to include the concept of reliability as one of the criteria for establishing eligibility under the Freight Gateways Program, which was a small funding set-aside for multimodal freight projects. It is the kind of change that affects few people, but in a substantial way. This made it an effective means of delaying the process while the small number of affected parties debated its merits.

Once staffers got their amendments drafted properly, they had to write in all the cosponsors (normally this could be done by Legislative Counsel but, given the compressed time period and cosponsors jumping on and off every few minutes, this had to be done by staffers themselves). Then staffers were required to put a coversheet on each amendment, with a number title, and a quick summary. Then they had to make copies of each amendment for the rest of the committee. Standard practice is fifty copies per amendment, but the committee decided to make one hundred copies the requirement for this bill. This was most likely a hostile act intended to

FIGURE 2.3	Amendment to the Freight Gateways Program

AMENDMENT NO. _____   Calendar No.

Purpose: To modify the eligibility of projects for the Freight Gateways Program.

IN THE SENATE OF THE UNITED STATES-108th Cong., 1st Sess.

S. 1072

To authorize for Federal-aid highways, highway safety programs, and transit programs, and for other purposes.

Referred to the Committee on _____
                          and ordered to be printed

          Ordered to lie on the table and to be printed

AMENDMENT intended to be proposed by Mr. KENNEDY to
          the amendment (No. _____) proposed by Mr. INHOFE

Viz:

1	On page 2–14 line 25, after "congestion" insert the following:
2	
3	"system reliability"

---

push the endurance of the rebellious staffers. The irony of the fact that this was the *Environment* and Public Works Committee did not escape anyone as the rebels burned through reams of paper. If the rebels wanted to deluge them with amendments, committee staff were not going to make it easy.

It's not easy to imagine what one hundred copies of about fifty amendments of two to ten pages each looks like. But if you can, then take that image and multiply it by ten; that is how much paper was to be submitted for this markup. Most staffers figured they would just send them off to the copy center and they would come back all done. But by the time most staffers finished getting all of their amendments in order it was 10 p.m. the night before the Tuesday morning deadline. The Senate's copy center office closed at 11 p.m. and could not possibly get these huge jobs finished that quickly, nor could they do it the next morning. Staffers frantically called Kinkos centers all over Washington, D.C. Most weren't open twenty-four hours a day. The ones that were open could not do such a huge job so quickly. All the interns had gone home. Things were looking bleak for the rebellion.

Staff that had failed to submit enough of their amendments to the copy center in previous days had no choice but to use the machines in their individual offices. Senate offices are not exactly luxurious, and they do not feature the latest in copy machine technology. The machines in most offices had a sign above them that read something like "Do not make more than 10 copies on these machines. For a bigger job, please use the Senate Copy Center."

There was also something about a budget and saving money, but that did not matter at this point—staff attacked these poor machines with a vengeance. They abused and violated them and forced them into more continuous labor than they had ever seen in their long, tortured existence. As the night progressed and as *Monday Night Football* ended, the machines showed more signs of wear than either the Packers or the Eagles. They made a few mistakes and ran out of staples; a few paper jams were inevitable. But they persevered into the night, and when they were done, the machines had reluctantly spat out all the copies needed. Each Senate staff team had three large boxes full of amendments.

The next morning, acting on maybe a couple hours of sleep if they were lucky, Senate staffers borrowed interns to help them cart their amendments down to the committee's meeting room in the Dirksen Senate Office Building, across the street from the Capitol. The room was a chaotic overflow of dead trees. There was paper everywhere. White sheets of paper covered every available inch of table space in the room, and it was stacked several feet high in many cases. It was a display of pure waste—hours and hours of labor had gone into creating these amendments, most of which had the main purpose of ensuring that the bill never passed.

Later that day, after the committee staff had gone through cataloging what they had received, they sent all other staff a master list of amendments and called a meeting to go through them. Andy Wheeler, the committee's majority staff director, opened the meeting by noting that they had received almost four hundred amendments, which were fewer than the number predicted by *Congress Daily*, a congressional newsletter. He wanted the rebels to know that everyone on the committee staff knew what the rebels were up to and that they were prepared for this. He then said that they would be going through the list of amendments publicly at this meeting and he asked each staffer to indicate which amendments of those they had filed they were actually planning to offer.

Filing an amendment and offering an amendment is not the same thing. Any amendment can be filed, just as any bill can be dropped, with little political cost to the sponsoring member of Congress. Press releases can be issued on amendments filed, but chances are low that the press will pick up on the amendment on its own. As long as the member does not submit an amendment to murder all newborn babies, few are likely to notice. Offering an amendment, on the other hand, is a very public event. It requires the member to openly declare, in front of the public and members of the press, that they want to submit said amendment. Any senator or representative will be cautious about which amendments they decide to offer up for debate.

Despite this meaningful difference, Wheeler's tactic had not been anticipated. The rebel staffers knew that it would be unlikely that they could keep their individual senators in the markup long enough to offer fifty-plus amendments. They also knew that individual senators would risk irritating their colleagues if they adopted this strategy, but no other senators did. But staff had assumed that either (1) everyone would do it and thus their respective senator would not look bad, or (2) staff would notice that people were backing off and offer the amendments they cared about most.

Wheeler's tactic made it clear that he expected staff to refrain from offering too many amendments. In fact, if his tactic wasn't clear enough, he had one of his lieutenants stand up and say as much more directly. This was a tall man with a fancier suit who threatened that if a senator offered too many amendments, the committee would take away funding from that state. This was a rather effective, and surprisingly direct, threat. Staffers quickly scanned their lists and checked off the amendments they thought were most important and had the best chance of passing. Some tried to avoid revealing their hand by saying they were not sure which ones they would be offering. Some Republican staffers outright refused to say which amendments they would be offering, but they could afford to do that without fear of retribution. Dawn Levy displayed the most cunning response—she publicly announced that she would withdraw all of her amendments if her most controversial one was to be accepted. She knew this offer would be declined, but she wasn't going to reveal which amendments she was likely to offer and she wanted to show that she was willing to make a deal.

By the time the staff meeting had adjourned, the committee staff had greatly improved their chances of getting through markup on time and with a bill reported to the floor. They knew which amendments were likely to be offered, so they could prepare themselves for handling those amendments. They also had taken the rebels' primary main dilatory tactic off the table by threatening those who participated in it. The committee staff's final stroke came later that evening as staffers were working well into the night preparing the markup briefing for their senators. They sent around an e-mail letting each staffer know which amendments they had decided to accept without a fight.

Their choice of amendments to accept seemed somewhat random. Perhaps in their haste to accept amendments they had not fully considered their ramifications, or perhaps they knew they could eliminate some of the more controversial amendments in a House-Senate conference. Some amendments were innocuous and obvious candidates for inclusion in the bill, but others made more radical changes than most people ever could have expected. Staffers who actually cared about policy and saw their amendments incorporated were thrilled. What many rebel staffers didn't notice at the time was that they had just seen their potential delaying tactic reduced in impact even further. Each staff had seen the number of their amendments severely diminished, and they had to be careful about offering too many of those.

There are two conclusions one can draw from this. One is that the rebels had mostly been bought off and the price was cheap. For a few measly amendments, coupled with a few serious threats, they had found themselves in a position where they could no longer hope to derail the bill in committee. On the other hand, the rebels had successfully taken a bill in which they had had no input and incorporated dozens of amendments within a very short period of time. In the battle for control of the bill, they had made great headway, even if they still did not know the formulas in the bill.

Dawn Levy did not come so cheap. She was still mad, she had a few bullets left in the chamber, and she didn't give up easily. She knew her boss could show up and make as much trouble as he wanted and get away with it because he was the ranking member on Finance. She had lots of cosponsors on many of her amendments. The committee would risk being embarrassed if it didn't make a deal with her.

At about 11 p.m. the night before the markup the rebel staffers all received an e-mail from Levy. I have "sold my soul to the devil," she said. The committee staff had agreed to accept all of her amendments that had sufficient cosponsors in exchange for her boss leaving the markup after his opening statement. He would leave his proxy for his vote and still go on record for the amendments she had said he would cosponsor, but he would not try to delay the markup.

The rebellion was over and Dawn Levy had gotten almost everything she wanted. She, too, may have failed in halting the bill and getting access to the formulas, but she had played her cards about as well as was possible. She had effectively utilized both the committee staff and the rebel group to create power for her and put more of an imprint on the bill than anyone else. That is how a solid, loyal, and professional congressional staff member operates.

THE MARKUP

It has been postulated that twenty-somethings run the world. On the day of the markup of S 1072 this certainly seemed to be the case. That morning staffers accompanied their bosses from their offices to the committee room. Each one sat in a chair directly behind his or her boss, ready to help with anything necessary. Most staffers had prepared a briefing that included a list of all the amendments that were likely to come up, and how the boss should vote on them. They were written as "recommendations," but most senators weren't going to have the time, knowledge, or inclination to go the other way. Staff also told the boss what to say, by writing opening statements for the markup and for each amendment that they decided the boss should introduce. These were also included in the briefing books. Each staffer also remained alert to advise the boss how to respond to any impromptu developments.

Any committee meeting is intended to be a public spectacle. Many of them are broadcast directly on C-SPAN, which congressional staff can watch via their desk televisions. Members of the press abound, particularly at a high profile meeting such as this one. At a typical meeting, senators might waltz in when convenient, deliver a few talking points on their issue of choice, and then make a swift unseen exit. In fact, most committee chairmen employed a "first come, first served" rule with regard to speaking in order to discourage this sort of thing. This was no ordinary meeting however, and most every senator intended to be there for the duration.

Chairman Inhofe controlled the markup skillfully in order to get what he wanted, which was the quickest markup possible under the circumstances. He knew that he had to finish the meeting by about 1 p.m. to be able to maintain a quorum of senators for the final vote to order the bill reported to the full Senate. If the bill failed to pass that day, it was going to have to be held over until the next year. One key strategy Inhofe employed to this end was to go through the bill section by section and only accept amendments on one section at that time. Once a section had been "closed," no more amendments could be offered on it. This meant that senators who left the meeting could not offer certain amendments later if they missed their chance. It ensured that the meeting moved along swiftly. The chairman also was careful not to allow excessive debate, and he frowned upon any senator who was long-winded.

Staffers had no choice but to offer the remaining amendments that they cared about and thought had a chance to pass. The bloc of four stood strong, mostly with the help of other Republicans on the committee, and defeated all but a couple of the dozens that were offered. After all, committee staff knew which amendments were likely to be offered, and they were not likely to have allowed them to come to a vote if they thought they would pass.

Of note were some of the amendments that did not pass. The one low-income amendment from Clinton that, remarkably, had ultimately been agreed to by some rebel staff members was one that created a research program. Presumably this one was acceptable if people felt there was a chance their state could secure some of the research money. With some convincing and language changes (the staffer for Alaska's Lisa Murkowski wanted native tribes mentioned specifically, for example), there had been a few cosponsors. Nonetheless, it failed miserably when brought to a vote at markup. Apparently the senators felt the same way as their staffs on this issue.

One of the amendments would have passed except that one senator switched votes without informing the bill's sponsor, and another forgot which side to vote for. Switching votes was George Voinovich, a Republican from Ohio who had been a cosponsor of the amendment, but apparently his staffer changed her mind and advised her senator to vote the other way. Forgetting was Alaska's Murkowski. Of course, it was not she who forgot how to vote, but her staff aide. He had agreed to back it in a deal he had made previously, and his boss was listed as a cosponsor on the amendment when it was filed. But Murkowski voted against when it came up for debate in the markup. Such is how policy is made in the Senate.

It is remarkable how far one can progress in the U.S. government without even knowing what the United States looks like. At one point Senator Clinton of New York offered an amendment that would change the funding allocation formula for international border crossings. Border crossings were given money under the bill to improve roads or entrances at international borders, thus improving the flow of international commerce. When Clinton offered her amendment, Republican Craig Thomas of Wyoming was confused. What possible reason, he asked incredulously, does New York have to care about borders? With what "country," he pressed, does New York share a border? Clinton politely informed him that New York, in fact, borders Canada. Perhaps, she added, he should come and see it sometime.

As the markup wound to a close, Chairman Inhofe had clearly succeeded. He kept the meeting as brief as possible under the circumstances, and enough senators stuck around to ensure final adoption of the bill. The vote to send the bill to the full Senate was a landslide, with only two senators voting against it. The nays came from Bob Graham, a Democrat from Florida who was running for president, and Ron Wyden, Democrat of Oregon. Though members of the minority party, both were operating from positions of strength that allowed them to register a protest vote. Graham had the double advantage of being from a donor state, which Inhofe would likely take care of, and he had also previously announced he was retiring from the Senate upon completion of his current term. Wyden had just been re-elected in 2002 and was not concerned about re-election until 2008; highway funding was not a major issue for him. Both Graham and Wyden spoke with anger at the markup, expressing frustration with the fact that they were not being informed of the formulas for the bill. But these were the lone voices in opposition. The rest of the rebel group had capitulated. The vote to adopt was 17–2.

AFTERGLOW

After the markup the staff was in a daze. Phone calls poured in with people offering congratulations on the amendments that had passed, or even on those offered and rejected that showed solidarity with the cause. The "bicycle people" were particularly ecstatic. Their amendment, which increased funding for bicycle and pedestrian safety dramatically, was one of those few accepted by the committee staff before the markup. Martha Roskowski of America Bikes, the primary organization for the bicycle lobby, was so appreciative she reputedly offered to bear the children of the staff member responsible. He declined that offer but gladly accepted a T-shirt, lunch, and a homemade apple-raspberry pie.

The rebellion had failed to stop the bill and markup from proceeding, and unlike Dawn Levy, the remaining staffers had not been overwhelmingly successful with their amendments. Yet the strange thing was that they remained somewhat sanguine that the bill that had come out of committee probably wasn't actually going anywhere. There was still no financing mechanism, and there was a chance that a new chairman or administration would take over next November before the bill went anywhere, thus negating all of the work they had done.

In Washington sometimes you have to settle for winning one battle, or even just doing OK in one battle, knowing that the entire circumstances for the war and potentially even the side you were fighting on were likely to change. The rebel staff knew the bill would not have been the same without them, and that they had accomplished more as a group than they ever could have individually.

The big four, meanwhile, had accomplished their goal. They had successfully moved a bill through committee that, although based on President Bush's original SAFETEA, still contained many of their intended objectives. They most likely had an agreement with the Senate majority leader, Bill Frist of Tennessee, to allow the bill to come to the floor, and would submit a manager's package at that time with formulas for funding. The Finance Committee would then have to develop a method of paying for the bill on its own, and submit that as part of the manager's package.

Chairman Inhofe came out of the committee process looking good. He had sidestepped a committee fight on the Minimum Guarantee and overall funding levels, the two most contentious issues in the bill. He had completed the bill before Congress adjourned for the year, putting it in a position to be passed immediately in the New Year. However, the same fights he skillfully managed to avert in committee were about to resurface on the floor of the Senate.

NOTES

1. Thomas Weko, *The Politicizing Presidency: The White House Personnel Office, 1948–1994* (Lawrence: University Press of Kansas, 1995).
2. Norman Ornstein, Thomas Mann, and Michael Malbin, *Vital Statistics on American Congress* (Washington, D.C.: American Enterprise Institute, 2000).

CHAPTER 3

FLOOR FIGHT

For all the time and attention that members of Congress and their staffs devote to their work in the committees of Congress, there remains a special reverence when a bill goes to the floor of either chamber. When Congress is in session, C-SPAN will be covering the floor proceedings live, gavel-to-gavel, and every congressional office will have their office television sets tuned to either the House or Senate channel. At any point in the day, you can look at the screen and see—well, not much going on. Usually, some member of the House or the Senate is speaking, but there will be few others in the chamber except for the managers of the floor proceedings hovering at the front of the room.

Still, due deference must always be paid. In the Senate, in particular, there are many rules regarding the floor. No cell phones allowed, which means that staffers must either have Blackberries or rush outside to the bank of phones to communicate with staff back at the office. Even the most senior staff aides cannot get on to the floor without their names on a list submitted by a senator's office. After the doorkeeper checks the list to make sure you are permitted, you receive a special badge that allows floor access, but you must surrender that badge whenever you leave the immediate area. Once inside the chamber, you still encounter doors that are guarded and beyond which even staff are not allowed. Even dress code matters. Word among staffers is that Sen. Robert C. Byrd of West Virginia, the oldest member of the Senate and a man who embodies its values and tradition, has been known to admonish staffers who are wearing a sport jacket and tie without matching pants. The place is intended to intimidate and awe, and it does so successfully.

In theory, anything can happen on the chamber floor, but most of the time there are few surprises. Congressional staffers spend a good portion of their days monitoring the floor of their chamber, waiting for something exciting to occur. The House, with its strong partisan ethic and majority rule, rarely sees any interesting action at all on the chamber floor. The Speaker and majority leader typically know they have the votes before they bring a bill to the floor. (Or they are bringing a bill to the floor that they know will fail in order to score a political point.) There may be a few amendments of interest that could go either way, or in a very close vote someone could switch and change the outcome, but generally not much is going to happen that isn't expected.

Chances are there will be far more activity in areas of the Capitol building surrounding the Senate floor, where both members and staff linger. The rooms you don't see on C-SPAN are the above-mentioned phone bank and the separate Republican and Democratic cloakrooms. The cloakrooms do not actually contain any coats, but it is the place where staff file amendments and senators retire out of public view. It is, in many ways, the real center of the action.

FLOOR PROCEDURE

Above and beyond the informal rules relevant to the floor of each chamber, the legislative process is guided by clearly established formal rules about floor procedure. These rules vary across the two chambers, but some similarities also exist. One key difference is the role of the presiding officer. In the House, considerable political and parliamentary powers enable the Speaker to retain strong control over floor proceedings. The Speaker also possesses powerful discretionary powers that give him or her latitude over a host of floor proceedings, including the recognition of members to speak on the floor.

In the Senate, where the Constitution formally charges the vice president to serve as presiding officer, a president pro tempore from the majority party is designated to manage proceedings in the vice president's absence. Generally, the president pro tempore appoints another colleague to serve as acting president pro tempore, and this member may appoint another to do the same. The duties of presiding officer are thus rotated to junior members of the majority party who manage proceedings for about an hour at a time.

Presiding officers in the Senate have far less control over proceedings. In the Senate, presiding officers must always recognize members to speak in the order they seek recognition, with members of the majority getting alternating preference. The presiding officer may not participate in the debate without relinquishing the gavel to another senator. And where the House Speaker (or his designee) typically rules on points of order without challenge, the presiding officer's rulings on points of order in the Senate are frequently appealed, then referred to the full chamber for resolution by a majority vote. Floor procedure in the House is governed by a large and consistent body of formal rules and procedures. Because the Senate operates more informally, it has a smaller and less consistent body of precedents than the House, and these often change over time.

Procedures for floor debate also differ across chambers. In the House, debate is usually time restricted. There is a standard "one hour" rule for floor debate on most amendments, with a "five minute rule" limiting any single member's debate time. Special rules can impose even tighter restrictions on floor debate for less controversial measures. In the Senate, meanwhile, there are no restrictions on floor debate and unless a supermajority of sixty senators vote to invoke "cloture" and shut off a filibuster, senators can talk ad infinitum.

In the House, most measures are actually considered by the "Committee of the Whole," which is in fact the whole House membership meeting under different rules. Before a bill comes to the floor, members vote on a rule for floor debate that determines which amendments will be considered and under what terms. The rule is written by the Rules Committee, which by tradition is heavily stacked in the majority's favor and led by the Speaker's handpicked chairman. Bills are usually amended by section or title. Debate usually ends by a majority vote.

In the Senate, by contrast, bills may be amended at any time, there is no limit to the number of amendments, and, unlike in the House, there is no germaneness requirement (except under a few specific circumstances). Floor debate in the Senate ends when a member yields the floor and no other member seeks recognition.

For this reason, a Senate debate is moderately more exciting. The minority party actually retains some power and can filibuster at any time. Even absent a filibuster, the prevailing courtesy of an unlimited debate in the Senate typically means that any senator who wants to speak will be able to. Although these are called "debates," it is unlikely that in the modern era any senator has ever actually been swayed by what another senator says publicly. It's possible to make a deal on the floor or in the cloakroom that could change the outcome of a vote, but these are usually the result of private conversations.

Most of the time, activity on the Senate floor consists of one of two things: (1) a so-called quorum call or (2) senators speaking on whatever issue they feel like. Quorum calls, in which the clerk slowly reads off the names of senators in alphabetical order, are used simply to stall for time as senators conduct the actual negotiations that will determine whether an amendment or bill comes to a vote or is passed. To the outside observer, or even to most staff members, this looks like nothing at all. Watch C-SPAN sometime and you will see how often the chamber is shown with a tired-looking young senator presiding while waiting for things to happen during a quorum call.

When senators do rise to speak, this typically does not mean that actual legislation is being discussed, or that senators are engaging in any great debate. Most of the time it means simply that a senator is taking advantage of free television time to expound on whatever issue he or she feels like. This most often takes place during a special "morning business" period set aside for such speeches, but it can also occur when a bill is stalled pending negotiation. The bill at hand may be on transportation, but a senator will use whatever time he can consume to speak on the war in Iraq. Some senators are brilliant orators. They get up, make their point succinctly, and leave. They hold your interest and can make you care about their issue. Other speeches are different. There are the boring, pointless speeches a senator might give when there is not much happening on the legislative agenda. The senator typically has a point when he takes the floor, but loses it somewhere along the way. Or perhaps the point will be rediscovered later on. It is easy to fall into this trap because few, if any, other senators are seated at their desks to listen. A senator can lose his audience and never notice because he has no visible audience to lose.

There is also the high-and-mighty tirade one might hear from the Senate floor. This popular form of speech occurs when a senator wants to oppose a bill or amendment for a morally ambiguous reason, but claims to oppose it for another reason. This form was very useful during the highway bill because the primary reason anyone would oppose the bill was that the senator wanted the home state to receive more funding. The highway bill was one massive pot of money, and each senator was trying to increase the share for his or her state as much as possible. But taking to the floor and blatantly crying for more money does not tend to win over anyone from any of the other forty-nine states, so most senators will look for something else objectionable about a bill like this one. Fearful of retribution, minority party members were unlikely to vocalize demands or complaints. However, if they were Republicans and thought they could maneuver for a bigger piece of the pie, they might be more likely to rise and complain about some other matter.

As a last resort, there is the time-killing nothingness speech. Senators are known for using this method when engaging in a filibuster, but it actually comes into play at other times as well. In the modern filibuster, senators rarely have to talk at all. Unlike Jimmy Stewart in *Mr. Smith Goes to Washington,* or the record-holding Strom Thurmond during the civil rights debate in the 1950s and 1960s, no senator any longer has to read from a phone book or recite poetry to keep a bill from coming to a vote. The minority party today can often conduct a filibuster simply by showing they have the votes necessary (41 out of 100) to maintain it. Only occasionally will the majority leader attempt to break a threatened filibuster by actually forcing the opponents to speak indefinitely. This is when the time-killing nothingness speech comes in most handy.

These speeches are also useful when senators are awaiting the results of back-room negotiations that will allow legislation to move forward. Suggesting the "absence of a quorum," which triggers a quorum call, is a practical way to stall for time, but sometimes, in order to maintain focus on the bill at hand, senators will continue to speak about the bill instead of waiting around doing nothing.

THE TRANSPORTATION BILL

When the transportation bill, now numbered S 1072, came to the floor of the Senate in February 2004, there was a lot of stalling of both kinds. There were numerous quorum calls and longwinded speeches on other issues. For example, immediately following the bill's introduction, both Bill Frist, the majority leader, and Tom Daschle, the minority leader, made opening statements about the bill. Then Daschle proceeded to discuss this vital item of business:

> Mr. President, I congratulate a South Dakota native, Adam Vinatieri, on yet another Super Bowl–winning field goal.

The Senate then proceeded immediately into a period of morning business, wherein the first speaker was Bob Graham of Florida. Senator Graham was running for president at the time and used the opportunity to make a speech about the war on terrorism. He was not interested in discussing the highway bill at that moment, even though he sat on the Environment and Public Works Committee, which wrote the bill. He had bigger fish to fry.

Part of the reason that the Senate proceeded to discuss issues such as field goal kickers and the war in Iraq is that the highway bill itself was at an impasse. Even though it had been brought to the floor, it was done so with the understanding that passing it would not be perfunctory. When the bill was called up for floor debate, the big four's secret funding formulas were finally inserted. This was done under a Senate rule that allows the committee chairman—in this case Oklahoma's James M. Inhofe—to change the bill as much as he likes after the committee markup so long as he has the consent of the committee. He does not even have to take a vote on it.* Now that the formulas were in there every senator knew what each state would be receiving under the bill, and not every senator was pleased.

---

*Interview with Ruth Van Mark, Deputy Staff Director, Environment and Public Works Committee, October 18, 2006.

Just because a particular state fared badly under the bill, however, did not mean that the bill would fail. It would take at least twenty-one unhappy states or forty-one unhappy senators to derail this legislation in the Senate. Moreover, the opponents would have to be senators who thought that by voting against the bill, they would not harm their own state even further. Every senator knew that a vote against the bill put a state at risk for losing even more money during the House-Senate conference negotiations to follow (the conference committee is discussed in the next chapter).

Table 3.1 shows the funding distribution as proposed under S 1072. Note that the states that fared the poorest tend to be larger states that had done well under past bills and were now seeing their funding taken away. These included New York (Sen. Daniel Patrick Moynihan had written ISTEA), Rhode Island (Sen. John Chafee had been chairman when TEA-21 was reauthorized), and Pennsylvania (Rep. Bud Shuster headed the House Transportation Committee under both ISTEA and TEA-21). Connecticut, Wisconsin, and Hawaii were convenient places from which to take funding—each had two Democratic senators and had fared well under previous bills. The only stranger on the list of states negatively affected was New Hampshire. This state not only had two Republican senators, but also it was not a very large state. Taking funding away from New Hampshire and making it a donor state in order to get to a 95 percent Minimum Guarantee for the other donor states was kind of like robbing the poor to give to the rich. It may not have been intentional on the part of the committee staff, but it would prove to be a thorn in the side of the bill as it progressed on the floor.

THE EQUITY BONUS

The transportation bill can be thought of as a huge pot of funding that all states were striving to get their hands on, except that there were some rules regarding how much each state could hope to acquire. No one would be able to pass a bill, for example, that gave 50 percent of the highway funding to 1 percent of the roads, which is practically what would happen if the chairmen from Alaska and Oklahoma had their druthers. In practical reality, you must get a majority of the populous (House) and a majority of the states (Senate) to buy into your legislative solution in order for the bill to pass. The transportation bill did serve an actual purpose—building

	TABLE 3.1	Proposed Distribution of Funding in S 1072

STATE	PERCENT INCREASE	2004 RATE OF RETURN	2009 RATE OF RETURN	CHANGE IN RATE OF RETURN
Connecticut	10%	134%	99%	−35 pts
Hawaii	17	196	162	−33
New Hampshire	19	103	95	−8
Pennsylvania	20	115	97	−17
New York	20	117	100	−17
Rhode Island	24	204	182	−22
Wisconsin	25	97	95	−2
Oregon	27	95	95	0
Minnesota	33	95	95	0
Massachusetts	33	95	95	0
Maine	33	95	95	0
Iowa	35	101	97	−4
Alabama	36	101	101	0
Alaska	36	572	572	0
Arkansas	36	98	98	0
Delaware	36	168	168	0
Idaho	36	136	136	0
Montana	36	220	220	0
Nevada	36	99	99	0
New Mexico	36	109	109	0
North Dakota	36	205	205	0
West Virginia	36	159	159	0
South Dakota	36	222	222	0
Kansas	36	103	99	−4
Missouri	37	95	95	0
Vermont	37	185	185	0
Indiana	37	95	95	0
Michigan	37	95	95	0
Illinois	37	95	95	0
Utah	38	95	95	0
Wyoming	38	135	135	0
Washington	39	94	95	1
Tennessee	39	94	95	1
Virginia	39	93	95	2
Ohio	39	93	95	2
Mississippi	39	93	95	2
Louisiana	39	92	95	3
Kentucky	39	92	95	3
Georgia	39	92	95	3
North Carolina	39	92	95	3
South Carolina	39	92	95	3
New Jersey	40	91	95	4
Florida	40	91	95	4

(continued)

TABLE 3.1	Proposed Distribution of Funding in S 1072 *(continued)*			
STATE	PERCENT INCREASE	2004 RATE OF RETURN	2009 RATE OF RETURN	CHANGE IN RATE OF RETURN
California	40	91	95	4
Maryland	40	91	95	4
Arizona	40	91	95	4
Nebraska	42	102	99	−4
Texas	42	91	95	4
Oklahoma	42	92	95	3
Colorado	47	91	95	4
District of Columbia	51	359	346	−13
Average	35%	128%	126%	−2%

and maintaining roads—that if left unfulfilled could cause some serious public backlash. However, once a basic funding threshold is met, and certain reasonable levels of in funding distribution are achieved, members of Congress can fight over the remainder of the booty.

This is the origin of the Minimum Guarantee provision that was such a big battle in ISTEA and TEA-21. The Minimum Guarantee was a device that allowed the bill crafters to toggle the funding levels at the fringes in a way that could benefit their own states while still satisfying enough other members to win passage in both chambers.

This explains why the Minimum Guarantee was no simple legislative provision. One might think that such a provision would be written with one line in the bill mandating that every state must receive at least 90.5 percent (the rate in TEA-21) of its gas tax contributions. Unfortunately, it cannot be that simple because the money to bring every state's revenue up to 90.5 percent must come from somewhere. If there is a finite amount of money in the bill you have to take money away from some states to bring others up to 90.5 percent. Which states do you take from? And how much do you take from each? Inevitably, there are winners and losers here, and whenever that happens you are likely to get a complicated formula. A formula allows those in power to designate winners and losers to their liking, without making the choices seem blatantly political. Instead of writing into the bill that they will be taking money from, say, Connecticut to increase the take for, say, Oklahoma, bill authors create an obfuscating formula that accomplishes the same goal. That's why the Minimum Guarantee language was probably the most complicated provision in the entire TEA-21 bill. It was much more than a prescriptive paragraph or two in the bill's legislative language—it was a funding program in and of itself. In fact, it was one of the largest programs in the entire transportation law.

Even that, one might assume, could be relatively simple to achieve: Just create a new pot of money and give it to the states that needed enough to receive at least 90.5 percent of their gas tax contributions. Alas, that would not work either. Remember, the Minimum Guarantee was based on each state's *percentage* contribution to the Highway Trust Fund. If you gave money to one state, you would affect the rate of return received by every other state. This means that the formula not only determined winners and losers, it did so quite arbitrarily. Funding for the Minimum Guarantee program was apportioned using an incredibly complicated formula that included, at its core, a list of numbers, one for each state, that were carefully calibrated to favor some states over others. The actual formulas were as complex as they were irrelevant—the bill writers created them to mask how they were choosing winners and losers. They simply found a mathematical way to arrive at the numbers they wanted in the first place.

In S 1072, chairmen Inhofe and Bond had very different priorities than those previous bill-crafters (Moynihan, Chafee, and Shuster). Inhofe had explicitly announced a goal of raising the minimum rate of return to 95 percent. This was a very ambitious goal, and Inhofe's staff soon figured out that it could not easily be accomplished through the existing Minimum Guarantee mechanism. The previous committee staff had structured the formula with very different goals—indeed, they wrote it to a large extent to reward the states that Inhofe now wanted to punish. But to work within the existing framework, Inhofe's staff would have had to decipher the old formula well enough to manipulate it and make it work for them in several different directions. That proved to be more difficult and complicated than anyone bargained for. So rather than change the formula, the committee staff came up with something easier to manipulate—a brand new funding system whereby they could create their own set of winners and losers. They called it the Equity Bonus.

The name "Equity Bonus" reflects an improved marketing consciousness on the part of the donor states. Instead of Minimum Guarantee, which sounded like something a used car salesman might say, Equity Bonus seemed to promote fairness for the deserving. In fact, Inhofe attempted to make the donor-donee debate a question of equity and fairness from the start, as did others in his boat. He maintained that it was unfair for the donor states to receive less than they contributed to the trust fund. Essentially, he was asserting that it was unfair to distribute funds based only on need. His position flew in the face of logic, to no small extent. What could be fairer than distributing federal funds based on need? But Inhofe wanted to steer the debate away from highway and transit needs—the expense side of the ledger—and instead turn the discussion to the issue of fairness and equity of tax contributions. Donor states were being treated unfairly and inequitably with respect to trust fund distribution, he argued, even if this had absolutely nothing to do with their need for highway dollars. It was this sense of unfairness that the name "Equity Bonus" sought to bring home to donor state senators.

The most important aspect of the Equity Bonus was Inhofe's ability to toggle each state's rate of return for each year of the bill's six-year lifespan. That way he could bring every state up to 95 percent—as promised—though not necessarily right away. Bringing every state to 95 percent in year one would have been impossible under available funding levels. By moving it upward each year, Inhofe could achieve his goal while still putting together a passable bill. Bigger states, such as Texas and Florida, would be brought up to 95 percent in the sixth year of the bill because they would cost the most to make whole. Smaller states— Oklahoma and Missouri, to cite just two obvious examples—could be brought up to 95 percent more rapidly. This allowed Inhofe to reach his goal and stay within sight of the budget.

The interesting thing about the Equity Bonus was that it made the real political goal of the Minimum Guarantee much more explicit. Both provisions were intended to satisfy donor states while also allowing the allocation of federal funds to proceed in a manner determined by those in power. But while the Minimum Guarantee maintained the illusion of objectivity by hiding its formula from all but the most persistent legislative aficionados, the Equity Bonus put the bill writers' biases right out in the open. In fact, it practically eliminated a formula altogether and simply focused on what everyone wanted to know—how much would each state get to increase its funding and rate of return? The Equity Bonus outlined specific guidelines for when donor states would reach a 95 percent rate of return. It also provided a minimum rate by which funding for every state—donee as well as donor—had to grow. That would protect donee states from the kind of pillaging that could derail the bill.

To be sure, the Equity Bonus was not entirely transparent. Inhofe decided against actually naming certain states in the legislation, using a proxy system instead. Rather than explicitly naming the states to be shielded from cuts in the rate of their funding growth, the committee staff found various statistics that would identify them anonymously. States with low population and low population density were exempted from the cuts, for example. This made some sense; there was no reason to plunder small donee states to feed large donor states since the amount of funding in play was insignificant. However, the legislation also eventually used the price of gas as well as accident fatality rates as delineators. Although one could logically justify using these statistics, they were chosen for a reason—to protect the states Inhofe was choosing to protect. Obviously, he had ignored other delineators that would have generated a different funding picture.

BILL FINANCING

If it seems like the spending side of the bill required some fancy footwork, get ready for the tap dancing that went on to make the financing portion come together. As we discussed in Chapter 1, the revenue debate was a threshold issue for everyone involved—not least President Bush. Even if Congress could get the president to agree to a higher level of funding in the bill, declining revenues in the Highway Trust Fund meant that Congress could no longer rely on gas taxes to cover the cost of the bill for six years. To fund the bill at a level that would cover all the bases necessary to garner a majority vote, Congress was going to have to come up with some other source of funding.

One strategy already tried and failed was to pillage the Mass Transit Account to pay for highways. Dawn Levy's brainstorm had failed because there were too many strong transit voices still alive in the Senate, so the Finance Committee staff had to come up with another solution. They used all their ingenuity and tricks of the trade to come up with a hodgepodge of various revenue sources, none of which accomplished much on its own, but when loaded into one grab bag, they looked like they would make a difference. They were the following:

- **Gasohol Change.** A blend of gasoline and ethanol that has some arguable environmental benefits, gasohol at the time was being taxed at a reduced rate relative to regular gasoline. Also, a portion of the tax on gasohol was being transferred to the general fund instead of the Highway Trust Fund. Inhofe's bill proposed to maintain the reduced rates but ensure that all revenue from taxes on gasohol would go into the trust fund. Moreover, he proposed to cover the gap between the reduced rate on gasohol and the rate of taxation on normal gas by appropriating funds from the general fund.

- **Tax Evasion.** The bill included several strategies, recommended by the Department of Transportation, to combat fuel tax evasion. It also proposed continuing the Highway Use Tax Evasion program, which provides funds for enforcement efforts, to bring more scofflaws to justice.

- **Spending down the Balance.** Previous transportation laws had always assumed that revenues from the Highway Trust Fund would either match or exceed spending needs. Conventional wisdom among transportation experts presumed that it was wise to maintain a surplus balance in the trust fund, although no one ever knew what that balance would be in any given year (estimates ranged from $8 billion to $20 billion). S 1072 stipulated, for the first time, that this surplus would be spent down in order to fully fund the legislation. In other words, it cleared the way for spending more funds than current revenue projections would otherwise allow. The bill authors were able to get away with this because previous legislation had accomplished the opposite and spent less than projected revenues.

For a bill that totaled $318 billion, these new financing mechanisms were relatively small change. Although increased vigilance on tax evasion was politically innocuous, it was also the least valuable of the three strategies. The other, more lucrative strategies posed some political obstacles. The gasohol maneuver essentially meant taking money from the general fund to spend on highways. Spending down the balance was clearly a stopgap solution that could not be employed more than once. Neither of these strategies was popular, but most senators, even self-proclaimed fiscal conservatives, could accept them as long as their states were happy with their take from the bill. The problem was that there were those who still were not so happy.

SENATE DEBATE—OPPOSITION

There were precious few senators who could afford to oppose this bill. Democrats, in particular, were stuck between a rock and a hard place, so many of them were content to capitulate and be glad they got anything. They knew that their states' take from the bill could have been—and still could be—plundered by Republicans and that it would be very difficult to stop them.

This may seem odd because this bill was such a regional piece of legislation. One would think that regional coalitions would stay together and fight for their mutual interests. But there is a big difference between having the same interests, and having the same leverage with which to fight for those interests. Senators from Arizona and California, for example, had much in common in this bill. Both were donor states from the Sunbelt that had experienced rapid growth in the past twenty years. Both had high populations and relied heavily on automobiles over transit, which meant their citizens paid copious amounts of federal gas taxes. Both would stand to gain from an increase in the minimum rate of return from the trust fund.

Yet Arizona had two Republican senators, and California had two Democratic senators, one sitting on the Environment and Public Works Committee. This meant that Arizona had the leverage to wage this battle, and California had little incentive to step in and fight with them. Arizona could afford to take on the White House and Chairman Inhofe. Both the president and the chairman would want to see their Republican colleagues reelected in Arizona, and would not want to put their reelections at risk by raiding their highway funds. The president and the chairman, on the other hand, would not think twice about punishing California and slighting it on high-priority projects once the bill reached conference. California senators might be able to support Arizona when the bill came to a vote—maybe—but they certainly were not going to get up and start raising a fuss now, especially after California's Barbara Boxer had voted to approve the bill in committee.

Few other Republicans had reason to oppose the bill. The only senators who would stand in the way were likely to come from states that did not do well under the formulas. "Doing well" for the most part could be defined as growing their funding at the same rate as the average rate of growth for all states, or better. The big four had structured the growth rate of the bill so that most of the states below the average growth rate were represented by Democratic senators. However, the big four could not do this perfectly. The nature of the past winners and losers, along with the need to provide for some actual highway needs, meant that winners and losers could not be chosen individually. Unavoidably, it turned out, some Republican states took a hit. A look at the first Senate vote regarding the bill reveals a great deal about whose ox got gored.

The First Filibuster

Because the Senate majority leader has no way to strong-arm legislation through the chamber (unlike in the House), the Senate functions largely on the basis of comity and mutual accommodation. One of the main tools the majority leader uses to get things done on the floor is the unanimous consent request. He simply asks for unanimous consent to proceed to the next bill. While this means than any one senator can put up a roadblock, the minority leader and his colleagues typically put up no objection in order to avoid a roll call vote on such a minor point. They know they will need similar accommodations from their opponents if they ever win control of the Senate, and they also recognize that the majority leader could get the votes to proceed if he is determined to do so.

However, if senators want to make a point they can object to a "UC" request and force a vote on a motion to proceed. They may know that doing so will not stop the bill from moving forward, but at the very least they can stall the process and make it clear to the leadership that the states in question are not happy. The leadership then has to choose whether to accommodate the opponents in order to move the process along, or push through and make them pay for their obstructionism.

Once the details of the funding in the transportation bill became available, the senators who thought they got a raw deal were going to have to devise a strategy by which they could improve their lot. The average bill before the Senate divides along partisan lines. The majority party by nature is trying to push through its agenda, and therefore confronts the minority party doing what it can to thwart that agenda. The minority tends not to do annoying things like object to UC requests unless the bill to be debated is a hot-button issue on which they think they can win over public opinion. The same goes for a filibuster threat. Minority senators may rant and rave about a bill and how terrible it is for the republic, but they will be careful and selective about when they employ the few levers of power at their disposal.

The transportation bill was different. It was not as divisive along party lines as it was on regional lines, so a number of Republicans were opposed to the bill. Unlike their Democratic colleagues, they were not so reluctant to employ obstructionist tactics normally used by the minority side. They naturally wanted to avoid angering their party's leadership and the White House, but their first responsibility had to belong to their own constituents and to their own self-preservation, or else they might not have party leaders to anger. This meant that Republicans could object to Majority Leader Frist's first UC request on S 1072, namely that it come to the floor for debate and amendment. This objection meant that the Senate had to debate and vote on whether to consider the bill. The opposition used this debate to create their first filibuster, which, in turn, forced Frist to file a cloture petition to shut off debate. A cloture petition takes two days to "ripen," as they say in the Senate, meaning that the bill was temporarily put on ice right from the start even though it was clear that Frist had the 60 votes he needed to proceed.

You can tell a lot about the opposition to the bill by looking at the senators who voted against the cloture vote (it prevailed, 75–11, with 14 abstentions). Here are the states where senators voted "no," and the likely reason:

- **Hawaii.** Democrat Daniel K. Akaka voted against cloture, although fellow Democrat Daniel K. Inouye did not. Hawaii received only a 17 percent increase in funding, less than half of the bill average (35 percent). It is possible that Inouye, as a senior member of the Commerce and Science Committee, did not want to oppose the transportation bill, while Akaka, a more junior member, felt he could take a stand against something that would be bad for Hawaii.

- **Connecticut.** Democrat Christopher J. Dodd voted against cloture because Connecticut received the lowest increase of any of the fifty states (10 percent). The probable reason Joseph I. Lieberman, still a Democrat at that time, did not vote against the bill was because he was busy campaigning for president and thus was absent.

- **Wisconsin.** The state fared rather poorly under the bill with only 25 percent growth, prompting both Democratic senators, Russ Feingold and Herb Kohl, to oppose it.

- **Florida.** Though a huge donor state, Democrat Bob Graham was not planning to run for reelection (unlike fellow Floridian Bill Nelson, also a Democrat, who voted in favor of cloture) so he could afford to take a stand for Florida in the hopes that someone might pick him as a vice presidential candidate who might carry the state for the Democrats.

- **New Hampshire.** The state fared poorly under the bill with only 19 percent growth, and it is conservative enough to support politicians who object to pork-barrel spending on the basis of fiscal austerity. Both Republican senators, Judd Gregg and John E. Sununu, voted against cloture.

- **Texas.** Texas was a huge donor state and Republican Kay Bailey Hutchison could afford to fight for more, so she voted against cloture. John Cornyn, a GOP freshman who sat on Environment and Public Works, was unlikely to take up the same fight; he voted in favor.

- **Arizona.** Arizona was also a huge donor state, and Republican John McCain had consistently put himself forward as an opponent of large government spending bills like this one. He also had an eye toward future presidential aspirations. His GOP colleague, Jon Kyl, also voted against cloture.

- **Pennsylvania.** The state did very poorly (only 20 percent) growth, in part because it had fared disproportionately well in past years under House Chairman Shuster. Arlen Specter, a moderate Republican, voted against cloture. Rick Santorum, a more ideological conservative and a member of the Senate leadership, voted to shut off debate.

As this collection of opposition voters shows, an accidental coalition formed here among states that received low percentage increases in funding, typically donee states that had done well in previous bills (Connecticut, Pennsylvania, and Hawaii), and large donor states that could have done better (Arizona, Florida, and Texas). Democrats seemed more willing to vote against the bill if they were donee states than donor states— note that California, a very large donor state, saw neither of its Democratic senators vote against the bill.

The opposition lost the cloture vote on the motion to proceed, as they probably knew they would. They had demonstrated their anger, and their numbers included several Republicans, so they were still a force to be reckoned with. Nonetheless, they still needed a new strategy if they wanted to defeat the bill. They soon found one.

THE STRENGTH OF A RIDER

The opposition Republicans knew they would lose a filibuster, and they knew that all the debating in the world wasn't going to change that. They also could not adopt the strategy of adding more money to the bill because President Bush had threatened to veto a bill that exceeded his spending limit. Therefore, their only strategy was to go after their own colleagues in the Senate and make it difficult for them to continue with the bill.

They did this by offering an amendment to the bill. Not surprisingly, the impetus came from the one state that was being punished for no apparent reason: New Hampshire. Republican Judd Gregg led the charge. A former governor and future chairman of the Senate Budget Committee, Gregg was serving his second term in the Senate and was up for reelection in 2004. He rose to speak against the bill and condemned the fact that it allowed for spending out of the general fund, not just the Highway Trust Fund. He expressed his opposition along these lines in part because it seemed to carry more weight than if he had simply complained that New Hampshire was getting the short end of the stick. In fact, Gregg was a true fiscal conservative and felt responsible for protecting the Treasury against deficit spending. However, at the conclusion of his remarks, Gregg made a move that on its face had nothing to do with either New Hampshire's parochial interests or the nation's fiscal health. Quite suddenly, he offered an amendment entitled the "Public Safety Employer-Employee Cooperation Act of 2003." This clearly non-germane amendment seemed like it came from out of nowhere, but it certainly threw a wrench in the carefully laid plans of the GOP leadership.

Gregg was the current chairman of the Health, Labor, Education, and Pensions Committee. So he took this opportunity to propose an amendment that called for police officers and firefighters to be permitted to organize for the purposes of collective bargaining. His amendment had no relationship whatsoever to the transportation bill, though Gregg tried to act as if it did. He was able to offer the language as a "second-degree" amendment, which, under parliamentary rules did not have to be germane to the bill. This one surely was not.

The amendment effectively halted progress on the bill. Missouri's Christopher S. Bond observed that it was indeed irrelevant, but then discussed it no further. In fact, the merits of this particular amendment were never debated. Gregg probably did not intend for it to be discussed—he merely wanted to halt progress on the transportation bill.

The dilemma Gregg presented to his GOP colleagues was that the party leadership did not want to have to go on record for or against it. Philosophically, the last thing they wanted was to allow collective bargaining for policemen and firefighters. But politically, no Republican wanted to be on record opposing such a move. They could not be seen as anti-police and anti-firefighter, especially so soon after September 11 and certainly not in an election year. But neither could they vote for it. They were stuck. The Republicans could not allow the bill to go forward unless Gregg agreed to withdraw the amendment.

In many ways, this is what makes the Senate so entertaining to an impartial observer. Using the rules of the Senate, New Hampshire's Gregg had single-handedly derailed a $318 billion spending bill. In order for this bill to go any farther, Gregg and any other opposing Republican would have to be accommodated.

A WAITING GAME

With the bill temporarily on hold, Senate staffers could do little except wait. The initial flurry of excitement from seeing *their* bill finally come to the floor of the Senate had suddenly waned. That excitement was now replaced by boredom, from watching the World's Greatest Deliberative Body, as the U.S. Senate is widely known, fumble around while private negotiations took place behind closed doors.

The Republican leadership needed to find a way to quell the opposition and persuade Gregg to withdraw his amendment. In the meantime they had to keep something—anything—happening on the floor to make it appear that the Senate was conducting the nation's business. Chairman Inhofe pleaded with senators to come to the floor with their amendments, but no one would budge. Instead, Inhofe was reduced to discussing various portions of the bill to an empty chamber. Hour by hour, day by day, he would discuss another section of the bill and try to relate its importance to the C-SPAN audience. The only break from the inertia was another droning quorum call. There was little else he could do.

Senators' personal staffs were holding off on bringing amendments to the floor until they saw the results of the standoff. They did not want to put their bosses on the line making speeches for or against controversial amendments, only to find that the entire bill was going to be derailed or completely changed in back room negotiations. So, instead, they waited for several days, listening passively to Inhofe's speeches and waiting through countless quorum calls to see if anything might breathe new life into the bill's fate.

A few things did happen. Inhofe had some of his colleagues relieve him and speak on transportation issues relevant to their states but otherwise meaningless to the Senate at large. Various senators wandered into the chamber to bring up other issues, and the Senate meandered through other pressing issues. The Senate took time out to confirm a low-level judicial nominee by a 96–0 vote. There was discussion of the Iraq war intelligence, Medicare, Cuba, gay marriage, Mad Cow Disease, and District of Columbia schools. Meanwhile, staff continued to wait.

AN AMENDMENT APPEARS

Although the major impasse was still not resolved, two senators finally came up with an amendment that they could submit even before the core funding issues were settled. This was only because they had an amendment about policy, not funding.

In this case, two senators from the Environment and Public Works Committee put forward the amendment. They had held off on offering it in committee because their calculation was that they had a better chance of passing it on the floor. The bill would make primary seat-belt laws practically a necessity by withholding safety funding from states that did not pass them. Primary seat-belt laws enable police officers to pull a car over if the only driving infraction is that the driver is not wearing a seat belt. Many states have only secondary seat-belt laws—these allow a driver to be ticketed for not wearing a seat belt if the driver is pulled over for some other reason. Some data suggest that states with primary seat-belt laws have much higher compliance rates. A great deal of data suggest that most traffic fatalities happen to drivers not wearing seat belts.

The two senators offering the amendment, John Warner of Virginia and Hillary Rodham Clinton of New York, were ideal cosponsors. They both sat on the Environment and Public Works Committee. They were both from states that already had primary seat-belt laws and thus would not be seen at home as trying to regulate new laws for their own states. Finally, they were from opposing parties, giving the amendment a bipartisan flavor.

The political calculus in offering this amendment was simple. Neither senator had much to lose by offering it, since they could not be accused of partisan politics or of trying to secure more funding for their own states. Whether the amendment passed or failed, both would be seen as trying to do something for driver safety, and who doesn't want to be seen that way?

One might wonder why any senator would oppose such an amendment. The argument put forward against adoption was that states should take responsibility for their own safety laws—the federal government should leave this to the states. Of course, the entire transportation bill was full of regulations that withheld or distributed funding to states based on federal mandates, but none had come up for such a clear-cut vote.

This states' rights argument was most likely a front, but no matter. The amendment failed. To avoid a direct vote on the amendment, which might force senators to vote against safety, leadership pulled a routine procedural move: they moved to "table" the amendment, which is a parliamentary euphemism for killing it. In most senators' eyes, voting to table an amendment is more palatable than voting against it. Voting against this amendment would have put a senator on the record as opposing increased seat-belt use, and there were obvious disadvantages to that. Voting to table the amendment, on the other hand, could be construed as voting to postpone it until a later date, which is not quite as bad as opposing it outright. The fact is, however, that once tabled, an amendment almost never resurfaces. The Warner-Clinton amendment was tabled (killed) by a vote of 57–41.

MOVING FORWARD, FINALLY

The rebellious senators were in a good position. Time was on their side. The Senate leadership could not allow weeks of Senate sessions to go by with the bill on the floor and not moving anywhere. The bill's sponsors certainly did not want the bill to carry on for very long—indeed, it was important to them to get the bill done before the President's Day recess, which would begin on February 13. If the bill was not passed by that date, it would likely die. The rebels would win.

On the other hand, the leadership was not about to make peace with the rebellious senators immediately. They probably could have come out and given them a huge chunk of money for special projects right at the beginning, thus moving the bill forward. But they needed to drive the price down, and this took time. It was a game of chicken, where neither side stood to do well if no agreement was reached. That meant a compromise was both necessary and likely.

Unfortunately, we will never know exactly what that compromise was, because it happened at a very secretive, members-only level. It is very likely that New Hampshire's Gregg and the other rebellious senators were assured, however discreetly, that their states would benefit from allowing the bill to move forward. This may have been done with special projects money, or perhaps with some blatant vote trading. All we know is that the deal was done.

Once that happened, the floodgates opened. Leadership filed a petition for cloture on the bill, which, if successful, meant that debate on the bill would come to an end and any amendments would have to be germane to transportation. This forced senators to file their amendments rapidly. The vote to shut off debate, held on February 12, was a landslide, 86–11. Once again, we can glean some insight from the senators voting against cloture:

- **Nevada.** The state actually did very well under the bill and Democrat Harry Reid, one of the big four, played a large role in shaping the bill as ranking member on the Transportation Subcommittee. However, Republican John Ensign voted against the bill. One can interpet this to mean that Ensign believed he could take credit for Reid's parochial largesse while also taking a stand as a conservative Republican against pork-barrel spending.

- **Wisconsin.** Both Democrats Feingold and Kohl voted against cloture. Whatever deal other Republican opponents got was probably much better than what was offered Wisconsin, assuming Wisconsin was offered anything at all.

- **New Hampshire.** Gregg had led the rebellion and probably got a deal for himself, but even so he still needed to register discontent with the bill to be fiscally consistent. Sununu also voted against cloture in support of his state and fellow senator.

- **Texas.** Hutchison voted against, continuing to oppose a bill that she viewed as unfair to her donor state.

- **Arizona.** Kyl and McCain continued their opposition against both special projects and the perceived unfairness to donor states.

- **Pennsylvania.** Santorum did not vote against the original cloture motion on proceeding to the bill. Perhaps he felt it was wrong to obstruct debate in that case. But ultimately he could not vote for a bill that damaged Pennsylvania so badly. This time, both he and Specter voted against this cloture motion.

- **South Carolina.** Democrat Ernest F. Hollings voted against cloture. One explanation is that he was the ranking member of the Commerce Committee and disagreed with the safety provisions.

THE AMENDMENT FLURRY

Once the Gregg amendment was disposed of, floor action proceeded apace. Amendments began to pour in. The process was an interesting yet efficient one. Staffers would come down to the cloakroom with amendments they wanted their senators to offer. Then staffers from the committee, who were spearheading the bill on the floor, would decide if they could accept these amendments into the manager's package. If they did so, this would mean automatic acceptance of the amendments. Any amendments they refused to accept would die unless a senator wanted to force the issue and bring it to the floor for a vote. The senator and staff would have to calculate whether it was worth spending the political capital to force the entire Senate to vote on their amendment.

Sometimes a senator might decide to bring an amendment to the floor and discuss it, but then withdraw it without a vote. This would happen if the senator wanted to make sure it was discussed publicly, creating a "legislative history" for the idea, but knew it was going to be hard to win a majority vote. Other times there might be some negotiation on the amendment so that it could be accepted in the manager's package. Floor discussion or the threat of a vote could potentially help negotiations along.

The only three amendments brought to a vote were just the last vestiges of the rebellion, the sponsors trying vainly to make a point. The first amendment to come up, for example, was a simple attempt by the big donor states trying to boost their rate of return. It was sponsored by Texas's Hutchison, who was both a Republican and from one of the largest donor states, and thus the most logical person to offer the amendment. She was not afraid to go after the Interstate Performance and Maintenance account. IPAM, as you recall from the previous chapter, was an ambiguous and yet "untouchable" part of the bill that committee staffers had hinted would be used as a sort of slush fund for special projects. Hutchison's amendment called instead for distributing those funds to donor states.

The amendment was an ideal way for the donor states to express their displeasure with the bill. Winning approval from the full Senate was unlikely because everyone knew that committee leaders had earmarked the IPAM money for buying off key votes of recalcitrant senators from donor states. So donee states had absolutely no reason to support the amendment because they were not going to get any money from it anyway. Donor states would only be likely to support it if they thought they were going to do poorly when the time came to dole out special project money, or if they were big states like Texas and stood to gain substantially from this amendment. The only senators supporting Hutchison were from the very largest donor states (Texas, California, Florida, Wisconsin, Indiana, Michigan, and Arizona). The amendment fell in a landslide, 17–78.

Next up was another prong in the donor states' attack. If they were going to lose their rebellion, they certainly were going to gain whatever political mileage they could from taking a stand against the bill. Arizona's McCain raised a point of order against the bill on the grounds that its cost exceeded the limit allowed by the budget that Congress had approved earlier in the year. Supporters of the bill needed sixty votes to waive the budget rules and allow the bill to use a small amount of spending from general revenue as called for in the gasohol switch.

McCain calculated that it was worth it for him to take a principled stand against deficit spending and force senators to a vote. He knew he could make his point without suffering any serious consequences because of his stature in the Senate and popularity among the general public. Also, given his public opposition to special projects, he probably didn't care if his state was left out when it came to distributing the pork.

He also had to know that the vote would fail miserably. The Senate voted overwhelmingly to waive its budget rules, 72–24.

Following McCain was his fellow Arizonan, Jon Kyl, with a similarly themed amendment. Kyl would have reduced overall spending in the bill to the level deemed acceptable by the president ($256 billion). Getting senators to vote to reduce spending on anything, much less highways, would be an uphill battle and Kyl knew it. He also knew the Senate had already given its blessing to busting the budget, and the two cloture votes showed there was plenty of support for the bill as written by the committee. But he wanted to make the point yet again, and as a Republican from Arizona, he could afford to do so. Predictably, his amendment went down, 20–78.

Several other amendments were adopted underneath the radar as part of the bill manager's package. It worked this way: Committee staff would consider whether they could reasonably adopt an amendment without damaging their goals or angering a sufficient number of other senators. Then staff would run the amendment by the leadership and certain senators who refused to allow anything in a manager's amendment that they did not read personally. Committee staff would circulate the amendment among the Senate staff standing guard on the floor who might, if they could read it quickly enough, persuade a senator to object. The committee staff attitude at this point was to accept as many amendments as possible. They knew that these amendments would win votes for passage and, if any were truly objectionable, could be quietly dispensed with in conference.*

Deals were being made at a rapid pace as staff from the committee tried to accommodate as many senators as possible. In the end, very few staff members—and even fewer senators—could know exactly what was in the manager's package. There was nowhere near enough time to examine each amendment accepted. Much of the work and analysis that had come before in committee—crafting amendments with care and making sure that senators voted properly on each one—was now being thrown out the window. Instead, amendments were rapidly accepted as the clock ticked away. The vote on final passage had to happen soon before the Senate adjourned for the February recess, and staff was fighting against that deadline. In the end, most staff and their bosses had to take it on faith that their amendments were accepted into the manager's package, and hope that amendments they did not like were kept out.

Both staff and senators could harbor this faith because they knew their party leaders had incentive to help them out. For example, Nevada's Reid, who was the minority whip as well as ranking member on the Transportation Subcommittee, was not likely to sell out a Democratic senator and endanger that person's reelection chances. Reid and his staff were able to keep on top of all the amendments along with the Republicans. The only conflict that might arise was if Reid felt obliged to sell out another state for his own state's benefit.

Such an issue did arise. Reid decided to serve himself a bit of pork by shifting a small portion of the research funding in the bill from New York

---

*Interview with Ruth Van Mark, deputy staff director, Environment and Public Works Committee, October 18, 2006.

to Nevada. He did this simply by changing the name of the university receiving the funds, which were for earthquake-related research, from the University of Buffalo to the University of Nevada, Reno. It was a small switch of a relative small amount of money ($2.5 million), and no one would have noticed it except that officials from the University of Buffalo were wisely checking to make sure their money was in the bill. Reid had made the secretive switch during the committee markup via the chairman's package presented there. Now the New York senators had finally discovered it and wanted it reversed in the floor manager's package. Furious negotiations ensued. The parties reached a last-minute compromise, splitting the baby and distributing the money 50–50 between the two schools.

In the end, on February 12, S 1072 passed overwhelmingly, 76–21. The votes against it remained in line with the level of opposition that had existed all along. Congratulatory speeches were given all around as senators patted themselves on the back for finally completing the legislation. They were very happy with themselves. Of course, they all knew that everything could change in conference.

THE HOUSE BILL

The bill that Alaska's Don Young had wanted to push out of his Transportation and Infrastructure Committee was a huge challenge to the president. The chairman wanted to raise the gas tax and send a $375 billion bill to the House. This would have allowed him to scrounge up a ton of special project money for his state while satisfying both the donor and donee states. Unfortunately for Young, the president had put the kibosh on that idea post-haste.

The administration was so strong at that moment that the House, where party affiliation and loyalty matters to a much greater extent than in the Senate, was almost certain to adhere to the president's wishes. This meant, at a minimum, keeping the bill at a funding level low enough to prevent raising the gas tax. Keeping the funding level that low would make passing a bill with a 95 percent Minimum Guarantee very difficult. Majority Leader Tom DeLay, hailing from Texas, clearly wanted to push for the 95 percent benchmark but backed off in the face of White House threats. Chairman Young could care less about the Minimum Guarantee as long as he could secure more money than anyone else for high-priority projects. So he reached an agreement with DeLay to send through a bill, HR 3550, at $275 billion.

To be sure, $275 billion was a lot less than the $375 billion blockbuster Young had originally proposed. It was still more than the $256 billion put forward by the administration. The White House was threatening publicly to veto anything over their targeted level of funding, but $275 billion was so close that Young and DeLay figured they could get away with it. They proposed maintaining the Minimum Guarantee at the same level it had been under TEA-21 (90.5 percent). Donee states were baffled at their good fortune. They knew they did not have the votes to prevent an increase in the Minimum Guarantee, and could not understand how they had won.*

THE MINIMUM GUARANTEE

Of course, it could not be that simple. Tom DeLay did not earn the nickname of the "Hammer" because he let other people push him around. Even if it were the president who was doing the pushing, DeLay was not going to take it lying down. He worked with Young to include two provisions that kept hope alive for the donor states. Both were cleverly worded yet obviously self-serving at the same time.

The first concept was to fiddle with the "scope" of the Minimum Guarantee provision. When this concept first started floating around congressional offices, staffers struggled to determine what it could possibly mean. This is one of those strange instances on Capitol Hill where a provision is framed in such an odd manner that it isn't immediately clear what the intention of its creator might be. Even if the staff realized how clever it was, they still faced the difficult task of explaining it to their bosses. If their bosses could not understand it well enough to know why they should oppose it, the provision could survive.

The scope of the Minimum Guarantee program refers to which transportation programs would be included in the calculations of each state's minimum rate of return. Recall that other major programs to be reauthorized by the bill included the Surface Transportation program, inter-

---

*Interview with Amy Chiang, deputy chief of staff for Sherwood Boehlert, R-N.Y., October 17, 2006.

state maintenance, national highway system, and others. The Minimum Guarantee payout is determined, in part, by how many of these programs are included in the funding equation. Generally speaking, if more programs fall under the scope of the Minimum Guarantee, the donor states will do better because their payouts will be calculated based on more of the available funding in the bill.

Strangely enough, the House bill decided to move several programs *outside* the scope of the Minumum Guarantee. This seemingly favored the donee states, which would seem totally unnecessary in a bill that maintained the same rate-of-return requirement as TEA-21. The donee states had already gotten what they needed, so what were Young and DeLay thinking?

They were thinking that Minimum Guarantee is chump change compared to High Priority Projects. These are the soul of the transportation bill for House members. The Senate may show some disregard for pork-barrel spending, but only because a number of senators can afford to. House members live or die by special projects for their districts—or at least many of them perceive that to be true—and High Priority Projects are some of the juiciest pork projects around. The most money for special projects goes to the most powerful members of the House, and those same members get to decide which other members get a piece of the pie and how big a slice.

By taking High Priority Projects out of the scope of the Minimum Guarantee, House leaders were giving themselves more power to decide the winners and losers in the transportation bill. If donor state representatives complained about the 90.5 percent minimum, they could be mollified with a few more big projects and in the end come out even better than if they insisted on an increase in the minimum rate of return. By moving the High Priority Projects outside the scope, increases to its funding did not require accompanying increases in the overall funding to keep donee states whole. Members could be swayed for much less.

The second concept was to include a "re-opener" provision. This concept was far from subtle, and the White House did not take kindly to it. Recall that this bill was moving through Congress in early 2004, a presidential election year. There was no guarantee that Bush would still be in office come 2005. The re-opener automatically cut off all non-safety related program funding in the bill in 2005, effectively shutting down funding for U.S. surface transportation, if Congress did not act by then to make sure the Minimum Guarantee was increased. The provision even stipulated the levels of increase that were required: Minimum Guarantee had to hit 92 percent by 2006 and rise by one percentage point each year thereafter.

The provision was entirely dependent on the ability of the next Congress to find more funding to pay for the increases. But it was also clearly dependent on having another president in office. For obvious reasons the White House did not see this as a positive development and threatened a presidential veto based on this provision alone.

HOUSE DEBATE

House debate is very different from the Senate in that things move very quickly. There are no quorum calls. There is no time for the kind of rambling speeches that prevail in the Senate. Speakers are severely limited by time and need to be careful in choosing what they have to say. HR 3550 was brought to the House floor on April 1, 2004, less than two months after the Senate had passed its version.

As we've already seen from previous transportation bills, the official name for a piece of legislation is often cleverly—or too cleverly, if you are of that mindset—crafted. A good bill name forms an acronym that makes it easy to remember. Once ISTEA established the tea metaphor for transportation bills, bill sponsors could not contain themselves. Both ISTEA and TEA-21 scored high points for being easy to remember, both as acronyms and for mentioning positive things like "equity" in their names. However, the popular summer beverage has little to do with transportation or highways, so when SAFETEA came along, it added a new dimension to the bill and made for a resonant moniker.

Don Young didn't care much about that. He knew that this bill was not a marginal one that would stand or fall by its name. There was too much money at stake for Congress to pass up. He could call it COFFEE if he wanted to and it would still pass easily if the funding allocations were agreeable to enough members. Even so, Young wanted to put his personal stamp on the bill, so he decided to name it after his wife, Lu. He continued to hold onto the tea theme, so he came up with the "Transportation Equity Act—A Legacy for Users." That's right: TEA-LU.

During floor debate, House members spent much of their allotted time lamenting the fact that the bill was too small. Most representatives, especially the Democrats, would have preferred to defy the White House and put forward a bigger bill. But now that the Senate had passed a bill much larger than the $256 billion limit set by President Bush, House GOP leaders had to fall in line or risk embarrassing their leader in the White House.

What had taken the Senate two weeks took the House two days. On April 2, the bill passed easily on a 357–65 vote. There were several amendments along the way, as allowed by the Rules Committee, but any representatives hoping to change the outcome of the bill knew that their chances were slim to none. They also knew that the Senate had already passed a bill that got the Minimum Guarantee to 95 percent, if only by slight of hand. Members from donor states figured they would improve their lot in conference and that Tom DeLay would look out for them there, so they had little reason to attack the bill on the floor. Meanwhile, members from donee states figured that at least they had done better in this bill than in the Senate bill.

Opposition to anything in the House must be more cautious. Any rebellion by Republicans like the one in the Senate would have led to severe punishments. Only Democrats could have rebelled with impunity, but this was not a party-line issue and many Democrats were more than happy with what their districts would receive under the House bill. Rebellion would have required a large coalition of Republicans and Democrats from aligned groups of states. With Republicans more or less shoved out of the picture by party loyalties, and several Democrats happy with what they got, such coalition building was unlikely to emerge.

ON TO CONFERENCE

The House and Senate battles over the transportation bill illustrate some key differences between the two bodies. Certainly the Senate is slower, more deliberative, its members more independent. The House can move quickly, rolling over the opposition, and is more likely to go along with the ruling majority's party line. Both chambers managed to pass very large transportation bills, even if the House version was smaller and more aligned with administration policy.

The differing bills that emerged from the House and Senate were the respective bids of each chamber on what would eventually become the nation's surface transportation bill. Now negotiators from each side would have to get together to create one unified piece of legislation. The conference process, where the real bill would be configured, came next.

4

CONFERENCE

THE "THIRD HOUSE"

The U.S. Constitution requires bills to pass in identical format in both chambers of Congress before they can be sent to the White House for the president's signature. When differences between measures passed by each chamber must be reconciled, one option is to form a conference committee, where representatives from each chamber meet to iron out their differences. (See Appendix 1 for examples of how conference committees reconcile differences between the two chambers in the conference report it issues.) Roger H. Davidson, Walter J. Oleszek, and Frances E. Lee observe that most public laws clear Congress without conferences.[1] Indeed, roughly 70 percent of laws that are initiated in one chamber pass the other chamber without any changes. Twenty percent of measures shuttle back and forth between chambers until both agree on the final wording. Only about 10 percent of measures passed by Congress go through bicameral reconciliation by conference committee. Once there, however, conference committees can exert considerable influence over the eventual content of legislation. For that reason, they are an integral part of the legislative process. Some analysts go so far as to call conference committees "the third house of Congress."[2]

Despite the influential role conference committees can play in shaping legislation, these panels operate with far less transparency than other parts of the legislative process. There is no transcript of a conference committee's proceedings, for instance. Most of the real negotiations take place behind doors closed to the public and the news media. Often the real decisions are left to party leaders or their designees. And while the rules stipulate that conference committees must stay within the "scope" of the two versions of the bill they are considering, it is not uncommon for provisions to emerge out of a conference committee that were never really part of either. As one representative remarked about conference committees: "I don't think one person in a million has any appreciation of their importance and the process by which they work. Part of the explanation, of course, is that there never is a printed record of what goes on in conference committee."[3]

Davidson and Oleszek argue that conference bargaining can be classified in four ways. Most conferences are *traditional* conferences; these bring members face-to-face to haggle and negotiate to reach agreements. In *offer-counteroffer* conferences, one chamber's delegation suggests a compromise proposal and the other side discusses it privately and then returns with its own variation. Large conferences typically splinter into smaller units, or *subconferences*, to reconcile discrete parts of a measure. Finally, *pro forma* conferences resolve differences informally, generally by sub rosa negotiations between conference leaders or their staffs.[4]

Conference committees operate under each chamber's rules and precedents. They generally cannot reconsider items that both chambers have already agreed to, nor are they supposed to write new laws by inserting provisions that neither chamber had previously considered. As Davidson and Oleszek observe, however, parliamentary rules are not self-enforcing, and either chamber can waive or ignore them.[5] Reinforcing the potentially powerful role of the conference committee, Sen. Arlen Specter of Pennsylvania remarked, "[conference committees are where] the work is concluded. Everything else which is done is really of much less significance than the conference, where the final touches are put on legislation which constitutes the laws of the country."[6]

For most of Congress's history, the proceedings of conference committees were secret. In recent years, both chambers adopted rules changes that provided for greater transparency and openness in conference committee discussions. Despite these reforms, private bargaining sessions still permeate conference negotiations,[7] and conference committee meetings remain the most opaque part of the entire legislative process. Yes, staff and members often meet behind closed doors during the markup and floor debates proceedings, and some of these private meetings can result in large changes in the proposed legislation. But the outcomes of these private meetings can be amended or overturned by the full committee or during final floor debate before moving on to the next stage of the process. By contrast, the conference committee's final report goes back to each chamber for an up or down vote, but it cannot be amended. By this stage in the process, it's very difficult (though not impossible) to reverse course. Once a conference agreement is reached, both chambers will almost always pass the resulting bill rather than kill the bill or send it back to conference for further changes.

Unless the president decides to veto the bill—something George W. Bush had never done by the time the transportation bill reached conference—the bill would become law as passed out of the conference committee. So the conferees have enormous power because they essentially craft the terms of what the final law will be.

Referring to a conference committee in the singular tense is actually a bit of a misnomer. The conference is really two committees, one from the House and one from the Senate. Each committee votes by majority rule on whether to accept changes to its version of the bill. It is a challenging and difficult process, especially in a case like this one where the bill is huge and the stakes even larger.

APPOINTMENT OF CONFEREES

The first step in forming a given conference meeting is the appointment of the conferees. This determines who actually gets to sit at the table and vote on each decision put before the committee. The majority party in each chamber controls the appointment of conferees, though its decisions must be put to a vote on the floor. This means that there are two things to fight about even before conference begins. First, there is the issue of how many members of the minority actually get to sit on the committee—the ratio of majority to minority members. Second is the issue of which members jockeying to become conferees will get the prized assignment.

By the time the 2004 transportation bill was ready for conference, a lot of bad blood had built up on the question of minority representation. The last large piece of legislation to go to conference had been the Medicare Prescription Drug Improvement and Modernization Act of 2004.

This bill, which provided prescription drug benefits to Medicare recipients, had created severe tension between the two political parties, particularly in the House. Democrats felt they had been excluded from the conference process because majority Republicans in the House and Senate essentially negotiated the final agreement in private meetings among themselves. Even though SAFETEA-LU had been a strongly bipartisan bill since its inception, Democrats were still wary that they would be shut out this time around as well.

Democrats in the House were accustomed to this kind of treatment. They had been excluded from most processes since 1995, when Republicans took control of that chamber for the first time in forty years. This time around they briefly called foul when Speaker J. Dennis Hastert of Illinois put some of the most vulnerable House members—those who could potentially lose their seats in November—on the committee.[8] Republicans barely felt the need to defend themselves against this charge. Of course they were trying to use this bill to improve their reelection chances! This was the House, after all. (See Appendix 2 for a complete list of House conferees.)

The Senate was a little different. Democrats had controlled the Senate briefly under the Bush administration when Jim Jeffords had switched from a Republican to an Independent in 2001. They had recently tasted power and felt that when they were in charge briefly, they looked out for the interests of the minority party (of course, they had little choice in this matter given that the House and White House were both Republican at the time). Moreover, the Senate tends to be a more bipartisan place than the House due to the increased rights of the minority party and Senate tradition of comity. But Democratic senators felt they, too, had been slighted during the final conference stages of the prescription drug bill, and they did not want to get rolled again.

So Senate Democrats chose to take their stand during the appointment of conferees on the transportation bill. Like most processes in the Senate, the appointment of conferees is typically done by unanimous consent. If necessary, the Senate majority leader could force a roll call vote on his conference appointments and be fairly confident of his ability to prevail. But Senate tradition usually prevents this course of action. Most senators in the ruling party, knowing full well they could be members of the minority party after the next election, would prefer to make conference appointments that satisfy the minority party, if that is in any way possible.

But that proved to be a tall order this time around. Recall that the transportation bill passed the Senate in February 2004. Then it passed the House in April. Yet it was not until July that conferees would be named from the Senate side. Over the intervening six months Senate Majority Leader Bill Frist and Minority Leader Tom Daschle were negotiating over the ratio of majority-to-minority representation on the Senate side of the conference committee, trying to find a solution that would meet the comfort level of each side. This long delay put the conference committee in a difficult position once it finally convened, with a tight timeline to finish the bill. In the end, Frist and Daschle agreed on a ratio of eleven Republicans to ten Democrats. This was probably the best outcome the Democrats could possibly have conceived. Of course, this bill was less about party and more about regions, and Frist probably recognized that. He may have been concerned about setting a precedent for future bills, but in the end probably decided that he could always change his mind in the next go-around.

As for which senators would get an appointment to the conference, this was purely an intra-party discussion, with each party leader making the final decisions on the makeup of his respective delegation. There were certain givens regarding committee appointees. Obviously all of the big four would be appointed. But there had been three committees involved in the production of this bill on the Senate side—the chairmen of Finance and Banking committees wanted appointments, too. On the House side, the Transportation and Infrastructure Committee had seventy-five members, and clearly not all of them could be appointed. Even the Highways, Transit, and Pipelines Subcommittee had fifty-five members. Whittling these numbers down was a difficult task. The final appointments are listed in Tables 4.1 and 4.2.

As these lists show, it was a powerful group, almost all of whom had earned their appointments based on their positions of power in Congress. In the Senate, everyone except North Dakota's Kent Conrad (a senior member of the Finance Committee but not the most senior), was in the highest-ranking position possible, such that no one of greater seniority on this issue was missing from the conference committee. Daschle

TABLE 4.1	Senate GOP Appointees to the SAFETEA-LU Conference Committee (108th Congress)

APPOINTEE	EXPLANATION
James M. Inhofe, Oklahoma	Chairman, Environment and Public Works Committee
Charles E. Grassley, Iowa	Chairman, Finance Committee
John McCain, Arizona	Chairman, Commerce and Science Committee
Don Nickles, Oklahoma	Chairman, Budget Committee
Richard C. Shelby, Alabama	Chairman, Banking, Housing, and Urban Affairs Committee
Trent Lott, Mississippi	Chairman, Commerce Subcommittee on Surface Transportation
Christopher S. Bond, Missouri	Chairman, Environment Subcommittee on Transportation
John W. Warner, Virginia	Senior Republican on Environment and Public Works Committee
George V. Voinovich, Ohio	Next most senior Republican on Environment and Public Works Committee
Orrin G. Hatch, Utah	Senior Republican on Finance Committee
Mitch McConnell, Kentucky	Senate majority whip

TABLE 4.2	Senate Democratic Appointees to the SAFETEA-LU Conference Committee (108th Congress)

APPOINTEE	EXPLANATION
Tom Daschle, South Dakota	Senate minority leader
James M. Jeffords (I), Vermont*	Ranking minority member, Environment and Public Works Committee
Harry Reid, Nevada	Ranking member, Environment Subcommittee on Transportation; minority whip
Max Baucus, Montana	Ranking member on Finance Committee
Kent Conrad, North Dakota	Senior Democrat on Finance Committee
Paul S. Sarbanes, Maryland	Ranking member on Banking, Housing, and Urban Affairs Committee
Ernest F. Hollings, South Carolina	Ranking member on Commerce and Science Committee
Bob Graham, Florida	Senior Democrat on Environment and Public Works Committee
Joseph I. Lieberman, Connecticut	Next most senior Democrat on Environment and Public Works Committee
Barbara Boxer, California	Next most senior Democrat on Environment and Public Works Committee

*James M. Jeffords was an Independent who caucused with Senate Democrats.

and Mitch McConnell of Kentucky, the assistant majority leader, were the only two members appointed to the conference committee who were not members of the committees with jurisdiction over the bill. But increasingly, party leaders were playing a more active role not only in assigning conferees, but also in shaping the final outcome of major legislation. So they often made sure they had a seat at the table to boost their leverage in the bicameral bargaining process.[9]

CONFERENCE PROBLEMS

As meetings began between the House and Senate conferees, the parties involved had every reason to believe that they could complete the task at hand. Although it was an election year, there was strong industry pressure to complete the bill, and passing the transportation bill is usually helpful for most incumbents. If compromises could be reached on the funding levels, the remaining differences in the bill were thought to be marginal.

Conference began with committee staff on both sides presenting interminable "walk-throughs" of the bill. The Senate Environment and Public Works staff explained each component of their bill, and the House Transportation and Infrastructure staff explained each component of their bill, and the differences were highlighted. These walk-throughs seemed almost pointless, given that the major differences were obvious to everyone. Most staff and their bosses were not concerned with how much fewer research dollars were allocated in one bill compared to the other. These little battles could be fought on the sidelines. The real battle, as it had been from the beginning, was overall funding. Until the funding issue was resolved, few staff members saw the need to bring up any other negotiating points.

Unfortunately, the funding issue was not going to be resolved easily. One would think that picking a number between $318 billion (Senate) and $275 billion (House) would have been relatively simple. "Splitting the difference," as conference negotiators often like to do, and settling on $296.5 billion might have worked, for example. However, in this case, matters were complicated by the *third* party involved in these negotiations—the White House.

The fact that both the executive and the legislative branches were under control of the same party, and the fact that the party held together strongly, meant that it was unlikely Republicans in Congress would pick a fight with the president. The party had stuck together so strongly that Bush had yet to veto a single bill. This was the spring of 2004, when Bush's approval ratings were rather low, and members of Congress were in a precarious position. If they piled on the president and fought with him on this bill, this would likely produce one of two results: (1) Bush would be reelected anyway and punish those who had fought him or (2) Bush would be defeated and Republicans in Congress would lose substantial power anyway. Therefore, the only way that Congress was going to fight the president hard on this one would be if they really thought their own jobs would be in jeopardy if they did not do so.

Luckily for all Republicans involved, not much turnover was expected in Congress. The Republican incumbents quickly realized that it was in their interest to compromise with the president. He wanted a smaller bill, closer to his original funding level of $256 billion. For Congress, passing a smaller transportation bill would be better than passing no transportation bill at all. If they could get anything at all done, it would look good for everyone involved.

Despite this incentive, it was difficult to get anything done because there were still sufficient numbers of conferees who continued to believe that they could get a higher number. The House members were constrained strongly by their loyalty to their party and the president. In fact, a representative of House Majority Leader Tom DeLay attended all conference proceedings to make sure that House GOP conferees toed the line and kept the total spending down. However, senators did not fall into line so easily and soon frustrated DeLay's efforts. The problem was that many senators had no problem with the idea of sending a bill to the president to veto. Certainly the Democrats had no problem with it, but even some Republicans, such as James Inhofe himself, thought nothing of putting the president in the position of having to choose whether to veto the bill. Unlike the House, where Republican members saw themselves beholden to the titular leader of their party, Senate Republicans acted much more independently and thus felt free to pass whatever number they chose.[10]

At one point, the battle between DeLay and the Senate conferees became explicit when DeLay accused Inhofe of committing the ghastliest of sins in the eyes of fellow Republicans—a tax increase. Despite the fact that there was no tax increase in the bill, DeLay insisted that "they [the Senate] want to kill jobs by raising taxes on the one hand, and then use federal money to create jobs on the other. It doesn't work."[11] This kind of rare intra-party fighting signaled that something was very wrong, and that the conference was in trouble.

On the other hand, the Senate was constrained by the fact that its total was drastically higher than what the president had in mind. As noted above, senators fancy themselves as independent from the president, and were not as willing to defer to him. They also wanted a bigger pie. Not only were they willing to defy the president on his veto threat, but they were willing to publicly proclaim their success in negotiations with the White House. When DeLay and the White House signaled that they might be willing to accept $299 billion, Inhofe bragged, "When the White House comes up three times as far as we came down, I would say that is a successful negotiation. We went down 6 percent; they came up 17 percent."[12]

The president did not appreciate this behavior and did not want to look like he had been rolled. The result: gridlock.

Newspapers and textbooks often refer to gridlock in Congress as being the result of two different parties disagreeing over how to proceed. This case shows that getting agreement on legislation can be very difficult even within the same party. If the Republicans could have reached common ground among themselves, they could have passed a bill at whatever number they wanted. But they could not. Harry Reid of Nevada was happy to kick the Republicans while they were bickering among themselves. He blamed Rep. Don Young for failing to buck the White House, saying that his predecessor as House Transportation chairman, the infamous Bud Shuster, "wouldn't back down for a second."[13] This was a particularly blunt criticism because Shuster was a Republican, so Reid was essentially praising another Republican for doing a better job than Young. The problem was that some Republicans agreed with Reid's assessment.[14]

The Democrats, seeing an opportunity with the way the conference negotiations were progressing, were happy to take advantage. Conference meetings had been proceeding as planned, with walk-throughs and talk of working out the differences in the bill. But the Senate Democrats sensed weakness in the Republicans' inability to agree on a number.

They announced that they would no longer participate in the conference until an overall sum was agreed upon. They noted that the Senate Republicans had all backed a Senate bill that was much larger than anything the administration was proposing. Why should they now change their minds? Also, it made little sense, they noted, to argue over anything else in the bill until an overall number had been determined. Democrats knew that Republicans did not need them around in order to get a bill done, but then, Democrats certainly did not need to waste their time negotiating a bill that was going to change as soon as a funding number was agreed to.

Also, the Democrats probably saw that they at least had a shot to take over the Senate and perhaps influence the bill more substantially in the next Congress. This gave them little incentive to compromise in late 2004. Instead they publicly berated Republicans for failing to get the bill done. Besides humiliating Young by comparing him to Shuster, they decided to blame Inhofe for his public compromises on the overall funding level. They said he had failed to consult the Democrats on these compromises in blatant disregard for what he had agreed to do before the conference began.[15]

Republicans, realizing that blaming themselves publicly probably wasn't the best strategy, tried to fight back. They accused Harry Reid of being "committed to killing the bill."[16] Inhofe also cried foul, asserting that the Democrats were using the bill for political purposes when it was supposed to be bipartisan and untainted by election-year posturing.[17] The Democrats could simply sit back and laugh at this attack. It is pretty hard to accuse the minority of obstruction when they can so easily be ignored, as was the case here. The real issue was the gulf between the Senate and the White House, and everyone knew it.

Senate Chairman Inhofe made one last-ditch effort to resolve the problem. He was the one with the most at stake, yet he was also the one who could most afford to take a gamble. House Chairman Young could hardly be the one arguing for the higher Senate number given that his committee and the House as a whole had gone on record for a bill at a much lower number. Inhofe was the one who could resolve the crisis if he could come up with a compromise number that worked for everyone. If he could not do so, the bill would be lost.

Inhofe called for an emergency meeting of the conference committee on July 20. His staff dimmed the lights and booted up a laptop for a

PowerPoint presentation. Dramatically, and with all the requisite build-up, a number appeared on the screen: *$301.5 billion.* This was the compromise that Inhofe felt he could live with, and that could potentially start the whole process up again. This was the chance to keep going. All of the nation's transportation policy, all the potential federal spending for the next six years, was now hanging on that one number.

As Inhofe himself later conceded, however, "That's when things did fall apart."[18] The number appeased absolutely no one, and was met with derision rather than elation.[19] It was still way above anything the White House saw as acceptable, and it was well below what the Senate was looking for. Once this last-ditch attempt had failed, the conference committee lost any steam it had remaining. Although publicly Inhofe and Young both said they held out hope for passage, everyone could see the writing on the wall.

By September, Senate Republicans decided to officially close negotiations by introducing a six-month extension of the existing surface transportation bill.[20] This extension—longer than any of the previous stopgap extensions that had kept the transportation dollars flowing while Congress negotiated the new reauthorization measure—would ensure that the bill would not be dealt with again until the next Congress convened in January 2005. The Republicans and the White House had essentially decided that there would be no bill. Not this year anyway.

The truth is that transportation is never a signature national issue. Bush was not going to win the election based on transportation—he could only lose it if it came out looking fiscally irresponsible and full of pork-barrel spending. The administration strategy, in the end, was to hold fast and prevent the bill from hurting them.

PICKING UP THE PIECES

During the fall of an election year, lawmakers on Capitol Hill are frequently preoccupied with election-related activities. In a presidential election year, this intensifies. Most people are out on the campaign trail, including many staffers who often help other candidates from their own party if their bosses are not running. To a large extent, the business of the nation is temporarily on hold.

For the staff of the Senate Environment and Public Works Committee, this particular election season was a time of disillusionment. The years of sleepless nights and endless negotiations that they believed would result in the passage of a transportation bill had instead ended up with nothing.

All the staffers could do was to drown their sorrows in the coffee shop underneath the Russell Senate Office Building across the street from the U.S. Capitol. They would need that coffee because they were soon going to have to go through the entire process again. The new Congress could not simply pick up where the other had left off in conference. The 109th Congress would have to start all over again. Like the movie *Groundhog Day,* the entire frustrating and Byzantine process would have to be relived one more time come January.

Until then, transportation staff enjoyed their hiatus. Those not involved in election campaigns spent short days in their offices, enjoying actual time for lunch somewhere besides the Senate cafeteria. They reintroduced themselves to their families and the gym. They dressed in casual clothes and went to happy hours. When Congress is out of session, the Hill is a fun place to be.

Eventually, though, the staffers had to return to their desks and to reality. Before the new Congress showed up, they would need to prepare a new bill for consideration in committee. The new bill would have to be priced to move, as the saying goes, because the pressure from industry groups was going to be immensely higher than ever as the short-term extensions of current law increasingly constrained road-building activities.

Meanwhile, as Election Night results poured in, the president would be reelected for a second four-year term and Republicans would increase their majorities in both the House and Senate. There would be no major changes in the key power centers of transportation policy, and now it was in everyone's interest to get this bill back up in the new Congress and finished as quickly as possible. Given all their experiences over the past two years, neither the members nor their staffs could ever be sure that this would be enough to get a bill passed. But they would have to try just the same.

NOTES

1. Roger H. Davidson, Walter J. Oleszek, and Frances E. Lee, *Congress and Its Members,* 11th ed. (Washington, D.C.: CQ Press, 2008), 267.
2. Ibid., 205.
3. Quoted in ibid., 206.

4. Ibid., 206.
5. Ibid., 267.
6. Quoted in ibid., 267.
7. Ibid., 269.
8. Shweta Govindaranjan, "Vulnerable GOPers Get Transportation Seats," *The Hill*, June 8, 2004.
9. Davidson, Oleszek, and Lee, *Congress and Its Members*, 206.
10. Isaiah Poole, "Amid Highway Fracas, an Unbowed Young Works to Bring Spending Bill to Fruition," *CQ Weekly*, July 10, 2004.
11. Isaiah Poole, "DeLay, Inhofe in Spat over Highway Bill," *CQ Weekly*, June 26, 2004.
12. Isaiah Poole, "Highway Bill Still Tangled in String of Extensions," *CQ Weekly*, September 25, 2004.
13. Poole, "Amid Highway Fracas."
14. Ibid.
15. Poole, "Highway Bill Still Tangled."
16. Jonathan Kaplan, "Senator Inhofe Delivers an Ultimatum," *The Hill*, July 21, 2004.
17. Poole, "Highway Bill Still Tangled."
18. Isaiah Poole, "Reid Stalls Highway Measure; Lame-Duck Action Unlikely on Compromise Price Tag," *CQ Weekly*, November 13, 2004.
19. Jeffrey Squires, interview, 2006.
20. Poole, "Highway Bill Still Tangled."

5

BACK TO THE DRAWING BOARD

TEA-21, the 1998 law that had been authorizing all spending on surface transportation in the United States expired in October 2003. The first attempt at reauthorizing that legislation, SAFETEA, died its slow and painful death in advance of the presidential election in November 2004. Now a new Congress and the same president had been elected and the process of reauthorizing the bill could begin again. One might wonder, what had been happening with transportation spending during that time?

Transportation spending had not been interrupted at all. It was just continuing at a lower level than what members of Congress would prefer. The spigot was also flowing with legacy preferences for the states that had led the ISTEA and TEA-21 writing in 1992 and 1998, respectively. With very little fanfare, at regular intervals, Congress had continued to reauthorize the previous legislation with temporary, stopgap measures that simply extended existing funding levels and previous funding formulas. There was a five-month extension in October 2003 and a sixty-day extension in April 2004. Finally there was the kiss of death—an eight-month extension in September 2004. This last stopgap measure signaled to everyone that Congress had accepted the fact that it was not going to pass a new bill before the election.

These extensions represented an accidental victory for many states. States that had both Democratic leadership and donee status were likely to benefit from keeping TEA-21 in place. This meant they also had a chance to do better with SAFETEA if Democrats took control of either chamber in November. In the meantime Democrats got the benefits of the same rate of return that had been negotiated when they had more power.

An important distinction to make here is that the transportation bill is solely an authorization bill.[1] This is one of the peculiar realities of how Congress spends money. Authorization bills, which are the responsibility of the authorizing committees such as Senate Environment and Public Works and House Transportation and Infrastructure, set the terms for how money is allocated but, for the most part, they only establish ceilings and floors for the actual amount of money released from the Treasury. The actual spending authority in any fiscal year must be approved through annual appropriations bills, which are under the control of the House and Senate Appropriations committees. This meant that spending could continue under the stopgap extensions—so long as Congress passed the annual appropriations bill for the Department of Transportation—but Congress could not increase spending beyond the previously authorized ceilings. Congress as a whole was chomping at the bit to spend more money for highways, and the new leadership was eager to put their stamp on the spending. Both Rep. Don Young and Sen. James Inhofe, as we have seen, had waited years to become chairmen of their committees so they could deliver highway dollars to their states. They were bound and determined not to wait any longer.

And if you think members of Congress were chomping, you should have seen the transportation industry. Billions of dollars were not being spent on transportation because of the delay in reauthorizing highway programs. This affected not only states and their transportation networks, but also directly impacted contractors, construction workers, cement companies, trucking companies, and dozens of other purveyors of equipment related to road construction. These businesses and their associations were often strong contributors to congressional election campaigns, and they expected to be repaid handsomely on their contributions back in the 2003 and 2004. Consider that the transportation industry as a whole—individuals employed in the industry and political action committees—contributed more than $51 million to congressional candidates in the 2003–2004 election cycle.* In fact, the transportation industry ranked twelfth in the 2003–2004 election cycle in terms of total contribution to congressional candidates. Most of those contributions—74 percent—were directed to Republicans (see Figure 5.1). In the 2001–2002 cycle, Don Young had received more money from the transportation sector than any other candidate running for congressional office—a total of $348,518 (see Table 5.1, pages 130–131). Young raised another $360,000 from the related construction sector in 2002. It was now 2005 and the industry—as well as the country—was still operating on a transportation bill written in 1998. Vested interests were not amused.

Staff and senators had been working on this bill since late 2002. Committee hearings on the reauthorization had started even before that. Everyone was exhausted and ready to be finished with the thing. Early ambitions had crumbled, strong stances had weakened, and people were sick of fighting over the transportation bill. The president was in a second term and Congress was a full two years away from the next election. This was just the kind of political climate during which a bill like this could actually be passed.

MARKUP REDUX

Despite an overwhelming desire by many powerful parties to get the bill done quickly and without a lot of fuss, the entire sausage-making process had to start up all over again. The 109th Congress, which convened in January 2005, started with a clean, blank slate, just like the 108 Congresses that came before it. So the 109th Congress could not consider the bill S 1072, passed by the Senate in 2004, or HR 3550, passed by the House in 2004, because those bills were creatures of the 108th Congress that was in session for the two calendar years of 2003 and 2004. Once the 108th Congress adjourned for good at the close of 2004, any bill that had not been passed and signed into law by the president was tossed into the dustbin of history. The new Congress could try to re-create what its predecessor had

---

*Center for Responsive Politics. Based on contributions of $200 or more. Excludes Levin funds to state and local party committees. *http://opensecrets.org/industries/indus.asp?Ind=M*. Accessed on June 22, 2007.

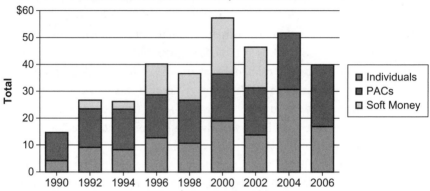

Individual, PAC, and Soft Money Contributions

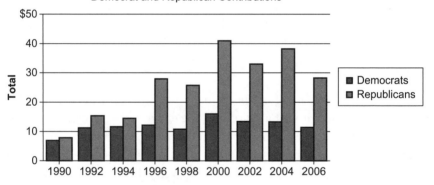

Democrat and Republican Contributions

Source: Center for Responsive Politics, www.opensecrets.org.

Methodology: The numbers on this page are based on contributions of $200 or more from political action committees (PACs) and individuals to federal candidates and from PAC, soft money, and individual donors to political parties, as reported to the Federal Election Commission. While election cycles are shown in charts as 1996, 1998, 2000, etc., they actually represent two-year periods. For example, the 2002 election cycle runs from January 1, 2001, to December 31, 2002.

Notes: Soft money contributions to the national parties were not publicly disclosed until the 1991–1992 election cycle, and were banned by the Bipartisan Campaign Finance Reform Act following the 2002 elections. Figures for 2004 and 2006 election cycle do not include donations of "Levin" funds to state and local party committees. Levin funds were created by the Bipartisan Campaign Reform Act of 2002.

tried to write into law, but the same procedures we described in Chapter 2 had to be followed once again: A member had to introduce a bill in each chamber, each bill had to be referred to the committees of jurisdiction, in which each had to schedule a markup and take a vote to send the bill back to the floor, where it had to be passed, and, once again, reconciled with the other chamber's version.

It's a laborious and painstaking process, to be sure, but one that has its protective benefits for both the nation and members of Congress. For one thing, this system ensures that newly elected members get an equal say in any legislation that moves through Congress. The system ensures that voters who have decided to send a new representative to Washington also theoretically get a say in the legislation that a new Congress writes.

But for practical purposes, the system also meant that the newly convened 109th Congress could not simply resume where the 108th Congress had left off and pick up with the House-Senate conference negotiations. Even if it would have been simpler to appoint replacements for those on the conference committee who were no longer in Congress, and then push the bills forward from there, it was not allowed under the rules.

The 109th Congress was still run by Republicans, but there were some key changes from the 108th that affected the new bill. The House saw relatively little shuffling. The main change came in the position of minority leader, where Richard Gephardt of Missouri was replaced by Nancy Pelosi of California. Not only is the role of minority leader relatively less important in the House anyway, but Gephardt had hardly been involved the first time around because he was preoccupied for much of late 2003 and early 2004 with his unsuccessful campaign for the Democratic presidential nomination. For the most part, the major power players—Speaker J. Dennis Hastert of Illinois, Majority Leader Tom DeLay of Texas, Transportation Chairman Young of Alaska, and the committee's ranking Democrat, Jim Oberstar of Minnesota—were all in their same positions.

In the Senate, Inhofe was still the chairman of the Environment and Public Works Committee and Christopher S. "Kit" Bond was still the Transportation Subcommittee chairman. But Harry Reid of Nevada had replaced Tom Daschle as the Democratic minority leader after Daschle lost his race for reelection in South Dakota to challenger John Thune. This meant that Reid had to relinquish some responsibilities, so he gave up his

TABLE 5.1	Top Recipients of Transportation Sector Contributions, 2002 and 2004 Cycles		

2002 CYCLE

Rank	Candidate	Office	Amount
1	Don Young, R-Alaska	House	$348,518
2	John D. Dingell, D-Mich.	House	286,590
3	Elizabeth Dole, R-N.C.	Senate	284,684
4	Ted Stevens, R-Alaska	Senate	281,341
5	John Cornyn, R-Texas	Senate	259,100
6	Norm Coleman, R-Minn.	Senate	225,840
7	Max Cleland, D-Ga.	Senate	224,006
8	James M. Talent, R-Mo.	Senate	221,278
9	Gordon H. Smith, R-Ore.	Senate	221,195
10	James L. Oberstar, D-Minn.	House	210,220
11	Max Baucus, D-Mont.	Senate	198,590
12	John L. Mica, R-Fla.	House	193,250
13	Roy Blunt, R-Mo.	House	189,305
14	Richard A. Gephardt, D-Mo.	House	186,200
15	Joe Knollenberg, R-Mich.	House	186,040
16	John Thune, R-S.D.	Senate	179,300
17	James M. Inhofe, R-Okla.	Senate	179,127
18	John E. Sununu, R-N.H.	Senate	174,960
19	John D. Rockefeller IV, D-W.V.	Senate	163,800
20	Lindsey Graham, R-S.C.	Senate	161,500

committee seat and his position as ranking minority member on the Transportation Subcommittee, allowing Max Baucus of Montana to move up the ladder on that panel. Moreover, Thune got a spot on the full committee, as did newly elected Republicans David Vitter of Louisiana, Jim DeMint of South Carolina, and Johnny Isakson of Georgia. Reid's committee spot went to newly elected Barack Obama, Democrat of Illinois.

Despite all the reshuffling, a key aspect of the reconstituted committee was that Harry Reid's staff stayed on even though Reid himself had left. Many times committee chairs and ranking members will hire their own staff members to work on the committee. Reid had made sure that his staff stayed on the committee staff when he left to become minority leader. This ensured that even though Max Baucus was technically the new ranking member, Reid maintained a strong hand in the markup process. Reid's staff made it possible for the big four of 2003–2004 (Inhofe, Bond,

2004 CYCLE

Rank	Candidate	Office	Amount
1	George W. Bush, R	President	$4,884,893
2	John Kerry, D	President	742,566
3	Mel Martinez, R-Fla.	Senate	380,612
4	David Vitter, R-La.	Senate	333,583
5	Christopher S. Bond, R-Mo.	Senate	323,350
6	Don Young, R-Alaska	House	321,789
7	James DeMint, R-S.C.	Senate	317,633
8	John Thune, R-S.D.	Senate	295,956
9	Lisa Murkowski, R-Alaska	Senate	291,000
10	Arlen Specter, R-Pa.	Senate	267,515
11	Richard Burr, R-N.C.	Senate	261,599
12	George V. Voinovich, R-Ohio	Senate	260,981
13	J. Dennis Hastert, R-Ill.	House	259,231
14	Johnny Isakson, R-Ga.	Senate	232,050
15	George R. Nethercutt Jr., R-Wash.	Senate	225,749
16	Tom Daschle, D-S.D.	Senate	220,263
17	Richard A. Gephardt, D-Mo.	President	211,680
18	James L. Oberstar, D-Minn.	House	205,139
19	Russ Darrow, D-Wis.	Senate	200,500
20	John D. Dingell, D-Mich.	House	199,100

Reid, and Jim Jeffords of Vermont) to hold onto the agreements they had reached in the previous Congress.

This time, however, the cat was already out of the bag on the pivotal funding question. The big four could not possibly try to force through a bill without revealing the individual state funding levels, since their proposed levels had already been revealed in the previous legislative cycle. So this time, they decided just to put forward the same funding formulas and hope it would pass muster in the refashioned committee. With four freshman GOP senators on the panel, all hailing from the House, where dissent was rarely tolerated by the ruling party, the big four felt confident of moving their bill through the committee without a hitch.

The Environment and Public Works Committee released its bill, newly numbered S 732, in early March, which is relatively early in a legislative session. The new bill was identical to the bill that had passed the Senate a year earlier, except that the total funding level had been dropped from $318 billion to $284 billion. This rather substantial decrease was a direct result of threats from the White House. President George W. Bush could no longer realistically threaten a veto of anything over $256 billion—not after the Senate had passed a $318 billion bill the previous year. He was willing to compromise again this time, but he would be the one to outline the terms of the compromise. His staff settled on the figure of $284 billion.

The enforcement mechanism for the White House was the House and Senate leadership. Senate Majority Leader Bill Frist of Tennessee informed Inhofe that no bill above $284 billion would be allowed on the floor for consideration. This was new. Last time, prior to the election, the Senate had willfully defied the president, debating and then passing a bill that wildly overshot his veto marker. Now, in Bush's lame-duck second term, the Senate GOP leader was cowing exactly to his demands.

Frist's behavior can be explained by the fact that Frist harbored presidential ambitions of his own, and George Bush had just been elected in a more decisive manner than his first time around. If Frist wanted to have a chance at the 2008 nomination, he assumed he would need Bush's support. Caving in on this issue was probably an easy choice. He had no worries about the wrath of voters in his home state, where he was not running for reelection and where voters would likely support him in a national election even with a few less highway dollars. As we have pointed out before, transportation spending was not a hot-button *national* issue that voters used to determine their choices for president. So Frist had zero incentive to defy the president at this juncture in his political career.

Meanwhile, Bush's new bottom line for the highway bill also meant that Inhofe had to cave on his most pronounced and publicly defined goal—raising the minimum rate of return to 95 percent of each state's contribution to the Highway Trust Fund. Inhofe knew that at 95 percent, the potential harm would be too great for too many donee states if there was only $284 billion to go around. He had to compromise for now. So he settled for raising the rate to 92 percent, to be phased in gradually over the life of the six-year bill. Ironically, his goal was ultimately undone by the GOP White House, not the largely Democratic donee states.

Still, Inhofe and his staff were not going to give up that easily, no matter how tired they were. They had withstood years of lobbying from the trucking and construction industries on the importance of this bill. They had countered various insurgent attacks from within. They had one last trick left in them and they decided to play it.

Frist had required that they bring the bill to the floor with a price tag of $284 billion. He said nothing about what could happen after that—in fact, he had little control over what would happen after the bill reached the floor. Inhofe and his staff planned to have the chairman submit an amendment on the floor immediately boosting the size of the bill.

What is interesting about this plan is that it was not hidden from Frist, and therefore was probably apparent to White House officials as well. It was openly discussed among committee members' personal staffs. The spirit of the ruling from the White House seemed completely irrelevant here. As long as the bill was kept at the lower level before it got to the floor, Frist would be protecting himself for his planned future presidential run.

Of course this induced speculation among donee state staff members that, along with the increased amount of funding, could come an increase in the Minimum Guarantee. Such a maneuver would be equivalent to what had happened in the previous Congress, when the formulas were never voted upon by the committee. It could have provoked outrage and a rebellion, despite blandishments from committee staff that the formulas were not going to change. But there were two big reasons why no rebellion fomented this time around. One was that everyone was tired and ready to move on. The cost of doing nothing had grown higher, and there was no new Congress around the corner to bail anyone out. The other, perhaps bigger reason was that although Max Baucus was now ostensibly part of the big four, his star staffer, Dawn Levy, had long since departed for a higher-paying job in the private sector. Without Levy leading the charge for the minority staff, there was no driving force for rebellion. There was little more that anyone else could find the energy to fight about.

Finding Something to Fight About

It is often remarked, about senator's offices as well as any other office in public or private life, that leadership comes from the top down. Workers imitate their bosses in attitude, work ethic, and their general approach to their jobs. Most staff members working for senators on Environment and Public Works had little idea what Kit Bond was like as a human being, but if they were to guess, based on his representation by committee staff, they probably would have been very scared of him.

Ellen Stein was Bond's lead staff member on the committee. She was originally from New York City, but you would never have guessed it because she seemed to have adopted a slight Missouri accent. She was very smart and very tough, and quite clearly very annoyed with something most of the time.

It was Stein who informed the minority staff that Majority Leader Frist would not allow any bill to come the floor at higher than $284 billion. Therefore, any amendment submitted in committee that aimed to increase the funding in the bill would be viewed as a "poison pill." What she meant by this is that both committee staff and their bosses would be very angry, since any amendment to increase funding would make them look awful in the eyes of Frist and the White House. Stein was none too subtly threatening to take her anger out on an offending state's funding for high priority projects. If such an amendment were to pass, the bill would either die or provoke a fight among majority Republicans about bringing the bill to the floor. If the amendment were to fail, the big four would have to publicly vote against greater funding for a bill on which they had fought to increase funding for the past three years. This put Inhofe and Bond in a double bind. They were willing to be Frist's and President Bush's lap dogs, but they were not willing to announce it publicly.

The problem was, this time around, that the committee staff actually had to face up to the possibility of amendments on funding and formulas. Last time, by keeping funding and formulas out of the bill marked up in committee, they had bypassed a huge fight (they created a different one, but that was one they could win). This time, they faced the distinct possibility that the committee members could override their leadership on either funding levels or formulas, or both. That was the last thing committee staff wanted. Even if the funding levels and formulas already arrived at were compromises, they were compromises reached by the leadership. Formulas were their last vestiges of power over the bill. Committee staff had to fight to protect them.

The committee went through a similar process the last time, except without a massive rebellion full of excess amendments. Committee staff met with senators' personal staff and went through the amendments their bosses were planning to offer in order to see if any could be accepted before the markup. In the case of the new senators on the committee, this was a useful exercise—for the alumni of the last markup, however, it was a little pointless. The alumni merely came forward with a pared down list of the same amendments they had put forward last time, hoping to see if maybe this time they could be accepted. Many of the amendments that had been submitted last time were already in the bill, and there was no particular reason why the ones that had been rejected by committee staff last time would be accepted this time.

Ellen Stein in particular grew frustrated with this process. The typical tone of the committee staff was calm—this was encouraged by their leader, Ruth Van Mark, who never seemed to lose control at all despite years of late nights and countless battles over this one bill. Even when they were getting ready to chop off your hand, the committee staff would speak pleasantly. They might say, for example, that your state was going to get the shaft and your boss's election chances destroyed if you messed with them, but they would say it in a subtle and pleasant manner.

Stein was the bad cop to Van Mark's good cop. She did not mince words. Unlike Van Mark, she was losing patience with the entire process. This time, when staff discussed their amendments, she was on the attack. Last time staff had just rejected or accepted amendments, without explanation. This time, Stein tried to actually argue against the amendment. Her strategy presumed that the person submitting the amendment did not know what was good for his or her own boss and state. It presumed the person submitting the amendment did not know how to do his or her job. It also accomplished very little, because Stein was unlikely to "win" such an argument and persuade the staff member to withdraw the amendment.

A good example was an amendment submitted by one office to aid low-income communities by encouraging research into how transportation policy affects them. As discussed in Chapter 2, other staff reacted to these amendments with incredulity even when they were *trying* to find as many amendments as possible to gum up the works. Now that the amendment was being submitted in good faith, because it was intended as an actual change in the law, Stein was completely baffled. She argued with the Clinton office staff members trying to submit the amendment, telling them that there were already plenty of provisions in the law to protect low-income individuals. Even her compatriots on the committee staff looked at her with surprise because of the way she attacked fellow staffers on this amendment. She took this tack with every amendment submitted up and down the line.

Stein may have been tired of dealing with the laboriously slow process of representative democracy. Or perhaps she was just feeling combative. Regardless, what is notable is that her demeanor had a lasting effect on the outcome of this bill, and thus national transportation policy. Because of this Senate staffer's clout and attitude, perhaps some amendments were rejected due to her antagonism, or perhaps some were not even submitted. Either way, her personality held sway over policy in no small way.

Marking Up a Marked-Up Bill

Congress, and especially the Senate, loves procedure. Procedure makes the government go around in many ways. If not for procedure and strict adherence to it, those in power would find it infinitely easier simply to roll over the opposition. Procedure keeps them from doing that without at least working at it. There is a procedure for everything, as this book has already described in detail. There is a procedure by which a bill is submitted, a procedure for how it is to be considered, and a procedure as to how it can be changed. All of these procedures are rules designed to keep the government functioning in a fair and equitable manner. By not allowing anyone to skip any steps in the prescribed process, even in the interest of time, the government intends to avoid intense corruption and favoritism.

It is beyond the scope of this book to explore whether all of these procedures actually accomplish their goals. However, there is no question that these procedures introduce complexity, make shortcuts difficult, and make legislation time consuming. The transportation bill was a prime example. The bill had gone through a laborious process of writing, negotiation, amendment, and more negotiation for more than a year. Yet all of this work was not enough because Congress changed its composition.

New members of Congress had been elected, and they too must have a say on the nation's transportation policy. Therefore, there had to be another markup.

This time, however, the markup process moved in a relatively smooth manner. Senators were not angry about being kept in the dark on funding formulas because this time the formulas were in the bill. Donee states had to be happy that the minimum rate of return was down to 92 percent, even if some of them harbored concerns that it might not stay there. Donor states were not thrilled with the result, but if Chairman Inhofe, who had once proclaimed 95 percent as his No. 1 goal, was himself being forced to compromise, there was little they could do.

The last markup had been a combative, tense experience wherein each senator attempted to put his or her personal mark on the bill. This time, a substantial number of amendments were up for consideration, but nothing compared to the last time. Most of the new committee members were too new to the game to even start in with amendments. That left the old guard to resubmit their previous amendments—ones that had not yet been discarded somewhere in the process.

A few of these amendments were discussed during the markup, but mostly everyone was cordial and tried not to push anything too hard. Sen. Thomas R. Carper, a Democrat from Delaware, submitted an amendment to include passenger rail ridership in the calculation of transit ridership for the purposes of a travel and emissions model. The amendment was too complicated for the other senators to understand. In fact, it was not even clear that Senator Carper understood it in any great detail. The chairman asked for clarification from Federal Highway Administration officials attending the meeting, and even they could not say for sure that they understood the impact of the amendment. In the end, Carper withdrew his amendment due to the confusion, but it was certainly a friendly and jocular debate, with senators able to laugh at themselves for not really understanding what was going on.

There were close votes on some amendments. The donee states, fearing a 95 percent minimum rate of return might actually emerge once the bill reached the floor, tried to boost minimum annual growth levels compared to the last transportation bill for all states. Recall the "equity bonus," which built in a minimum percentage increase in funding for all states over their funding levels in 1998 under TEA-21. The intention here was to create a floor for growth, so that no state would see its transportation funding decimated entirely. That percentage was set at 10 percent for the first year of the new bill—so, for example, funding for the state with the lowest growth, Connecticut, would have to go up by at least 10 percent that year. The percentage growth guaranteed to the lowest growth state increased each year, and several states besides Connecticut would eventually hit that floor throughout the life of the bill. Therefore, increasing the floor for spending growth would mean increasing the minimum amount of funding guaranteed to the lowest growth states (the donee states).

These donee states wanted to pass an amendment that raised the floor from 10 percent to 15 percent. The basis of their argument was that all state transportation needs were growing—for donee states no less than for donor states—and therefore they should not be expected to grow at a rate that was so much lower than everyone else. They noted that, at currently proposed rates of funding growth, they were growing slower than the annual rate of inflation, which meant their funding was decreasing in real terms.

These were exactly the kinds of deal-breaking amendments that Inhofe had been trying to avoid when he submitted the bill the first time without any formulas. He knew that, if the committee turned against him, substantial portions of the formulas could be re-written by the other members of the committee instead of him.

The donee states tried to push their amendment, sponsored not surprisingly by Democrats Hillary Rodham Clinton of New York and Joseph I. Lieberman of Connecticut, by pointing out that no state would lose any funding under its terms. They were able to assert this bit of double-logic by employing a piece of legislative magic: They included language saying that amendment would only go into effect if more funding were added to the bill. They did not have to specify how or where that funding would come from, just that the minimum annual increase for each state would not take effect unless someone found a way to increase the total pie. That way, members could vote to increase the minimum growth rates without having to gore the funding allocations of anyone else. Given that everyone expected more money to be added to the bill once it reached the floor, it was not an idle proposal.

The donee state amendment amounted to little more than stating the following: "If there is more money added to the bill, we get it." It was dressed up cleverly to sound as if it was promoting equity, and there was certainly some logic to why it might have been good national policy. But in reality it was just another way of trying to get more funding.

The way that Clinton and Lieberman went about introducing this amendment was also interesting. The Clinton team had submitted several amendments for the markup that each called for raising the floor to a different percentage (15 percent, 20 percent, and 25 percent). The Clinton team knew that they might at least want to attempt to raise their percentage funding growth in committee. Lieberman's staff, despite representing the state with the lowest possible funding growth, had not submitted any such amendment. They may have believed that it would be fruitless. Nevertheless, when the Clinton team decided to actually introduce one of these amendments in committee, they wanted a cosponsor and naturally turned to Lieberman. But Lieberman's staff pointed out that the amendment would be more agreeable to all if it did not take funding away from anyone. Thus both senators' staffs agreed to change the amendment so that it only would apply if additional funds were to be added.

This meant that the amendment language had to be changed. But rather than simply submit a new amendment, staff from both offices agreed that Lieberman would offer a second-degree amendment. Second-degree amendments are an interesting loophole in procedure that permits senators to offer something at the last second that no one will have known about previously. Such amendments do not have to be submitted prior to the committee meeting, and thus can be kept secret from committee leadership. They are amendments to amendments, and therefore can only be submitted if relevant to another proposed amendment.

In the committee markup, Clinton and Lieberman each played their roles and made it obvious that they had planned this together. Senator Clinton offered her amendment, and Inhofe leaped to criticize. He argued that such amendments were dangerous and threatened to unravel the entire bill. If they started meddling with the formulas, he argued, where would it end? What he was really saying is that he wanted it to end with him. He and the rest of the big four had decided on the formulas, and so there was no point in trying to change them. They would be deciding what to do with any extra money that they would be adding. But then Lieberman came in with his second-degree amendment as planned. His method of introduction was quite lighthearted for an amendment that was essentially proposing to change the most contentious part of a $300 billion bill. As part of his introduction he said, "This amendment shall only take effect in the event that the contract authority in this bill is greater than $189,871,080,648, blah, blah, blah. Okay. Let me round it off to the nearest. It is $190 billion."[2] Prior to markup, Clinton's and Lieberman's staffs lobbied the staff of the other senators they thought they might be able to swing. They could tell that many of the staff were not buying it. Although senators might not have been able to see how the amendment could be damaging to donor states, their staff members could. Inhofe's coalition held. Only the minority Democrats were willing to vote for the amendment, and some of those Democrats were donor states with staff smart enough to recognize that the amendment would hurt them if it actually passed. The amendment failed on a 13–5 vote, but that does not mean it failed to accomplish anything. Those proposing the amendment almost certainly knew it would fail—they also knew that they would get credit for trying. They could return to their home states and boast that they had fought the good fight against the Republicans to get more funding for their respective states, but that it was not enough. This was about as much of a victory as they could hope for.

BACK TO THE SENATE FLOOR

The committee approved S 732 and reported it back to the floor in late March of 2005. Considering that there was a congressional spring recess in between, it was brought to the floor rather rapidly at the end of April. In some ways, the bill did not face the opposition it had the last time through. There was no major rebellion, as virtually the entire Senate was eager to get the thing over with as quickly as possible.

On the other hand, even under these circumstances, the bill took a while to get through. There was still a great deal of dead time during which negotiations took place behind the scenes. Even under the best of circumstances, this bill contained too big a pot of money to simply be zipped through the Senate without scrutiny.

The first thing that happened, as planned, was the introduction of a "manager's amendment" (Inhofe's prerogative as chairman of the committee of jurisdiction) that immediately boosted the total amount of funding for the six-year bill to $295 billion, from the $284 billion ceiling that Bush and Frist has insisted upon. As usually happens in the Senate, where committee chairmen are careful to protect each other's prerogatives, the manager's amendment brought no discussion and no vote. It was accepted by "unanimous consent."

Frist scheduled a cloture vote right away to speed things along. Although there was no threat of a filibuster per se, cloture closes off the bill to non-germane amendments from senators who might hope to ride this train to final passage with all manner of unrelated issues. The roll call on cloture showed just how diminished the donor-state opposition had become. Seeing their Minimum Guarantee drop all the way to 92 percent, senators from donor states were certainly not supportive of the bill overall. However, only three donor states voted against the legislation at this point—New Hampshire, Arizona, and Texas—all with Republican senators.

The opposition from the donee states also evaporated. Yes, Pennsylvania, Connecticut, Wisconsin, and Hawaii were all still doing poorly. But they could at least point to their funding growth with some degree of satisfaction. Their decline in growth was not nearly as significant as it would have been if the Minimum Guarantee for donor states reached 95 percent by 2009.

That left the large donor states as the only remaining opposition. Florida and California, the two other large donor states, both had reason to stay out of the fray—there were three Democrats between them along with one freshman Republican. No one in that group was going to raise a ruckus and risk retribution from Inhofe and the leadership.

Meanwhile, there were other delays brewing in the Senate that were completely unrelated to the transportation bill. The president's reelection had emboldened a Senate Republican majority and they wanted to approve some of the more controversial judicial nominations that the Democrats had filibustered in the previous session. There was an on-going debate, which reached national proportions, about whether the Democrats should be able to block Bush's nominees through their threat of the filibuster. Though the nominations were all for appellate courts, the fight became a partisan crucible in the Senate because everyone was keenly aware that there could soon be a vacancy or two on the sharply divided U.S. Supreme Court.

The judicial debate consumed the Senate, the national political parties, and all of Washington. Both parties seemed willing to put the highway bill and all other Senate business on hold in order to make their points on judicial nominations. Fearing that Majority Leader Frist would try to muscle the nominations through by arbitrarily deploying a highly contested parliamentary maneuver, dubbed the "nuclear option," Democrats began using delaying tactics on every aspect of routine Senate business. For instance, Senate rules require chairmen to get unanimous consent from the full Senate to conduct committee meetings while the Senate is in session. Democrats blocked those requests, bringing the real action centers of the Senate to a halt. This tactic was meant to demonstrate to the Republicans how far the Democrats would go to protect their right to filibuster. Meanwhile, Republicans gladly took time away from the highway bill and committee meetings to debate why the president was right to insist on his nominees for the federal bench, and why the Democrats were wrong to obstruct his choices. If not for the judicial nominations issue, the highway bill might have passed the Senate in a matter of days.

AN AMENDMENT ON TOLL ROADS

When debate on the highway bill finally resumed, most of the amendments submitted and voted on this time around involved marginal issues that attracted a small amount of public debate. The Senate covered issues such as storm water runoff, bicycles and pedestrians, and construction contracting. Behind the scenes, however, senators and staff engaged in constant debates and procedural maneuvers in an effort to get certain amendments into the bill.

For example, the committee chairman, who manages the bill when it comes to the floor, has a wide degree of latitude on what amendments to accept, and Senate rules can help him do so even when others might want to debate the issue. One particular procedure often used to insert amendments this way is by unanimous consent, known throughout the Senate simply by its acronym, UC. When a senator offers an amendment on the floor, the bill manager can agree to accept the amendment by UC and then put out a notice to all senators that such a procedure is about to occur, giving any other senator a chance to object if he or she chooses to do so.

The reality is that very few senators pay attention to bill as it's being "debated" on the Senate floor. Few even watch it on television in their offices. They stay close enough to make it to the floor when a roll call is announced, but otherwise they leave the actual legislating to the bill managers and key committee members. So once a floor manager agrees to take an amendment by UC, it is unlikely to be blocked. In order to block it, a senator must (1) hear about it, (2) care enough to object to it, and (3) succeed in objecting. Each of these steps is more difficult than one might assume.

In order to hear about the amendment, an individual senator's aides must be notified that such an amendment is going to come up. The majority and minority leaders will notify all legislative directors and chiefs of staff immediately, and these people then must relay that information to their legislative assistants in charge of the issue. If someone is in a meeting without a Blackberry, or doesn't notice somewhere along the line that this issue is important to the boss, they are out of the loop.

Next, the legislative assistant must convince the senator that it's important to object to the UC request. If the senator is the only person objecting, this is putting a great deal of political capital on the line because that senator will be personally responsible for slowing down the entire Senate. An objection to a UC request may only serve to force an extra roll call vote, and votes take forever and keep senators in session longer. No senator wants extra votes if they can be avoided, so the legislative assistant had better be sure this is a big enough issue to warrant objection. Sometimes several senators will want to object and there will be no problem if one of them acts for the group. But for one senator to object alone, knowing that the amendment can most likely be passed by ninety-nine other votes, is quite a burden to bear.

Finally, a senator may agree to offer an objection, but that doesn't mean it will actually happen. The senator has to get approval out to the aide, who must call down to the leadership in the Republican or Democratic cloakroom just off the floor. Someone, a party leader or a bill manager, must be on the floor to lodge the objection on behalf of the senator wishing to object, unless of course the senator is willing or able personally to rush over to the chamber very rapidly. Typically it will be the minority leader or the ranking member on the committee who will object on behalf of his colleague (the majority is less likely to object to UC requests). However, if the minority leader does not want to object—say, for example, he or she has a vested interest in the amendment or the bill, then the party leader might choose to ignore an objection request even from a party colleague.

The fact that the minority leader might disregard his party colleague's needs may seem incongruous, but it happens. It was poised to happen on the highway bill because Harry Reid, now the minority leader, was previously head of the subcommittee that helped write the bill. Reid felt the bill was his to play with on the Democratic side, and if he told his colleagues they should accept something by UC, he probably thought that he was doing what was best for them.

This issue came up with respect to an amendment on tolling. Tolling plays a strange role in the politics of transportation. Like gas taxes, no politician wants to go out and support the imposition or increase of tolls. Tolls are perceived by politicians, probably because they are perceived this way by the public, as even worse than gas taxes. People don't notice gas taxes. They are taken not from the consumer, but from the producer. Consumers typically have no idea what the federal or even state tax is on a gallon of gasoline. But they tend to know how much they are paying at a tollbooth because it is printed in huge block letters everywhere, and they sometimes have to reach into their pockets to get it.

The designers of the interstate system were so acutely aware of the tolling sensitivity (this was before EZ Pass and other automatic withdrawal technologies, when tolling was more obvious and caused more delay) that they actually prohibited tolling on any portion of the interstate.

This prohibition remains in effect today, since no politician would dare attempt to repeal it. The portions of the interstate that are tolled are all either segments that existed before the interstate system and were grandfathered in (such as the Pennsylvania Turnpike and the New York Thruway), or were part of a pilot program under TEA-21.

The TEA-21 pilot was probably the first sign of recognition in the federal government that gas taxes would not suffice indefinitely as a revenue method for funding road maintenance and construction. As discussed previously, the trust fund engine is losing steam, primarily because increased fuel efficiency in cars means consumers are not buying as much gas, but also because of stagnating gas taxes. Politicians' reluctance to increase gas taxes, coupled with the advent of hybrid and other more fuel-efficient vehicles, spells trouble for the Highway Trust Fund as a system of financing federal highways. In fact, the bill before the Senate in 2005 would put the trust fund into a negative balance before the end of the measure's six-year life—and that bill was at a reduced number from the one passed by the Senate a year earlier.

Therefore, whether the federal government takes action or not, the states were probably going to have to start using tolls more frequently as revenue from the Highway Trust Fund dries up. Interestingly, states also were beginning to find that tolls were useful as a method of relieving traffic congestion, in a way that constructing more roads was not. Successful experiments with "peak pricing" in London and to a lesser extent in New York indicated that charging high tolls during peak driving hours could alleviate congestion. Building more lanes and roads was not only more expensive, but probably less effective at accomplishing the same task.

The prohibition against using tolls on the interstate makes it impossible to use peak pricing to reduce congestion in many urban areas of the United States. Think of the most congested road in a given city, and it is quite likely you will think of an interstate highway. These are the places that people might even be most open to tolling, but it is prohibited by federal law.

TEA-21 attempted to find a remedy to the problem by allowing states to participate in a pilot program to toll their interstates for congestion-relief purposes. No state had succeeded in implementing such a program since its inception, although Virginia did apply for the authority to do so and its state department of transportation has been very aggressive in advancing such a program.

Meanwhile, it happened that Texas was busy debating within the state government about building its next-generation transportation system. In the Texas tradition, officials there had decided to ignore the federal government and press forward with their own program. There was an intense debate brewing in Texas between those who thought the system should be financed through tolls, and those who opposed tolls. Sen. Kay Bailey Hutchison, a Republican from Texas, was in the latter camp. She decided that the highway bill was a ready-made vehicle to keep her state from going its own route.

Hutchison crafted an amendment essentially repealing the pilot program for all states except Virginia. This would mean very little for most states, but would provide her with a platform by which she could make a statement against toll roads. Virginia's senators accepted the amendment because they were exempted, and it was presumed by leaders of both parties that no one would have a problem with it. The amendment was adopted by unanimous consent.

But it turned out that Virginia was not the only state that wanted the ability to toll its interstates. Legislative assistants who knew that their state transportation departments favored tolling were taken completely by surprise by the Hutchison amendment. Moreover, transportation policy advocates, of which there were at least a few among congressional staff, had long recognized that peak price tolling was probably the only potential long-term solution to congestion. They might have been able to persuade their senators to vote against such a blanket prohibition—or at least to ask Hutchison to exempt their states along with Virginia. The few staff members who cared raced down to the floor to protest, but it was too late. Once the amendment had passed, no one was going to do anything about it.

Something in the system had failed. It may be that the minority leader didn't care whether anyone in his caucus might have objected to the UC request. It is also possible that legislative directors in those Senate offices failed to act quickly enough. The end result was, strangely, one that no one particularly wanted except Hutchison, and even she didn't care which states were exempted as long as it wasn't Texas. Sometimes the system just breaks down.

Legislative staff complained to their bosses, who probably complained to the staff of Minority Leader Reid. It was his responsibility to give any senator a chance to object, and it appeared he had not done so. But there was no real consequence for him, as this particular amendment was perceived as not being that big of an issue in the grand scheme of things in the U.S. Senate. But it is a telling episode in the way public policy is made in Washington. Perhaps, someday down the road, this is how we will explain to our grandchildren why traffic is so terrible.

SENATE BILL PASSAGE

Compared to the action on this bill the last time out, the Senate floor was a hotbed of activity. With no rebellion to stall the bill, senators continuously came forward to offer amendments. They were interrupted by the ongoing debate regarding judicial nominations, and even on occasion for other discussions, but not because the transportation bill itself faced any obstacles. More likely these interruptions were allowed while bill managers negotiated behind the scenes with amendment sponsors. Despite the fact that hundreds of amendments were offered, there were only seven roll call votes on substantive amendments. This means that many senators saw their amendments incorporated by unanimous consent, or withdrew their amendments without a vote.

One particularly interesting amendment that did come to a vote was put forward by Republican George Allen, the junior senator from Virginia. Allen was very junior compared to his GOP colleague, John Warner. Senator Warner was the chairman of the Armed Services Committee, a war veteran, and former Navy Secretary. He was first elected in 1978, had played a very strong role in previous transportation bills, and was widely respected in the Senate at the time. Senator Allen, by contrast, was still in his first term.

Recall from Chapter 3 that Warner, along with Senator Clinton of New York, had offered an amendment in 2004 to require states, as a condition of receiving highway safety funding, to pass so-called primary seat-belt laws. Primary seat-belt laws allow police officers to stop a motorist if the only driving infraction is that the driver is not wearing a seat belt. Many states have only secondary seat-belt laws that allow drivers to be ticketed only if they are pulled over for some other reason. The bill already provided funding incentives for states that enacted primary seat-belt laws. The Warner-Clinton amendment would have also withheld funding from states that failed to do so—it sought to create a stick in addition to the carrot already in the bill. It was ultimately rejected.

This time around, Senator Allen, in a move that did not show tremendous tact or deference to his senior colleague, offered an amendment to eliminate the carrot. He did not want any incentives for primary seat-belt laws. He argued that primary seat-belt laws contribute to racial profiling, and that the federal government should not be involved in state issues like this one. His amendment would have changed the bill so that incentives could be provided for states that reach certain seat-belt usage rate levels, regardless of whether they actually enacted a primary seat-belt law.

The policy merits of Senator Allen's amendment are debatable. Although primary seat-belt laws are the only method of increasing seat-belt use that has proven effective, there was nothing in Allen's amendment to prevent states from enacting them. His language simply would leave the decision to the states regarding how they wanted to increase seat-belt use. So far as it goes, this is a perfectly reasonable point of view.

But one has to wonder why Allen would be the one to bring this forward. He was directly challenging the senior senator from the same state and same party with an amendment that did the opposite of what Warner had publicly advocated. Whatever reason Allen had for offering the amendment surely could have been accomplished by simply supporting it if it were to be offered by someone else.* The most likely explanation here is that the Virginia Department of Transportation wanted the amendment and Allen, a former Virginia governor, wanted to oblige. His staff probably failed to consider how it would look for him to challenge Warner directly in this way. The amendment failed 14–86.

---

*Senator Allen's lack of judgment would be underscored a year later, when he fell from potential presidential candidate to defeated senator in a close race that ultimately gave the Democrats the Senate. His loss in that race was generally attributed to several gaffes on his part as well as substantive policy issues.

Before the final bill could pass, there was one last gasp of rebellion. Yet this episode was very different than what had come before, and exposes the different points of view present in those opposing the bill. Many of the opponents of the bill, such as the senators from New Hampshire and Arizona, had expressed dismay at the overall size of the bill. They had complained that the bill was an example of excess spending, and that it busted the budget. It also happens that these states were donor states that did not fare as well as they would have liked. And both had two Republican senators.

There was another set of opponents to the bill who joined forces with this group but argued differently. These senators did not argue for fiscal discipline, but expressed direct concern that their states were being treated unfairly by not getting enough money. They were barely mincing words on the issue.

This last rebellion was constructed only to cater to the first group. It was never intended to seriously alter funding in the bill to favor other states, or derail the bill until a new funding formula could be produced. It was intended solely as a statement against the amount of funding in the bill and in favor of fiscal responsibility and administration policy.

It came in the form of an amendment from Jeff Sessions, a Republican of Alabama. His amendment sought to cut $11 billion from the bill in order to bring it into line with both the budget and the president's original request. Sessions could afford to make the argument for fiscal discipline because Richard Shelby, the other Republican from Alabama, chaired the Banking, Housing and Urban Affairs Committee and was in perfect position to ensure their state would receive plenty of transit funding. Sessions' amendment was more than a favor to the administration— he was clearly providing, for himself and other Republicans, a platform to oppose the "excess" spending in the bill. The amendment was defeated soundly, 16–84, but a look at "yea" votes reveals a great deal:

Brownback, R-Kan.	Gregg, R-N.H.
Burr, R-N.C.	Hagel, R-Neb.
Coburn, R-Okla.	Hutchison, R-Texas
Cornyn, R-Texas	Kyl, R-Ariz.
DeMint, R-S.C.	McCain, R-Ariz.

Enzi, R-Wyo.   Sessions, R-Ala.
Frist, R-Tenn.   Sununu, R-N.H.
Graham, R-S.C.   Thomas, R-Wyo.

First, note that every senator voting for this amendment was a Republican. This suggests that they wanted either to prove their conservative credentials or curry favor with the administration (or both). Second, note how few states are represented—the sixteen senators came from only ten different states—and they tended to be among the most conservative; only one state represented here had a Democrat in the Senate, and he (Ben Nelson from Nebraska) was one of the most conservative members of his caucus.

Finally, notice that Majority Leader Bill Frist also voted for this amendment. This was quite exceptional. This amendment essentially proposed to alter the most important national element of the bill—its funding level. This bill was a pie full of money, and Session's amendment would have decreased the size of the pie. Under normal circumstances, there was is no way on earth that the majority leader would allow a bill to pass that he fundamentally disagreed with, and there was nothing more fundamental to this bill than its overall size. Yet Frist, after allowing the bill to come to the floor and knowing that it would almost certainly pass, voted for an amendment to change the size of the bill. This suggests that the vote was actually orchestrated by the majority leader, who at the time had clear presidential ambitions, so that he could go on record as supporting the Bush administration and a fiscally responsible transportation bill.

The final vote on the transportation bill was, as usual, overwhelming. The vote was 89–11, meaning that even fewer people voted against passage of the final bill than voted for the Sessions amendment. The "nays" did include two Democrats—both Wisconsin senators (Russ Feingold and Herb Kohl). Perhaps the minority leader did not satisfy their parochial needs with enough special project money, but that is conjecture. The other nine votes were made up of the usual suspects who had all voted for the Sessions amendment. Sessions, for his part, voted for passage. Then there was Bill Frist: He may have wanted to decrease the funding in the bill, but it would have been unwise for him to vote against the bill on passage. He nodded "yea" for the $295 billion budget buster.

BACK TO THE HOUSE FLOOR

This time, the House and Senate were not playing around with different funding levels and bids and negotiations. The pressure from contractors and industry groups had reached a boiling point; these groups did not care about fighting for more money—they just needed a bill and the authority for states to build roads. So both House and Senate had marked up their respective versions and came to each chamber floor with a $284 billion price tag. Keep in mind that for the House this represented an *increase* rather than a decrease in the bill's proposed funding level.

With this increase, one might expect that House members would move to raise the Minimum Guarantee for donor states, or perhaps adopt the Senate's equity bonus model to make sure those states got some funding protections. Yet they did not. Despite the presence and clout of Texan Tom DeLay, the powerful majority leader from the biggest donor state of all, House leaders made no move to increase the Minimum Guarantee. The donee states could not believe their luck.

Of course, it was not all luck. DeLay knew that in order to pass the Senate, the conference version of the bill would have to satisfy at least thirty states in order to win sixty votes and survive a filibuster. And he also knew that any filibuster would not come from Democrats, whereby DeLay and the Republicans could accuse them of obstructing government business. A filibuster, if it were to materialize at this stage of the process, would be bipartisan and thus make everyone in Congress look bad, especially if it killed the bill. Given that Republicans were just then decrying the evils of filibusters over judicial nominations, doing anything that would set up for a GOP-led filibuster of the transportation bill was probably a bad idea for the House.

DeLay also knew that the real issue for the House was not the Minimum Guarantee as much as the so-called High Priority Projects. House members were eager to bring home as much targeted spending to their districts as possible, and it would be Republican incumbents who stood to benefit most. DeLay could make more hay out of the "scope" of the highway bill than with the Minimum Guarantee.

Recall that scope refers to language that stipulates which programs in the highway bill fall under the Minimum Guarantee umbrella. If a program falls under that umbrella, as almost all programs did under TEA-21, its funding levels are used in the calculation of the Minimum Guarantee. States receiving more money under any given program will therefore receive less from the Minimum Guarantee because they are likely to already meet the criteria for 90.5 percent rate of return. If a program is not under the scope of the Minimum Guarantee, then states receiving lots of funding under that program will not see their rate of return affected.

Given that Republicans controlled the House and were planning to provide their Republicans with lots of High Priority Project funding, they could effectively increase funding for Republicans only if they simply removed the program from the scope of the Minimum Guarantee. They would be providing plentiful benefits to Republican districts without penalizing the overall funding for those states. It was very confusing to anyone but transportation funding experts, which means it was a clever and potentially successful plan.

Donee states were unsure what to do. First they had to figure out what this proposal meant for each of them. This was actually very difficult to do at the time. There was no real way to evaluate this proposal because no one knew for sure what was going to happen with High Priority Projects. They would ultimately be decided in conference with the Senate.

The House took two days to debate the transportation bill (now HR 3) before voting to pass it and send it to a conference with the Senate. The vote was 417–9.

CONFERENCE

The conference experience could not have been more different this second time around. The two versions of the bill arrived in conference with everyone on both sides exhausted. Staff would have preferred indentured servitude to working on this bill any longer. Members of Congress, having recently been through an election, had lost the gusto they once had for fights on this bill and were ready to move on to something new. This time there was no election on the horizon to bail anyone out. An agreement had to be reached.

One way this conference was the same as before was in the appointment of the conferees. Although the names had changed to some extent, the spirit had not, as both parties gave seats on the committee to members in need of some special project money. (See Appendix 3 for a complete list of conferees.) For example, Rob Simmons of Connecticut, a Republican, was facing the closure of a military base in his district that would mean the loss of ten thousand jobs. With his state already trending Democratic, Speaker J. Dennis Hastert assured him of a spot on the conference committee, despite the fact that more senior individuals could have been given the seat.[3] Democrats played the same game with their seats, and even had the last laugh: Simmons would eventually lose his reelection bid in 2006 by eighty-three votes while the Democrats held all of their seats and regained majority control of the House.

As it turned out, the two "sides" in this conference were not all that far apart. The House came in with the White House–favored number of $284 billion, whereas the Senate came in with $295 billion. The gap was small, but what is most interesting about it was that House negotiators were in a perverse negotiating stance. They were in the position of arguing for a lower cost, when the reality was that they would have preferred the larger bill. We know that because the House, which had not been all that different the year before, had already passed a larger bill the year before. They were compromising on this bill to appease the president. They would argue on behalf of their new legislation in order to continue to support the White House, but their hearts wouldn't be in it.

A typical scene played out in the opening proceedings of the conference committee. With ninety-three appointed conferees, there were more opening statements than anyone would care to hear. Eager to do some actual negotiating on the bill, Senators Grassley and Baucus, as well as House Ways and Means Chairman Bill Thomas, left the meeting.[4] They went out to perform the actual work of the conference committee, which was finding a number between $284 billion and $295 billion. Opening statements are always meaningless, but this act put an exclamation point on that fact.

The determining factor in finding a number between $284 billion and $295 billion would be who had greater power—Congress or the president. The president had staked out a strong position by saying he would veto anything over $284. But there was likely to be room to negotiate there. One thing was clear—the bill would not move forward unless both parties agreed on a number that would not be vetoed.[5]

Not much is known about the particulars of the backroom negotiations that delivered a final compromise number. Here is what we do know—Congress won. Not that you would know that by looking at the actual number, which was $286.5 billion. That was the number that was ultimately broadcast through the news media, the number that made it appear as if Congress had mostly caved to the president. After all, the median between 284 and 295 is 289.5. The number that Grassley, Baucus, and Thomas came out with was $3 billion less than that. The president would appear to have thrown his weight around. Sure, he approved a number slightly higher than he said he would, but he appeared to have won the negotiation.

In fact, he had won only in the sense that the nominal cost of the bill was $286.5 billion. But in fact, the actual amount of spending in the bill was almost guaranteed to be $295 billion. That is because of a little legislative trick inserted into the conference agreement that ordered $8.5 billion in contract authority to be "rescinded" in the final year of the bill (fiscal 2009).[6] That's right. Congress would pass a bill that simultaneously authorized $295 billion in spending over six years and took back $8.5 billion in the final year. Of course, everyone involved knew that this last little provision could easily be eliminated by a future Congress after the president left office, or at least long after he would care. By the time 2009 came around, everyone in Washington and the states would be so invested in the highway projects already under way that Congress would be hard pressed not to fork over the final $8.5 billion. More immediately, this slight of hand also enabled members to send news releases trumpeting the fact that the bill they voted for would deliver $295 billion for state transportation projects, since that was the actual number written in the bill.

It was an incredibly well-crafted, if disingenuous, solution. Everyone got the result that each wanted. The president got something close to his $284 billion marker, senators got a big enough pie to make enough of the donor states happy, and House members got all the special projects they could hope for. The actual decision on how much to spend, well, that was essentially deferred, as it had been almost every step of the way in this bill's tortuous life. At the beginning of this entire transportation bill reauthorization process one might have postulated that eventually everyone was going to have to agree on a final number when the bill was completed. This would have been akin to declaring that the sky is blue. Strangely enough, this turned out to be incorrect, which indicates that, in some ways, Congress is capable of writing the law so that the sky does not, in fact, have to be blue.

FINAL FINAL PASSAGE (FINALLY)

The actual final passage of any bill is often uneventful. The real issues are hammered out in conference committee and, unless the opponents feel that they really need to take every opportunity to demonstrate publicly against the bill, it is likely to sail through both chambers without incident. This was the case with SAFETEA-LU, yet the two chambers of Congress used the opportunity of clearing the final bill very differently.

Both chambers took final votes on the bill on July 29, 2005, the last day of the legislative session before the month-long August recess. Also, the bills were the very last bills to be passed in each chamber on that last day of the session. It is likely that leadership in both the House and Senate figured that if there was any remaining opposition to the bill, it would be discouraged by senators and congressman who just wanted to catch their flights home as soon as possible. This sounds like a meaningless tactic, but it is used more often that one might think. The days before a long recess are often used to pass numerous bills in a short period of time.

The House took the opportunity of final passage to allow members a few more speeches. Some of this was just the usual platitudes about how great the bill was. Typical catchphrases such as, "This is truly a great day for the users of our Nation's transportation infrastructure," were thrown around.[7] The point of such rhetoric as this, one could argue, is that everyone in the country uses the transportation infrastructure. Therefore, the speaker was saying that this was a great day for everyone in the country. It is likely that very few people knew at the time that July 29, 2005, was such a great day for them.

There were lots of thanks and self-congratulations to go around. Chairman Don Young specifically thanked over forty people by name. Thus began a cavalcade of speakers who played prominent roles in developing the bill, each thanking their staffs and one another. Even the Speaker of the House took the floor to congratulate everyone. In doing so, he helped to perpetuate one of the greatest myths with respect to the transportation bill:

I think of the hours of days every week that commuters sit on clogged Interstates, intersections, commuter highways, and the waste of American energy and productivity; this bill will begin to help that issue. As a father, I can think of all those hours that families sit on those Interstates slowly moving along, and kids say, "Daddy, when are we going to get there?" Maybe with this bill, we may have to answer that three or four less times in our lives.[8]

It would have been a challenge to attend a hearing, markup, or floor session of Congress regarding the transportation bill and not hear something along these lines. Members of Congress know that traffic congestion is a problem that every American can identify with, and that almost anyone would love to see something done about. They loved to pretend that the transportation bill would do something about it.

Ask any transportation planner and they can tell you how to solve traffic congestion. The answer is not, as SAFETEA-LU did and does, to build more roads. It is not even, as SAFETEA-LU did and does, to build more public transit systems. It is certainly not, as SAFETEA-LU primarily does to this day, to build pork-barrel projects in the districts of prominent members of Congress.

Actually solving traffic congestion takes a wide variety of strategies, but the most obvious one is to charge drivers the marginal cost of their trip. This is most often done, in theory, by charging a toll to drivers that varies by time of day. By charging users more during times of heavy traffic demand, it is possible to ensure that any given roadway can provide consistent, free-flowing traffic. The revenues can then be invested back into infrastructure, particularly into alternatives to single occupancy vehicles.

This strategy is not as politically infeasible as it once was. London recently implemented a congestion charge for its central business district, and New York City charges peak hour tolls on the bridges and tunnels leading to and from New Jersey (Mayor Michael Bloomberg recently proposed expanding that program significantly as well). There are several high occupancy toll (HOT) lanes nationwide that charge peak hour tolls to ride in traffic free lanes.

There are some provisions in SAFETEA-LU that encouraged the development of peak road pricing. They provided some exemptions to the law against tolling on the interstate system, and provided for a few pilot programs that encouraged the use of tolling on non-interstate roads. But these provisions were few and resided primarily in the unfunded portion of the bill. Most of the bill still contains money for asphalt, which, if anything, is likely to increase traffic congestion. Building more roads without appropriate zoning can lead to more sprawled development and more traffic. SAFETEA-LU, on balance, probably created more traffic problems than it solved.

Of the speakers that day, only one rose to voice opposition to the bill. That was Rep. Jeff Flake, a Republican from Arizona, who had earned a reputation in the House as a deficit hawk and opponent of pork-barrel spending. He briefly criticized the earmarks and excessive spending in the bill, and was essentially ignored by the speakers who came before and after him. Flake's opposition was a very small pebble on the road to the finish line.

One House member, Democrat Anthony Weiner of New York, took the opportunity to proudly list all of the earmarks for New York City. His pride was probably not unrelated to his bid for the Democratic mayoral nomination. Despite taking credit for tens of millions of dollars for New York City, he lost the primary. The bill itself did not fail. As before, it passed by an overwhelming majority, 412–8.

The Senate was in much more of a hurry. There were no speeches, no congratulations, nothing at all. Majority Leader Frist brought the bill to the floor as the eleventh and final vote of the day. He did not even mention the purpose of the bill, referring to it only as the "highway conference reported bill."[9] The final vote was taken and in the end, only four senators opposed the bill (ninety-one voted for it). If you can predict the "nay" votes and the three states they represent, you are an astute and observant reader. They were:

Cornyn, R-Texas
Gregg, R-N.H.
Kyl, R-Ariz.
McCain, R-Ariz.

This group was not much of a surprise. Arizona showed remarkable consistency in both House and Senate in opposition to this bill, with two

House members and two senators voting against. Texas had previously lost three different votes against, but Senator Hutchison, who had been a strong and vocal opponent in the earlier stages, voted in favor in the end.

Voting against final adoption of the conference report was a bold statement. Even the most determined opponents were likely to be assuaged at some point with a few pieces of pork. Or else they may have hated the bill but were happy to take credit for the good stuff in it at the end. Anyone still voting against the bill had actual principles and consistency in their opposition to wasteful spending. Most telling, though, is that of the 535 combined members of the House and Senate, only twelve legislators went on record against the bill.

NOTES

1. Although funds for most federal-aid highway programs can be committed by contract authority without appropriations from general revenues, some highway programs receive budget authority through appropriations acts as do most other federal programs. Thus, the appropriations act is a key part of the fiscal process as it relates to highway funding. For details see Diana Evans, *Greasing the Wheels: Using Pork Barrel Projects to Build Majority Coalitions in Congress* (New York: Cambridge University Press, 2004), and www.fhwa.dot.gov/reports/fifahiwy/fifahi04.htm.

2. Senate Committee on Environment and Public Works, *Transcript of Business Meeting,* 109th Cong., 1st sess., March 16, 2005. The $190 billion figure is lower than the entire bill because this represents only the amount for highways (not transit). The Environment and Public Works Committee had jurisdiction only over this portion of the bill.

3. Peter Savodnik, "Vulnerable Legislators Picked for Highway Conference Panel," *The Hill,* June 8, 2005.

4. Isaiah Poole, "Crunch Time for Highway Bill Deal," *CQ Weekly,* June 13, 2005.

5. Chris Cillizza, "Veto-Free Steak May End Soon; Dynamic Different in 2nd Term," *Roll Call,* June 27, 2005.

6. Tom Kuennen, "After Record 12 Extensions, Congress Passes Surface Transportation Bill," *Expressways Online,* August 10, 2005, www.expresswaysonline.com/expways.

7. Don Young, R-Alaska, *Congressional Record—House,* July 29, 2005, H7571.

8. *Congressional Record,* July 29, 2006.

9. Bill Frist, R-Tenn., *Congressional Record—Senate,* July 29, 2005, S9418.

6

PASSAGE AND POLITICS: THE AFTERMATH

BILL SIGNING

President George W. Bush signed the Safe, Affordable, Flexible, and Efficient Transportation Equity Act: A Legacy for Users (SAFETEA-LU) on August 10, 2005. August is an odd time to sign a bill. Congress is not in session; President Bush is typically in Crawford, Texas; and most of Washington shuts down. Of course, the bill was not signed in Washington, D.C. It was signed at a Caterpillar plant in Montgomery, Illinois.

The timing and location of this bill signing, like most major political events, was not an accident. Although the bill passed the House and Senate on July 29, there were many people, including the president, who wanted to make an event out of the bill signing. Therefore it could not be signed immediately but had to be scheduled for a specific date that worked for all parties. In order to delay the signing until that time, Congress also had to pass yet another short-term extension of TEA-21 the same day it passed the new bill.

The bill was signed into law in the home district of House Speaker J. Dennis Hastert. The Speaker may not have played a particularly large role in the transportation bill publicly, but his machinations behind the scene were surely crucial. The Speaker's needs were clearly not overlooked; after all, Hastert's Illinois district was rewarded with the third-highest number of special projects totaling more than $300 million. The Speaker was a logical choice to benefit from the signing location. Oklahoma or Alaska, the homes states of the two top committee chairmen, could also have

President George W. Bush signs the Transportation Equity Act surrounded by members of Congress, with Speaker of the House Dennis Hastert to the right, on August 10, 2005.

been chosen, but favoring either James Inhofe or Don Young would have been seen as a slight to the one not chosen. House Majority Leader Tom DeLay of Texas also had a Senate counterpart in Tennessee's Bill Frist. But the titular head of the Senate is the vice president, as stipulated by the Constitution, and that role is largely ceremonial. The Senate majority leader rules the roost in practical, operational terms. But for ceremonial purposes, Speaker Hastert outranked Frist.

At the ceremony, President Bush paid special tribute to Hastert, telling the crowd, "The best words that I've recently heard were these: Denny Hastert is running for office again." Bush also mentioned the $207 million Prairie Parkway connector, which would join two major highways in the growing region outside Chicago. It was going to be built in Hastert's district as a result of an earmark in the bill.

The choice of a Caterpillar plant spoke to the Republican Party's attempt to make this bill about jobs as much as possible. Caterpillar makes many of the machines that are used to construct highways. Bush could have held the ceremony at a company that actually builds the high,. but then he would not have been able to rally a bunch of blue-collar workers with his sleeves rolled up, which is exactly what he did.

One has to wonder whether there was a memo sent out regarding the dress code for that event, or whether everyone just knew what to wear. It was probably the former, given the Bush administration's reputation for missing no beats in presidential photo-ops. Almost everyone at the ceremony, from Sen. Barack Obama (Illinois's representative on the Environment and Public Works Committee) to Richard Daley (the mayor of Chicago) and Norman Y. Mineta (Bush's secretary of transportation) was wearing the official outfit—light-colored shirt, no tie, shirtsleeves preferably rolled up. One might think that this was just because the ceremony was outdoors in the middle of August, except that several of the other attending officials wore jackets (but no tie, of course). The image they were attempting to project was clear—we are working people just like you and we will all benefit from this great bill we have put together for you.

The ceremony represented everything that every major politician had worked for with respect to the bill. They each had the opportunity to trot out their favorite parts for special tribute. President Bush spoke eagerly about how the bill did not require raising the gas tax. He listed all of the accomplishments of the bill that he liked, including job creation, economic progress, and safety improvements. Then he asserted that the bill, "accomplishes goals in a fiscally responsible way," adding with unmistakable emphasis: "We are not raising gasoline taxes in order to pay for this bill." Applause followed. At the very least, the Caterpillar workers believed what the president said.

Those who have read this text, however, may disagree strongly with the president's bald assertions. Some might credibly argue that a more fiscally responsible course of action would have been either to pass a bill that could be covered by expected revenue, or to raise gas taxes to cover the true cost of the bill. As you now have seen, the bill that Congress passed and the president signed came in at a compromise funding level that allowed some general fund revenue to supplement the Highway Trust Fund, as a substitute for raising the gas tax. Although this funding switch was masked by the change in rules governing ethanol, the legerdemain could not hide the fact that a major change in fiscal policy was going to take place. In point of fact, this bill was going to cost more than the trust fund budget would provide for. Whatever you call that, it would be hard to argue that it fit the definition of fiscal responsibility.

Moreover, one could argue that raising the gas tax would have been a fiscally responsible thing to do even if general funds had been required as well. Raising the gas tax also had the potential to reduce driving. A reduction in driving could have potentially reduced the need for highway funding while also reducing the need for foreign oil and cutting down on pollution. A gas tax increase could therefore have reduced several strains on the federal budget.

But these are policy arguments that were not really on anyone's mind at this bipartisan love fest. What Bush probably meant by "fiscally" was "politically." There is no question that this bill was politically responsible. No legislator would be crucified for not passing a gas tax increase. Few politicians would be punished for failing to bring home enough bacon. It was a "safe" transportation act, for the politicians most of all.

Yet even the safest bill can cause political trouble. Members of Congress had been so caught up in fighting over the total amount in the bill and how to pay for it that they forgot to keep their eye on aspects of the legislation that could be problematic. (We return to these below.) Politicians often put themselves in danger when they get so caught up in the inner workings of Washington that they forget what the results of these machinations look like and mean to the outside world. Unfortunately for them, the news media eventually points these out to them.

PRESS TIME

In some ways, news coverage of the transportation bill was what every staff member had been working so hard for (recall the importance of credit claiming and advertising). Every fight that had been waged, every amendment submitted, and every vote placed, all had been in an effort to put out a positive news release showing how well a given member of Congress had performed for his or her state.

The fact that President Bush signed the bill into law in August did little to distract media attention from the players involved. In fact, it may have had the opposite effect, boosting coverage at a time when relatively little else was going on. The bill signing was just an opportunity for the president, party leaders and committee chairmen to get some national attention. The local news outlets had been alerted months before whenever a member could tout a benefit he could bring home with this bill. In fact, there was local coverage on the transportation bill before the bill even came to the floor of either chamber of Congress.

Members often use this trick in their press releases to get the most credit possible for anything they do. If a member only issued a statement when bills became law—that is, when Congress had in fact done something—they would get very little attention from the news media. Instead, they will issue a new press release for every incremental action. When the bill passed the committee, every member on the committee issued a statement detailing what he or she had been fighting for in committee. When the bill passed the floor, or a particular amendment was even submitted on the floor, out came another press release. Ditto when the bill passed the floor again after conference. The public and the news media often fail to distinguish between what is passed by a committee, one chamber of Congress, both houses—what is *proposed* through legislation—and what becomes the law of the land upon the president's signature. This confusion between the verbs *would* and *shall* not only means that it is easy to get credit for doing the same thing multiple times, but also that one can take credit for something that actually gets cut out or dies at a later stage in the process.

Locally, the bill had played well. In truth, it was hard for it to fail. No local editorial writer is likely to complain about too much funding for transportation projects. The worst that could happen is that a newspaper might run a story showing how the local elected official failed to bring in as much money as his or her predecessor. Since most of the press releases for this bill came out just after the election, this was of diminished concern. Also, as the voting showed, it was only a concern for a small minority in Congress.

Nationally, however, trouble was brewing. Congress and the White House had spent two years fighting over this bill, primarily over its size. During that time, the White House had worried that an expensive bill could be perceived as excessive spending. Despite Congress' overwhelming appetite for pork, the White House consistently fought to keep spending down. Administration officials and their allies in Congress had battled it down from a $375 billion proposal by Don Young to the $318 bill passed by the Senate and then finally down to the $286.5 billion eventually signed by the president. The White House probably figured that if they kept the overall spending number in check the public would accept the bill as a job-creation engine that would help improve their daily commute. They did not count on the possibility that the public might actually look at how the money would be spent.

The bill did not necessarily create huge headlines at first, but from the start the news media was drawn to the issue of pork-barrel spending. Take a look at this short blurb from the *Pittsburgh Post-Gazette*. Keep in mind that Pennsylvania did very poorly under the bill compared to past years:

> *President Bush yesterday signed the six-year, $286.5 billion transportation bill, saying it would ease traffic congestion, create hundreds of thousands of jobs and impose stricter vehicular safety standards that will save lives.*
>
> *But critics said the legislation was stuffed with unnecessary and expensive projects that benefited only members of Congress seeking hometown support.*
>
> *The bill, the first major transportation spending measure since 1998, pays for projects from fiscal years 2004 through 2009. The previous highway bill expired Sept. 30, 2003, and Congress repeatedly passed funding extensions for current projects until it could agree on new legislation.*[1]

That was the entire article. Only three paragraphs and none of them mention any local issue for Pennsylvania. The first paragraph is just reporting on what the president said at the signing ceremony. The third paragraph is some basic information on the bill. It is the middle paragraph, which voices the objections of the "critics," that is important. Notice that the criticism is not of the total amount in the bill or of the Equity Bonus provision that boosted spending for some donor states, but rather of the "expensive projects" larded through the bill.

The critics were taxpayer advocacy groups such as Taxpayers for Common Sense (TCS) and the Cato Institute. TCS is a non-partisan watchdog that analyzes how the government spends tax revenue, and Cato is a libertarian think tank. These organizations raise hell with virtually every bill that passes Congress, but this time things were a little different. The story of super-lobbyist Jack Abramoff's shenanigans had recently broken, and Majority Leader Tom DeLay had recently been indicted in Texas on alleged campaign finance violations. The press and the public were already wary of congressional abuse of taxpayer funds, and the transportation bill only served to put another spotlight on that problem.

Nonetheless, in the summer, it seemed that this bit of anti-pork sentiment might just be a small blip on the anti-politician radar screen. The transportation bill would be signed, people would grumble about pork-barrel spending, and then everyone would move on. But the story lived, due in part to one special project and a now-infamous phrase identified and coined by the Taxpayers for Common Sense. They called it a "bridge to nowhere." The project was for a bridge connecting an airport on Gravina Island to Ketchikan, Alaska, which has a population of 14,000. The price tag: $223 million.[2] Newspapers and radio and TV news stations picked up the story and spread it all across the country. Late-night talk show hosts made jokes about it. The merits of the project, if there were any, were lost in the discordant ratio of cost to population benefited. By the time Congress returned from its August recess, almost every member felt pressure to deal with it. By October, the *New York Times* was referring to the bridge as the "notorious bridge to nowhere."[3]

The press picked up on the "Bridge to Nowhere" because, once exposed to the light of day, it was an easy mark. Yet a more rigorous analysis of the earmarks in the transportation bill shows that Alaska's Don Young was hardly the only pork-barrel offender in this bill, and that some other powerful transportation people got off rather easy as a result of the attention thrown Alaska's way.

Table 6.1 shows the top ten states in terms of overall funding for High Priority Projects in SAFETEA-LU, ranked by the total value of those projects. Right off the bat, one might expect that the most populous states would receive the most funding for earmarks. From a logical perspective, more populous states have greater transportation needs, and from a political perspective, they have more representatives in the House. Indeed, of the ten states listed, only three are not in the top ten in population nationwide. In fact, aside from those three, the other states fill the top echelon of the nation's population rankings, one through seven.

TABLE 6.1	Earmarks in SAFETEA-LU			
State	Value of Earmarks (in billions)	Number of Earmarks	Population Rank	Per Capita Value
California	$2.65	547	1	$ 73.34
Illinois	1.33	330	5	104.20
Alaska	1.00	120	47	1,506.79
New York	0.99	494	3	51.42
Texas	0.75	231	2	32.81
Missouri	0.73	97	18	125.86
Pennsylvania	0.71	423	6	57.12
Florida	0.69	232	4	38.79
Ohio	0.67	245	7	58.44
Oklahoma	0.57	66	28	160.66

Sources: Taxpayers for Common Sense, www.taxpayer.net/Transportation/safetealu/states.htm; U.S. Census Bureau, Population Estimates Program, http://factfinder.census.gov/servlet/GCTTable?_bm=y&-geo_id=01000US&-_box_head_nbr=GCT-T1-R&-ds_name=PEP_2005_EST&-format=US-9S.

The three states not in the top ten in population all come with easy explanations for their presence on this list, and if you have read the first few chapters in this book, you can probably explain it yourself. Don Young of *Alaska* was Transportation Committee chairman in the House, Sen. Kit Bond of *Missouri* was Transportation Subcommittee chairman in the Senate, and Sen. James Inhofe of *Oklahoma* was Environment and Public Works chairman in the Senate. Alaska's per capita funding of over $1,500 is particularly striking. It shows an impressive effort and willingness on the part of Don Young to secure funds for his district, which encompasses the entire state. Compared to Young, Inhofe was rather reserved in his pursuit of earmarks.

We can speculate about the relative ranks of the other states on the list as well. Illinois is ranked second despite being fifth in population, which is very likely related to the fact that Illinois was home to House Speaker Hastert. Texas is ranked below New York despite having more Republican representation; this may be due to the rebellion that Sen. Kay Bailey Hutchison helped fuel in the Senate on behalf of the large donor states, as well as the indictment of Tom DeLay. Texas had the lowest per capita earmarks of any state in the top ten.

It is also telling to note states at the bottom of this list (not shown). The District of Columbia, with no voting representation in Congress, ranked an unsurprising last along with the U.S. Territories that share the same status in the House. But the lowest ranked state is—you guessed it—New Hampshire. In the end, Sen. Judd Gregg was punished severely for his rebellion. Also at the bottom were Arizona and Wyoming. Arizona's John McCain spoke vehemently against the pork in the bill while playing a large role in the fight against passage, and Wyoming is the nation's least populous state.

THE COBURN AMENDMENT

The "Bridge to Nowhere" joined the DeLay indictment and Abramoff affair as symbols for what was wrong with Washington. And it became a rallying cry for the strong backlash against the bill. Fiscal hawk Tom Coburn, Republican senator of Oklahoma, seized the opportunity when the annual transportation appropriations bill came to the floor in the fall of 2005. (Recall that SAFETEA-LU was an authorizing bill—this bill addressed actual appropriations for provisions in the legislation not funded by contract authority.) He offered an amendment to move $75 million from those Alaska bridges to hurricane relief in New Orleans (this was less than two months after Hurricane Katrina). Sen. Ted Stevens, elder statesman of the Senate (he helped bring Alaska to statehood) and the chamber's president pro tempore, famously took the floor to defend Don Young's earmarks. He threatened to resign his Senate seat if the amendment were adopted. "These bridges," he said, "are necessary." His Senate colleagues did not dare to disagree.

The papers were eager to report the rhetoric of the irascible Stevens, but they mostly ignored what James Inhofe had to say. Inhofe was chairman of the committee of jurisdiction and thus partly responsible for allowing the bridge earmark to go into the bill. As such, he was also under attack from his home-state GOP colleague, Coburn. Inhofe had to choose whether to support the other senator from his own state, or defend the principle of earmarking in the transportation bill. The choice was very easy:

Mr. President, I do not have a better friend than my colleague from Oklahoma, but it does not mean we always agree with each

other. I have had a policy in voting for amendments on bills that
I have adhered to for a long time, and it is if a senator has a bill
or an amendment that takes authority from an elected official
and places it in the hands of an unelected bureaucrat and it does
not save money, then I think it is not good policy. Unfortunately,
I think that is what this does.[4]

Inhofe was insisting that earmarking better serves the public because it gives authority over individual projects to elected officials
rather than functionaries in the Transportation Department. He was
being somewhat disingenuous, given that he just steered through Congress a transportation bill where the vast majority of $286.5 billion in
new spending authority would be controlled by "bureaucrats." But Inhofe had to oppose the Coburn amendment because he had $570 mil-
lion worth of earmarks for Oklahoma, which he knew would be at risk
if he took on his fellow senator's earmarks. He probably also knew that
the primary reason that Coburn could afford to make a public spectacle of Stevens and Alaska over the "Bridge to Nowhere" was because,
politically, Coburn could not lose. If the amendment failed, Oklahoma
would still have that $570 million and even Coburn would get some of
the credit for it. If it passed, he would look like a benevolent crusader
against pork and probably still retain most of the pork for his home
state.

Stevens spent much of his time ranting about how, in 37 years of service, he had never seen one state try to take money from another state in
the Senate. But Stevens actually made one argument that had legitimate
transportation planning theory behind it. He used his advancing age and
long perspective to wage a more effective argument when he said:

I remember as a young man in California when someone sug-
gested there ought to be a bridge, what we call the Golden Gate,
over the San Francisco Harbor. People said: You can't do that.
That is a bridge to nowhere. I remember those words, "a bridge
to nowhere," a bridge up in Marin County where hardly any-
body lived. It was a place for cows and ranchers. Today what is
it? It is a thriving part of the great state of California.[5]

Of course, this argument has its own holes, in that Alaska, due to its remote geographic location, may not be as suitable for future development as the Bay Area of northern California. However, the fact is that transportation planning often involves channeling future development through infrastructure, and this is a legitimate point of view. It probably was not the argument that won over his Senate colleagues, however. More likely, it was threatening statements like, "I come to warn the Senate, if you want a wounded bull on the floor of the Senate, pass this amendment."

The Coburn amendment was overwhelmingly rejected, 15–82. Most senators knew where their bread was buttered and had no interest in declaring war on earmarking. A look at the senators voting in the affirmative is, as usual, revealing. Also note that McCain, usually a champion of the fight against pork and earmarking, was absent from the voting.

Allard, R-Colo.	Feingold, D-Wis.
Allen, R-Va.	Graham, R-S.C.
Bayh, D-Ind.	Kyl, R-Ariz.
Burr, R-N.C.	Landrieu, D-La.
Coburn, R-Okla.	Sessions, R-Ala.
Conrad, D-N.D.	Sununu, R-N.H.
DeMint, R-S.C.	Vitter, R-La.
DeWine, R-Ohio	

Other than Louisiana's Mary Landrieu, who had to vote for the amendment because it provided funding for her home state, which was currently recovering from a major disaster, there were only three Democrats who voted with Coburn. Everyone else was a conservative Republican. Even when the elimination of pork-barrel spending was pitted against hurricane relief, most members of the Senate were still afraid to challenge one of their most powerful members and one of their most cherished prerogatives.

DONOR/DONEE AND THE FORMULA FIGHT

The donor/donee issue is as old as the concept of a federal government. In the transportation bill, it is perhaps more transparent than in other cases because the bill consists of the naked division of an enormous pot of money collected from the states. Chairman Inhofe began this round of fighting on the issue by announcing a goal of increasing the minimum rate of return to 95 percent. He ultimately failed to accomplish that goal, but he did boost it to 92 percent from the TEA-21 rate of 90.5 percent.

After all the fighting and wrangling over this issue, the question remained: Who were the real winners and losers? (Donor and donee states under SAFETEA-LU are indicated on the map on page xx.) There are two ways to measure this. The first is to look at the changes in rate of return for each state. This can tell us which elected officials could go back home and point to their increased rates of return on the transportation bill. Table 6.2 shows the top ten states in that category.

The first thing to remark about the list in Table 6.2 is that there are only two states on it that were actually donor states under TEA-21 (in 2003)—Arkansas and Missouri. Otherwise, each appears to be a state with relatively low population that saw its rate of return increase irrespective of the Equity Bonus. Their rates probably increased simply because the size of the bill increased as vehicle miles traveled in the state increased. None of these states show substantial political connections within the transportation bill framework except for Montana (represented by Democratic senator Max Baucus) and Kit Bond's Missouri.

TABLE 6.2	Top Ten States, by Increasing Rate of Return		
State	2003 Rate of Return (under TEA-21)	2009 Rate of Return (last year of SAFETEA-LU)	Difference
District of Columbia	335.54%	425.03%	89.49%
Vermont	183.40	206.43	23.04
Wyoming	133.51	151.89	18.38
West Virginia	158.36	169.31	10.95
Idaho	134.84	143.78	8.94
Montana	218.42	227.10	8.69
Arkansas	96.91	105.44	8.52
Alabama	100.39	106.91	6.53
New Mexico	107.79	114.22	6.43
Missouri	91.55	97.80	6.25

Source: Federal Highway Administration, 2006, www.fhwa.dot.gov/reauthorization/rta-000-1664ar.xls.

Bond probably had something to do with getting Missouri on this list, but Montana is likely more of an accident given its small population and how little funding it would have taken to get it to grow even more.

Therefore, we know that the donor/donee fight did not result in major increases in the rate of return for most donor states. The vast majority of donor states increased by the minimum required, from 90.5 percent to 92.0 percent. This is not surprising given that the minimum is exactly what everyone was fighting over. We might learn more from examining actual growth in funding, which we will do in a moment. Before that, however, it is worthwhile to examine the losers in this battle. The ten states in Table 6.3 showed the most dramatic diminishing returns.

The first thing that must jump out at anyone examining this chart is the fact that Alaska is at the bottom of this list. Of all states in the union, Alaska showed the largest decrease in the rate of return under this bill. This might seem surprising until you notice that Alaska still has the highest overall rate of return of any state, by far. Don Young could not have been very concerned about his state receiving only $5.26 for every dollar sent to Washington instead of $5.67. Those numbers are meaningless for him (and for South Dakota, too) because for small states like

TABLE 6.3	Change in Rates of Return under SAFETEA-LU		
State	2003 Rate of Return (under TEA-21)	2009 Rate of Return (last year of SAFETEA-LU)	Difference
Minnesota	97.60%	92.00%	−5.60%
Pennsylvania	120.84	113.15	−7.69
New Hampshire	110.05	100.31	−9.74
Kansas	106.97	95.53	−11.44
Iowa	105.62	92.00	−13.62
Connecticut	142.72	128.49	−14.23
New York	124.88	109.61	−15.26
South Dakota	216.32	197.75	−18.57
Hawaii	208.46	175.26	−33.20
Alaska	567.34	526.85	−40.50

Source: Federal Highway Administration, 2006, www.fhwa.dot.gov/reauthorization/rta-000-1664ar.xls.

those, vast changes in the rate of return mean very little in terms of overall cash. And as we will see soon, they did very well in terms of overall cash.

The real losers here are the big states on this list because even small drops in rate of return mean big cash losses for them. These include Pennsylvania and New York, and to a lesser degree Minnesota, Connecticut, and Iowa. Pennsylvania and New York both knew that they were likely to take a hit in this category given the change in their past positions of power within Congress. The other states, however, do not seem to have much in common with respect to power or fighting on this issue. Some of these states were part of the rebellion in the Senate, such as New Hampshire and Pennsylvania, but many were not.

However, the rate of return was not the real issue. The real issue was how that rate of return affects funding. Therefore, to clarify this further it is necessary to examine the actual funding increases instead of the rate of return. The states in Table 6.4 experienced greater than average (the average was 30.32 percent) increases in overall funding relative to the last transportation bill (TEA-21).

TABLE 6.4	States with Greater Than Average Funding Growth from TEA-21 to SAFETEA-LU	

State	% Change in Funding from TEA-21
Colorado	46.75%
Minnesota	46.12
Arizona	40.66
District of Columbia	39.86
Vermont	39.40
Texas	37.42
Ohio	36.01
Indiana	34.66
California	34.30
Illinois	33.34
Florida	33.19
Virginia	31.86
Maryland	31.58
Oklahoma	31.51
North Carolina	30.95
Utah	30.58

Source: Federal Highway Administration, 2006, www.fhwa.dot.gov/reauthorization/rta-000-1664ar.xls.

There are a few states on this list that we can point to as the centers of power in the reauthorization of the transportation bill. Certainly Vermont, which had Sen. James Jeffords as the minority leader on the Senate Environment and Public Works Committee; also Illinois, which benefited from Speaker Hastert; Inhofe's Oklahoma; and Minnesota, represented by Rep. James Oberstar, the ranking Democrat on House Transportation and Infrastructure. But the others seem somewhat misplaced. Arizona was one of the biggest critics of this bill, and Texas was very busy complaining about its rate of return. The District of Columbia does not even have voting representation in Congress, yet it ranks fourth among all states in terms of funding growth. Something strange is going on here.

We can solve this mystery in part by remembering how this bill distributed the funding for the core highway programs. These formulas, presented in Chapter 1 as part of TEA-21, did not change under SAFETEA-LU. As an example, recall the formula for the Surface Transportation Program (STP), the largest of the core highway programs with $32.5 billion in funding over the six years of the bill (11 percent of all funding):

25%	State percentage of total lane-miles on federal-aid highways
40%	State percentage of total vehicle-miles-traveled on federal-aid highways
35%	State percentage of contribution to trust fund

This formula contains variables that were likely to change between 1998 and 2005. Lane-miles is probably the most constant of these three variables, but it is likely that states that are growing would have the greatest need for an increased number of lane-miles, and therefore are more likely to spend their highway dollars on building rather than maintaining roads. The other two variables are strongly linked to population growth—vehicle lane-miles and gasoline purchases both increase with population. Therefore, we might hypothesize that population growth could be fueling some of the increases in funding for the states that seem to grow the most under TEA-21.

TABLE 6.5	States with Above Average Population Growth, 2000–2005		
State	2000 Population	2005 Population	Percent Growth
Nevada	1,998,257	2,414,807	20.8%
Arizona	5,130,632	5,939,292	15.8
Florida	15,982,824	17,789,864	11.3
Georgia	8,186,816	9,072,576	10.8
Utah	2,233,198	2,469,585	10.6
Idaho	1,293,956	1,429,096	10.4
Texas	20,851,792	22,859,968	9.6
Colorado	4,302,015	4,665,177	8.4
North Carolina	8,046,491	8,683,242	7.9
Delaware	786,441	843,524	7.3
Virginia	7,079,030	7,567,465	6.9
Washington	5,894,140	6,287,759	6.7
California	33,871,653	36,132,147	6.7
Oregon	3,421,436	3,641,056	6.4
South Carolina	4,011,816	4,255,083	6.1
New Mexico	1,819,046	1,928,384	6.0
New Hampshire	1,235,786	1,309,940	6.0
Alaska	627,500	663,661	5.8
Maryland	5,296,506	5,600,388	5.7
Hawaii	1,211,537	1,275,194	5.3
Tennessee	5,689,262	5,962,959	4.8
Minnesota	4,919,492	5,132,799	4.3
Arkansas	2,673,398	2,779,154	4.0

Source: U.S. Census Bureau, 2006, Population Estimates Program.

As Table 6.5 shows, states that saw the greatest absolute population growth between 2000 (a midpoint year under TEA-21) and 2005 were some of the same states that saw the greatest growth in funding from TEA-21 to SAFETEA-LU. The average population growth nationwide was 3.7 percent. There are ten states that appear on both lists: Arizona, Florida, Utah, Texas, Colorado, North Carolina, Virginia, California, Maryland, and Minnesota. If we take out these ten states, as well as Vermont, Oklahoma, and Illinois, which clearly benefited from the power structure, we are left with three states: Indiana, Ohio, and the District of Columbia. Funding for D.C. is a strange bird that is decided not by political power or maneuvering, but rather by the recognition of Congress of its members' adopted city's local transportation needs. Therefore, the only real question that remains is why are Indiana and Ohio among the highest growth states in terms of funding, despite lower than average population growth and no specific place within the power structure?

It is difficult to provide a definitive answer to that question, but one good guess is to note that any large donor state was likely to see a substantial funding increase. Ohio and Indiana are the seventh and fifteenth largest states, and the fifth and twelfth largest donor states, respectively. California, Texas, Florida, and Illinois are the very biggest donor states, and they see major increases across the board.

The formula for how states actually succeeded in increasing their funding under SAFETEA-LU is very complicated, and it is unlikely that we could break it down into something simplistic, such as states with increased population growth or substantial political influence. Some would argue that the fighting, discussion, debate, and maneuvering described in the past few chapters played only a modest role in determining the winners and losers. Those with the ability to retain additional funding due to their position within the congressional power structure were generally able to do so. Those states that enjoyed population growth were likely to see substantial funding growth. And those states that were previously donor states and had substantial populations were likely to grow at high rates due to an across-the-board increase in the minimum rate of return.

In the end, the fights and interminable rounds of negotiation were mostly responsible for changes at the margins. Most of the actual results were created by circumstances largely beyond the control of any senator or representative, much less a given staff member. Nonetheless, if you asked any staff member if it was worth it, he or she would probably say yes, it was. And it is precisely this type of political maneuvering that members of Congress believe they were elected to do. They were just doing their jobs. Of course, producing results is what it's all about at the end of the day, but just fighting the good fight can go a long way on the campaign trail.

PORK-BARREL SPENDING AND THE 2006 ELECTION RESULTS

Congress rarely, if ever, enacts legislation that pleases everyone. Almost without exception, there will always be disgruntled parties and political foes who will keep the battles alive long after the last shots have been fired. In politics, this usually drags into the next election.

The midterm elections of 2006 were scheduled to take place more than a year after passage of SAFETEA-LU. If, as many believe, the electorate's memory is short term, then voters, if left to their own devices, were likely by November 2006 to have moved far past the highway bill and allegations of the egregious spending projects it included. But this was unlikely to happen. For one thing, members who had fought to deliver to their districts in the form of earmarked projects would trumpet the largesse on the campaign trail. This is precisely the kind of credit-claiming, discussed in Chapter 1, that congressmen live for. But even opponents had incentives to keep the electorate's collective memory of the process fresh. Poor performance in delivering for districts could fuel challengers' efforts to unseat incumbents, and Democrats, despite ferocious efforts to secure benefits for their own districts, could lambaste Republicans for uncontrolled spending and the record-breaking number of pork projects ultimately included in the bill signed by Bush.

To be sure, the 2005 transportation reauthorization reflected more than a three-fold increase in the number of earmarked (or "demonstration") projects, which amounted to a total cost more than double the 1998 reauthorization (in constant 1987 dollars).[6] Table 6.6 reveals the steady growth in both the total number of earmarked projects and the corresponding costs for transportation reauthorizations 1973–2005. The 1973 and 1978 reauthorizations included fourteen and eight demonstration projects, respectively, compared to 538 such projects in 1991, 1,850 in 1998 and 6,371 in 2005.

As the 2006 elections appeared on the horizon, the issue of excessive spending took front and center. Of course, as we pointed out in Chapter 1, it is difficult to tease out how this issue plays out among voters. It's a classic "tragedy of the commons" example: Everyone hates pork in general but they also prize their own pork projects. Still, the media picked up on the theme of out-of-control spending in Washington and ran with it. Editorial after editorial scolded Congress, and especially the key players in the reauthorization, for their reckless and irresponsible spending projects. The "Bridge to Nowhere" became a household name. In and of itself, the pet spending projects in the highway reauthorization would have probably held the attention of the public for only a short time. But the theme became part of a larger narrative fueled by other developments

| TABLE 6.6 | Growth in Number and Cost of Earmarked (or "Demonstration") Projects Included in Transportation Reauthorizations, 1973–2005 |

Year	Number of Projects	Total Cost (millions)
1973	14	N/A
1978	8	N/A
1982	10	$426
1987	152	1,400
1991	538	5,171
1998	1,850	6,516
2005	6,371	13,541

Sources: Diana Evans, Greasing the Wheels: Using Pork Barrel Projects to Build Majority Coalitions in Congress (New York: Cambridge University Press, 2004); data for 2005 added by authors.

Note: All amounts in 1987 dollars.

that lingered into the 2006 election cycle: the "culture of corruption" that threatened incumbents, but especially Republican incumbents, as Election Day approached.

The "culture of corruption" was a political slogan widely adopted by the Democrats in the 2006 election season to characterize the way Republicans were running things in the nation's capital. The phrase, originally coined by District Judge Frederick Motz while sentencing Gerard E. Evans, a Maryland lobbyist convicted in a fraudulent lobbying scheme, was taken up by Democratic Party chairman Howard Dean initially to link Sen. Bill Frist and the Republican Party to the Jack Abramoff lobbying scandal. The Abramoff affair eventually led to the investigation, conviction, or resignation of several lawmakers, lobbyists, Bush administration officials, congressional staffers, and businessmen. Democrats continued to use the phrase to link corruption and scandal to the Republican Party and pointed, as evidence, to the successive indictments or convictions of several high-profile Republicans, including former Majority Leader DeLay (indicted on charges of money laundering), Rep. Randy "Duke" Cunningham, R-Calif., convicted of accepting over $1.3 billion in bribes, and Rep. Bob Ney, R-Ohio, who pled guilty to accepting bribes while in office. To add insult to injury, a sex scandal that broke in September 2006 involving Republican representative Mark Foley of Florida and a 16-year-old male page led to his resignation—and allegations that Speaker Hastert tried to cover up the scandal. This further fueled the widespread perception of corruption in Washington and especially within the Republican Party.

Uncontrolled spending became part of the "culture of corruption" narrative in the 2006 elections. Even before the transportation reauthorization was signed into law, the *Washington Post* wrote that Republican leaders "simply saw the bill as a politically popular goodie bag for their members as well as special interests."[7] The article continued,

> *This pork platter of a bill, in other words, is a product of the corruption of the Republican Party—not necessarily the kind of corruption that sends politicians such as former congressman Randy "Duke" Cunningham (R-Calif.) to prison, but the corruption of the party's limited-government principles. The conservative revolutionaries who seized control of Congress in 1994 vowed to slash the size of government, but many of them quickly came to appreciate government's value as an ATM. Republicans have dramatically increased federal spending ever since, doling out hundreds of billions of dollars the government doesn't have. . . . Congress often seems to have devolved into a policy-free zone, where pork not only greases the wheels of legislation but is the very purpose of legislation.*

As the Sierra Club later put it in a newsletter reflecting on the 2005 transportation reauthorization, "Once an obscure bit of Beltway jargon, 'earmark reform' suddenly became the central symbol of Congressional corruption—a Bridge to Nowhere was something constituents could, and did, understand. It smacked of deep, profound rot—not principled conservatism or normal partisan bickering."[8]

Examples of pet spending projects, held up as evidence of politics over principle, were featured in countless media outlets after passage of the reauthorization. The "Bridge to Nowhere" was everywhere. On November 6, 2005, *Parade* magazine, one of the nation's largest with a readership of over 74 million, put a mock-up of the bridge on its cover (see Box 6.1). In the accompanying article, titled "Are Your Tax Dollars Being Wasted?" by David Wallenchinsky, the author asserted that "If all pork programs were miraculously suspended, the total would pay for about 18

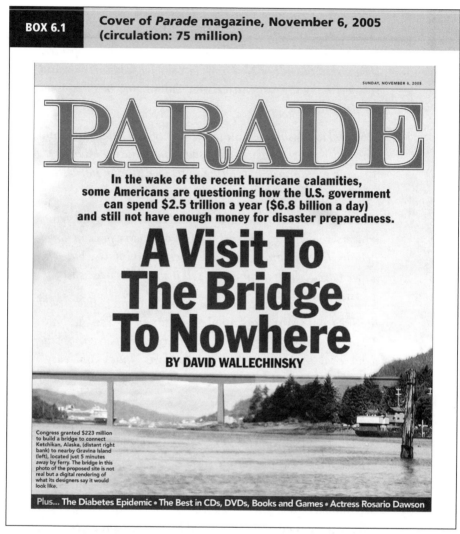

BOX 6.1 Cover of *Parade* magazine, November 6, 2005 (circulation: 75 million)

SUNDAY, NOVEMBER 6, 2005

PARADE

In the wake of the recent hurricane calamities, some Americans are questioning how the U.S. government can spend $2.5 trillion a year ($6.8 billion a day) and still not have enough money for disaster preparedness.

A Visit To The Bridge To Nowhere

BY DAVID WALLECHINSKY

Congress granted $223 million to build a bridge to connect Ketchikan, Alaska, (distant right bank) to nearby Gravina Island (left), located just 5 minutes away by ferry. The bridge in this photo of the proposed site is not real but a digital rendering of what its designers say it would look like.

Plus... The Diabetes Epidemic • The Best in CDs, DVDs, Books and Games • Actress Rosario Dawson

Note: The Gravina Island bridge, intended by local lawmakers to provide Ketchikan, Alaska, with hard-link access to the airport and to developable land, was decried by environmentalists opposed to road building in Alaska and Lower 48 critics of taxpayer waste as a "bridge to nowhere." This *Parade* magazine cover story brought the local project to national prominence.

percent of Gulf Coast recovery [from the Hurricane Katrina disaster], now estimated at around $150 billion." The article also enumerated several other examples of pet spending projects and asked readers, "Is there any defense for the following expenditures?" It went on:

- *$250,000 to connect two ski resorts in New York—North Creek Ski Bowl and Gore Mountain Resort—so they can compete better with resorts in Vermont and New Hampshire. If you lived outside of New York or New England, how would you feel knowing your taxes were subsidizing businesses in another state?*

- *$250,000 to Washington State University and Michigan State University for research to cut asparagus-industry labor costs by using mechanical harvesting to replace human harvesters. Why are taxpayers helping to eliminate U.S. jobs?*

- *$200,000 to Ocean Spray, a cranberry- and grapefruit-growers' cooperative, to market white cranberry juice in Great Britain. Ocean Spray cranberry juice is quite tasty, but why do we have to help the business sell its products overseas?*

- *$2 million to construct a parking facility at the University of the Incarnate Word, a Catholic institution in San Antonio, Texas. According to www.campusdirt.com, 58 percent of students said that off-campus parking was "quick and easy." Overall, parking at UIW was given a grade of "B"—without help from U.S. taxpayers.*

- *$70,000 to the Paper Industry International Hall of Fame in Appleton, Wisconsin, for construction and renovation. Is it just a coincidence that of the seventy inductees in the Hall of Fame, twenty-two were born in Wisconsin?*

- *$26 million to operate the Selective Service (draft boards) even though there is no draft now—and hasn't been any since 1973.*

- *$519 million in farm subsidies (1995–2003) to Riceland Foods of Stuttgart, Arkansas, a co-op with 9,000 members, the world's largest miller and marketer of rice. According to the Heritage Foundation, Riceland Foods receives more federal money in a typical year than all the farmers in twelve other states combined.*

- *$300,000 for a feasibility study for the world's first fully enclosed motor speedway, to be built in Ohio's Mahoning Valley.*

- *$150,000 to the Grammy Foundation to support Grammy Camp, where sixty high school students go to learn about the music business, including singing, songwriting, and engineering. (Tuition, room, and board are listed as $1,800.) Why are taxpayers helping the industry develop potential stars and other careers in the music business?*

- *$775,000 to the Biltmore Hotel in Coral Gables, Florida—part of a project to provide economic opportunity in areas of low or moderate income. (Coral Gables' per capita income is 19.6 percent above the U.S. average.) That would have been enough for 130 hurricane survivors to stay there for a month each at the luxury hotel's minimum rate of about $200 a night.[9]*

In the end, the electoral ramifications of pork-barrel politics and allegations of out-of-control spending reverberated into the 2006 electoral cycle—and beyond. To be sure, Iraq and national security were central—if not *the* central—issues in 2006. Against the backdrop of terrorism and the war in Iraq, government spending programs may have paled by comparison. Even so, outlandish spending seems to have exacerbated voters' perceptions of corruption and unethical behavior in Washington and contributed to the widespread view of irresponsible behavior on Capitol Hill. The president's approval ratings had plummeted well below 50 percent, and a majority of Americans—61 percent according to a Gallup Poll conducted just prior to the 2006 elections—were dissatisfied with the way things were going in the country. Congressional approval had similarly sunk. In an October 2006 Gallup Poll, only 23 percent of respondents approved of the job Congress was doing.[10] Surveys consistently cited concern about corruption as a key issue for voters leading up to the election.

These indicators were harbingers of things to come on Election Day. It was a challenging year for incumbents. In the general elections, twenty-two representatives and six senators were defeated at the polls. This was the greatest number of general election losses by incumbents since 1994; it had been more than a quarter century (1980) since more than six senators had lost reelection.[11] Clearly, the electorate's anti-incumbent sentiment was widespread in 2006. But it was also directed asymmetrically toward the parties. Democrats did not lose a single seat they were defending in either the House or the Senate in 2006—not even in open seat contests.

According to exit polls, scandals in government figured prominently in the minds of voters as they headed to the polls in November 2006, despite the other national preoccupations. Nearly three in four voters (74 percent) believed that corruption and ethics were at least "very important" issues in 2006. Of the main issues asked about in the exit polls—including Iraq, terrorism, the economy, values, and illegal immigration—a higher proportion of voters named corruption and ethics as "extremely important" (41 percent) than any of the other issues.[12] The Democrats' advantage over Republicans among voters who indicated that corruption and scandals were "extremely important" in their vote for the U.S. House in 2006 was twenty percentage points; 59 percent voted for the Democratic candidate compared to 39 percent who voted for the Republican.

In the end, the Democratic victory in 2006 was monumental. Republicans lost their majorities in both chambers of Congress, returning control of the legislative branch to the Democrats.

As we discussed in Chapter 1, the scholarly research on the impact of distributive politics on electoral outcomes is inconclusive. Despite the widely held belief among politicians that more benefits increase prospects for reelection, the empirical studies on the electoral effects of pork delivery have produced mixed results. While some analysts find evidence of a positive effect,[13] others find no relationship.[14] A recent study by Andrew Sidman and Maxwell Mak finds only weak evidence of a direct effect of distributive benefits on incumbent support.[15]

Despite the debate among scholars about the electoral impact of pork, there seems to be far greater consensus among pundits and politicians, at least with respect to the results in 2006. Earmarked spending projects may not have been singularly responsible for taking down individual incumbents or the Republicans in general in 2006, but the controversy around pork projects in the transportation reauthorization certainly did not help. Even if individual constituencies may have been thankful

for distributive benefits directed to particular districts, the overall perception of irresponsible spending penetrated the electorate. Moreover, it
is clear that key Republicans themselves attributed their losses in 2006
considerably to out-of-control spending. *USA Today* reported that the Republican loss of both chambers in Congress triggered a predictable round
of finger-pointing, bloodletting, and jockeying for position within the
GOP.[16] Republican representative Mike Pence of Indiana, pointing to
huge budget deficits and dispensing "oodles of pork," remarked that, "We
did not just lose our majority. We lost our way." Similarly, 2008 Republican presidential candidate John McCain told the conservative Federalist
Society soon after the election that the party lost the midterm elections
because its leaders had abandoned their principles on fiscal policy and
government restraint, inviting backlash from voters over what they saw as
widespread hypocrisy.[17] "I think [voters] rejected us," said McCain, "because they felt we had come to value our incumbency over our principle.
And partisanship, from both parties, was no longer a contest of ideas, but
an ever cruder and uncivil brawl over the spoils of power." In a speech to
party officials on the same day, McCain pointed explicitly to the transportation reauthorization:

> *Last year, a Republican Congress passed a highway bill with
> 6,371 special projects costing the taxpayers 24 billion dollars.
> Those and other earmarks passed by a Republican Congress in-
> cluded $50 million for an indoor rainforest, $500,000 for a teapot
> museum; $350,000 for an Inner Harmony Foundation and
> Wellness Center; and of course, as you all know, $223 million for
> a bridge to nowhere. I didn't see these projects in the fine print of
> the Contract with America, and neither did the voters.*[18]

Interestingly, analysis of the $24 billion worth of earmarked projects
included in SAFETEA-LU reveals that constituencies represented by
Republicans did not necessarily fare better than those represented by
Democrats in Congress. States with no Republican senators fared the
same or better in terms of earmarks as states with Republican senators.
Similar patterns emerge with respect to the level of Republican representation in the U.S. House by state.

This result illustrates two important points. One is that the transportation bill is different than other legislation because it is such a regional bill, and this makes it difficult for one party to garner all the booty. Instead everyone gets together and agrees that they all need sufficient numbers of special projects in order to get this thing passed, and thus partisanship is put on the backburner, even in such heavily partisan times. Those who do not play along with the game, such as fiscal conservatives sticking to their guns (New Hampshire's Judd Gregg, for example) are those who will not receive the benefits (this may account, in part, for why some states with Republican senators fared poorly). Such coalition-building strategies are common in Congress and had characterized negotiations over previous transportation reauthorizations.[19] The second key point is that somehow, despite the fact that the 2005 reauthorization, like those in the past, was more about politics than partisanship, Republicans took the blame for the excesses in pork-barrel spending. A big reason for that is that Republicans were in charge, and so they could not avoid the blame entirely, despite the fact that the majority party may grant earmarks to minority party members strategically, precisely to try to avoid any such backlash.[20] It is also true, however, that Republicans tend to boast that they are fiscal conservatives, so it seems more hypocritical for them to be seen bringing home the bacon by the truckload. Everyone expects the Democrats to play the pork-barrel game, but when Republicans do it, people take offense.

Perhaps this is why political pundits traced Republican losses in 2006 back to the pork-barrel problem, too. Conservative columnist George Will wrote on November 9, 2006, "At least Republicans now know where 'the bridge to nowhere' leads: to the political wilderness."[21] Even so, Will did not credit pork as the main problem for Republicans in 2006, even though it exacerbated the party's problems:

> Of course the election-turning issue was not that $223 million bridge in Alaska, or even the vice of which it is emblematic— incontinent spending by a Republican-controlled Congress trying to purchase permanent power. Crass spending (the farm and highway bills, the nearly eightfold increase in the number of earmarks since 1994) and other pandering (e.g., the Terri Schiavo

intervention) have intensified as Republicans' memories of why they originally sought power have faded. But Republicans sank beneath the weight of Iraq. . . . The Iraq war, like the Alaska bridge, pungently proclaims how Republicans earned their rebuke. They are guilty of apostasy from conservative principles at home (frugality, limited government) and embrace of anti-conservative principles abroad (nation-building grandiosity pursued incompetently).[22]

On Capitol Hill, the importance of addressing concerns about earmarks was not lost on Democrats. The newly elected Speaker of the House, Nancy Pelosi of California, declared her intentions to open the 110th Congress in January 2007 with a new rule to require the identification of sponsors or earmarks, declaring, "There has to be transparency."[23] The House did pass a rule requiring the disclosure of earmark sponsors, but this does not appear to have slowed the flow of pet projects in Congress.

In his 2007 State of the Union speech, President Bush placed earmark spending front and center. The president mentioned earmarks second (after balancing the federal budget, ironically) in the speech, reflecting the priority he was placing on curtailing pet spending projects.

Next, there is the matter of earmarks. . . . The time has come to end this practice. So let us work together to reform the budget process . . . expose every earmark to the light of day and to a vote in Congress . . . and cut the number and cost of earmarks at least in half by the end of this session.[24]

BEYOND 2006: EARMARK REFORM AND THE 2008 ELECTIONS

Government spending and earmarks remain a central campaign theme for candidates moving into the 2008 presidential contest. By early 2007, Republican presidential hopeful McCain was leading efforts in the Congress to cut back on earmarks. Along with seven Republicans and two Democrats, McCain introduced the "Pork Barrel Reduction Act" in February 2007.[25] The bill would allow senators to raise points of order against earmarks that are attached to spending bills without having been approved by the relevant committee. Sixty votes would be needed to override the point of order and to keep the provision in the bill. The measure also would require that earmarks be described in detail and the sponsor identified.[26]

At the time of this writing, McCain, who remained a contender for the Republican nomination, was keeping spending controls at the forefront of his campaign for president and keeping the issue in the national spotlight. Asked in a Republican debate in California how he would be different from President Bush, McCain replied that he "would have vetoed spending bill after spending bill and pork barrel project after pork barrel project. . . ." Repeating this theme in a CNN debate in New Hampshire on June 5, 2007, McCain responded (to applause from the audience) with the following when asked how his positions differ from the Bush administration's:

> Spending. Spending, spending, spending, which led to corruption. We have former members of Congress in jail as we speak because of earmarking. We let spending get out of control. We presided over the largest increase in the size of government since the Great Society. And our constituents and our Republicans became dispirited and disenchanted. We've got to stop the earmarking. The bridge to nowhere, with 233 miles [sic]—a $233 million bridge to an island in Alaska with 50 people on it was the tipping point.
>
> I want to promise you, as president of the United States, I'll veto every bill that has a pork-barrel project on it. And I'll make the authors of it famous, and we'll get spending under control, and we'll stop the corruption in Washington.[27]

EARMARK REFORM AND THE PUBLIC

The general assumption, as we've argued above, is that the public doesn't like the idea of pork-barrel spending, but that they like pork projects delivered to their own districts. It's clear that politicians believe this to be true. Public opinion data confirm that earmarks are not generally held in high regard by the public at large. According to a survey conducted by CBS News and the *New York Times* in October 2006, 61 percent of American adults find earmarks to be an "unacceptable" practice. In the same survey, conducted October 5–8, 2006, 23 percent of respondents indicated that earmarks should be eliminated altogether, and 42 percent said that earmarks should be allowed but that the rules should be changed about how and when they can be added. Only 21 percent believe the system for adding earmarks should remain as it is now.

A survey conducted in June 1993 by Princeton Survey Research Associates suggests that Americans link pork-barrel spending to job loss in America. In response to the following question, most respondents rated pork as an important contributor to job loss: "(Many reasons have been given for the loss of jobs in this country over the past 10 years.) As I read from a list of government practices and policies, please tell me how important a reason each is for the loss of jobs. I'd like you to use a scale from 0 to 5 where 0 is of no importance and 5 is of the greatest importance. What about . . . too much government spending on unnecessary 'pork-barrel' projects—how important a reason is this for the loss of jobs in this country. You may pick any number from 0 to 5." Sixty-six percent of respondents chose "5," greatest importance.

Perhaps more striking is the widespread lack of knowledge about whether or not respondents' own representatives in Congress pursue pork projects. In the October 2006 survey described above, most respondents (51 percent) indicated they did not know (or they refused to answer the question) if their representative in Congress sponsors pork-barrel projects. Only slightly more than a quarter (27 percent) of respondents answered in the affirmative.

Americans overall appear to favor earmark reform. In a survey conducted by Bloomberg News and the Los Angeles Times in January 2007, 72 percent of respondents expressed support for legislation that includes provisions for the disclosure of earmark sponsors.

THE FUTURE OF TRANSPORTATION POLICY

For many of those in the industry, the impact of SAFETEA-LU on transportation is far more important than any impact on the elections. SAFETEA-LU was, by its nature, a marginal change from the TEA-21 bill that preceded it. The industry spoke virtually as one voice in the time leading up to the development of SAFETEA-LU, explaining that there was no need for fundamental change in how the bill was structured. They generally argued for more funding, but were willing to settle for less. They wanted some tweaks around the edges.

Those tweaks turned out to be somewhat damaging for the industry, such as the highway builders, trucking companies, and transportation engineers and planners. By not providing a well-defined structural change, the industry allowed Congress to continue to put a purely political imprint on the bill. The bill became less about policy or a vision for transportation, and more about fighting over a pot of money. (We acknowledge and summarize some noteworthy policy changes that were adopted in SAFETEA-LU. See Appendix 4 for details.) The result was the greatest number of earmarks in history. Also, the Equity Bonus program, which was intended to do nothing at all policy-wise and focused exclusively on the division of funds, became the largest program in the bill.

The dramatic change can be seen even in the first year of the bill. Figures 6.1 and 6.2 show the difference in funding in the core programs between 2005, the last year of TEA-21, and 2006, the first year of SAFETEA-LU. The comparison looks at the same six core programs under both bills and shows the share each program takes. Every program has a smaller share of the total under SAFETEA-LU with the sole exception of the Minimum Guarantee/Equity Bonus program. That program more than doubles in size from 9 percent to 23 percent.

Fortunately, one of the provisions in SAFETEA-LU created a National Surface Transportation Policy and Revenue Study Commission. This commission was created by an amendment from Senator Clinton at the behest of New York's Department of Transportation. The hope is that a blue-ribbon panel of experts will help move national transportation policy in the future toward a more needs-based approach. SAFETEA-LU was the epitome of a political approach, where those in power got more of the pie. New York, regardless of its political clout in Congress, stands to gain from a less political approach where funding is distributed based on needs.

This is true for any state where population is large, mass transit use is high, weather is cold, and infrastructure is old. Such states need additional funding to serve their large populations, build mass transit, repair roads damaged by snow and ice, and rebuild ancient infrastructure. They are currently denied that funding, in part, due to a political process that insists upon determining allocation in part by a state's contribution to

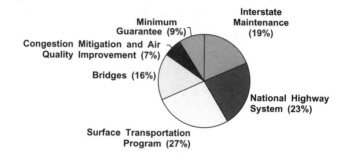

FIGURE 6.1   Funding of Six Core Programs under TEA-21, Fiscal Year 2005

Source: Federal Highway Administration.

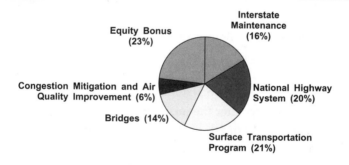

FIGURE 6.2   Funding of Six Core Programs under SAFETEA-LU, Fiscal Year 2006

Source: Federal Highway Administration.

the Highway Trust Fund. That contribution is directly correlated to consumption of gasoline, which is not necessarily something that should be encouraged.

The commission is also intended to solve the funding problem. SAFETEA-LU will be the first transportation bill to create a deficit in the Highway Trust Fund. This will happen in 2009 unless there are changes to the law. In fact, a recent report from the White House Office of Management and Budget (OMB) indicated that the deficit will be larger than originally predicted, due to the fact that higher than expected gas prices have been curbing fuel purchases.[28] Although a deficit does not necessarily mean that funding will be cut off, it does mean that the next reauthorization bill will have to rethink how funds are collected. The commission, which was created in part to solve this problem, will have to propose either a gas tax increase, an alternative source of revenue, or a reduction in the size of the federal transportation program. None of these options are very appealing to members of Congress, so it will be helpful to have a bipartisan commission publicly recommend them and provide members with some political cover. It is possible that with the weight of a commission recommendation behind them, the next administration could propose a dramatic change in transportation policy and funding that could actually have a chance for success.

CONCLUSIONS

At 6:05 p.m., the height of rush hour, on August 1, 2007, the I-35W Interstate highway bridge built over the Mississippi River in Minneapolis in 1967 collapsed. The bridge, along with at least fifty vehicles, plunged more than sixty feet into the river. At least five people were killed in the disaster, more than sixty were seriously injured, and thirty were unaccounted for several days after the incident.

In the immediate aftermath of the collapse, state and federal officials burst onto the scene, pledging millions to restore traffic flow, clear debris and begin repair work. First Lady Laura Bush was dispatched to the scene to console the victims' families, and President Bush told his Cabinet that, "the federal government must respond and respond robustly to help the people there not only recover, but to make sure that lifeline of activity, that bridge, gets rebuilt as quickly as possible."[29] Federal officials called on states to immediately inspect all bridges similar to the one that collapsed in Minneapolis.

All of these efforts were clearly too late to prevent a catastrophe of fatal human consequence. Within days of the disaster, reports emerged to reveal that Minnesota officials had been warned by the Department of

Transportation as early as 1990 that the bridge that collapsed was "structurally deficient," but officials relied only on patchwork repairs and stepped-up inspections.[30]

Promising $100 million to aid in the recovery and repairs, Minnesota's Democratic senator Amy Klobuchar remarked that, "[a] bridge in America just shouldn't fall down."[31] Indeed, it is precisely the type of maintenance intended to prevent such disasters that federal highway funds are supposed to be devoted to. But, as we have seen in this book, needs-based allocation schemes of federal highway funds are often abandoned in favor of more politically expedient divisions of the pie. Consequently, road conditions across America continue to deteriorate and structural infrastructure problems persist. A Federal Highway Administration report on the status of the nation's highways, bridges, and transit systems issued in 2006 indicates that over 15 percent of vehicle-miles of travel in the United States in 2004 occurred on roads with unacceptable levels of ride quality. Perhaps more disturbing, the same report indicates that 13.1 percent of the nation's bridges were "structurally deficient" in 2004, and that 13.6 percent were "functionally obsolete."[32] All in all, the report found that more than one bridge out of four in the United States was deficient.

Federal transportation reauthorizations are designed to address these needs. Not long after the Minneapolis bridge collapse, attention turned to Congress. Criticisms that the national legislators were negligent and that they had overlooked their responsibility to fund maintenance and repairs based on need began to mount. In the lead article on the front page, the *New York Times* reported on August 7, 2007:

> *Even as the cause of the bridge disaster here remains under investigation, the collapse is changing a lot of minds about spending priorities. It has focused national attention on the crumbling condition of America's roadways and bridges—and on the financial and political neglect they have received in Washington and many state capitals.*
>
> *Despite historic highs in transportation spending, the political muscle of lawmakers, rather than dire need, has typically driven where much of the money goes. That has often meant*

construction of new, politically popular roads and transit projects rather than the mundane work of maintaining the worn-out ones.

Further, transportation and engineering experts said, lawmakers have financed a boom in rail construction that, while politically popular, has resulted in expensive transit systems that are not used by a vast majority of American commuters.[33]

"The bottom line," argued New York senator Charles E. Schumer, "is that routine but important things like maintenance always get shortchanged because it's nice for somebody to cut a ribbon for a new structure."[34]

The 2007 Minneapolis bridge incident elucidates the importance of transportation policy in the United States. It reveals how dangerous it is for policymakers to turn a blind eye to need in favor of politics and pork. This is not to say that all pork-barrel spending is bad, or even that the 2005 transportation reauthorization was only about pork. In fact, we've seen that demonstration projects accounted for less than 10 percent of the overall cost of the legislation. But the process we've described in this book does shed light on the nature of the battles waged in Congress over highway funding, and the fact remains that many of these battles are politically motivated.

Of course, this comment does not distinguish transportation legislation. Lawmakers are constantly torn between supporting policies they believe are appropriate and policies that will help them get reelected; only on occasion are these one and the same. In that regard, the 2005 transportation reauthorization was typical, at least as an example of distributive politics.

Still, the main purpose of this book was not to make transportation experts out of readers (although we hope you've learned a lot about transportation in the process!). Instead, our main objective was to take you on a journey through the legislative process that is not unlike the path any other piece of legislation would be required to follow to become enacted into law. The substance of the policy and the nature of the debates may differ, but the process is identical. As such, some key observations about the legislative process persist.

To summarize some of these main points, we return to our initial emphasis on the Four Ps: power, process, policy, and pots of money (or price). Each of these ingredients matter tremendously in the lawmaking process as we've described it in critical ways.

Power Matters. One of the key insights that emerges almost instantaneously in the legislative battles we recount is the importance of power and clout. Powerful players—party and floor leaders and committee chairmen in particular—are able to extract greater policy concessions and benefits from the legislative process. Their control over important aspects of the process, including but certainly not limited to agenda-setting and appointment authority, enable them to shape the substance and even the outcome of legislative efforts. Diana Evans demonstrates that these key players in Congress often distribute particularized benefits at their disposal—such as earmarks, for example—selectively to win support for their policy preferences and to build majority coalitions in support of their priorities.[35]

Congressional leaders have strong incentives to retain strong control over project allocation decisions. The scholarly literature posits that district benefits are distributed strategically in order to gain recipients' support for their legislative preferences. Although there are limits to this quid-pro-quo, anecdotal and empirical evidence suggest such vote buying not only happens but that it also works.[36] Leaders will frequently distribute benefits, often in bipartisan fashion, to reward loyalty or even to punish defections.

Despite leaders' interest in controlling the funding distribution process, there is also another set of powerful actors who play a critical role in the policymaking process: congressional staff. The account of the 2005 transportation reauthorization we present is peppered with examples of the influential role often played by staffers in shaping congressional legislation and marshalling it through the legislative process, especially at critical junctures. With respect to earmark priorities, staffers enjoy a great deal of discretion. Although committee chairs and ranking members make decisions on requests for "big stuff," staffers will routinely make allocation decisions themselves on smaller projects.[37] One long-time staff director said he never brought 40 percent of project requests to the chair's attention and simply made the decisions himself.[38] The latitude that staff members typically exercise in making crucial policy decisions in

Congress is often overlooked by analysts, but the fact remains that staff members, especially senior staffers who possess a great deal of institutional memory, can also be powerful political players in the legislative process. We've seen, in the course of describing how the transportation bill became law, both the yin and yang of a staff aide influence. On the one hand, staffers are viewed as smart and hardworking with the potential to bring incredible expertise to the table. On the other hand, staffers can also be petty, inflexible, and too protective of their bosses. Nevertheless, as this book has shown, staff influence over the shape and substance of legislation cannot be overestimated. They can be the steam that powers the engine of a piece of legislation on its way to becoming the law of the land.

Process Matters. Legislative battles operate within established structural and institutional parameters in Congress. The fate of the transportation reauthorization we described in this book was, at several points, at least partly determined by the institutions—variations in chamber rules and norms for example—that the players must submit to. These structural parameters constrain actors and influence the bargaining process. Senate rules that preserve tremendous power for individual members (filibuster), for example, must be taken into account in the bargaining process. Relations with the executive branch, and the institutional mandates for bill enactment that require presidential support or veto override ability, are also crucial. The potential for, or threat of, presidential vetoes, for example, enable the executive to wrest policy concessions from Congress.[39] The story of the 2005 transportation reauthorization we tell here provides ample evidence to support this contention. The maze of structural and institutional features, through which any legislative proposal must navigate, serve to shape the compromises and decisions that ultimately determine its fate.

Policy Matters. It would be unfair and inaccurate to characterize policymakers as inattentive to policy details and interests. Members of Congress care greatly about the substance of policy issues and policy debates, often quite passionately, above and beyond their interest in distributive benefits for their districts. After all, lawmakers have policy preferences, and they will pursue these vigorously throughout the legislative process.

In addition, other crucial factors related to policy will induce members to act (or not). Ideology, partisanship, and public opinion can influence congressional action to a great extent. In the 2005 transportation reauthorization debates we've described, the main battles were not waged over ideology or partisanship, or even public opinion for that matter. But that does not mean these were absent from the scene. The public backlash partly in response to the "Bridge to Nowhere" and other earmarks in SAFETEA-LU in the 2006 elections and in the aftermath of the Minneapolis bridge collapse in 2007 ensure that such considerations are likely to be featured prominently in subsequent reauthorization debates. Still, policy preferences, as well as ideological and partisan commitments, are central components of the legislative process, even if they are not the primary engines of mobilization and activity in some policy areas, such as the one we recount in this book. It would be unwise and inaccurate to discount their relevance or importance even debates that are largely distributive in nature.

Price (Pots of Money) Matters. In Congress, as much as in life generally, everything comes at a price. Lawmakers are constantly faced with trade-offs that boil down to, for lack of better words, how much things will cost, who will pay for things, and at what political cost. For members of Congress, such financial considerations require a balancing act between policy priorities. In the 2005 transportation reauthorization debates, disputes over pots of money were the central point of contention. Even though attention to who gets what always permeates congressional legislation, emphasis on pieces of the pie takes on a whole new meaning in legislative initiatives that are primarily distributive, as the transportation reauthorization was. Few pieces of legislation—if any—feature the intense attention to distributional allocation of resources as prominently as the bill we tracked here. Oftentimes, fights over pieces of the federal pie are viewed favorably, especially by the beneficiaries. Yet critics contend that lawmakers' preoccupation with securing particularized benefits comes at a hefty price, giving way to *incrementalism* or only marginal legislative action. As the 2007 Minneapolis bridge collapse illustrates, such myopic congressional attention to big-picture policy can be catastrophic.

NOTES

1. *Pittsburgh Post-Gazette,* August 11, 2005, National Section, A-7.
2. Yereth Rosen, "How Pet Projects in Alaska Became Pet Peeve on the Hill," *Christian Science Monitor,* July 25, 2006. Another earmarked bridge in Alaska, named Don Young's Way by the committee chairman, was listed at $231 million and often called the same name.
3. Editorial, "Tom DeLay and the Bridge to Nowhere," *New York Times,* October 23, 2005.
4. *Congressional Record,* 109th Cong., 1st sess., October 20, 2005, S11636.
5. Ibid.
6. Diana Evans, *Greasing the Wheels: Using Pork Barrel Projects to Build Majority Coalitions in Congress* (New York: Cambridge University Press, 2004).
7. Michael Grunwald, "A 'Bridge to Nowhere'; An Overstuffed Highway Bill; A Teapot Museum; Pork by Any Other Name . . . ," *Washington Post,* April 30, 2006.
8. Sierra Club, "Looking Back on 2006," http://rmc.sierraclub.org/temp/lookingback.shtml (accessed June 22, 2007).
9. David Wallenchinsky, "Are Your Tax Dollars Being Wasted?" *Parade* magazine, November 6, 2005.
10. Paul Abramson, John Aldrich, and David Rohde, *Change and Continuity in the 2004 and 2006 Elections* (Washington, D.C.: CQ Press, 2007).
11. Ibid., 266.
12. Ibid.
13. R. Michael Alvarez and Jason Saving, "Deficits, Democrats and Distributive Benefits: Congressional Elections and the Pork Barrel in the 1980s," *Political Research Quarterly* 50, no. 4 (1997): 809–831; Steven Levitt and James Snyder, "The Impact of Federal Spending on House Election Outcomes," *Journal of Political Economy* 105, no. 1 (1997): 30–53.
14. Robert Stein and Kenneth Bickers, "Congressional Elections and the Pork Barrel," *Journal of Politics* 56, no. 2 (1994): 337–399; Robert Stein and Kenneth Bickers, *Perpetuating the Pork Barrel: Policy Subsystems and American Democracy* (Cambridge: Cambridge University Press, 1995).
15. Andrew Sidman and Maxwell Mak, "Pork, Awareness, and Ideological Consistency: The Effects of Distributive Benefits on Vote Choice" (paper presented at the annual meeting of the Midwest Political Science Association, Chicago, April 2006).
16. "Sound Bites, Sound Ideas: After the Voters Spoke on Tuesday, So Did the Politicians; Some of Their Quotes Said Volumes about This Year's Results," *USA Today,* November 10, 2006.
17. Adam Nagourney, "McCain Tells Conservatives G.O.P.'s Defeat Was Payback for Losing 'Our Principles,'" *New York Times,* November 17, 2006.
18. Quoted in ibid.
19. Evans, *Greasing the Wheels;* Frances Lee, "Senate Representation and Coalition Building in Distributive Politics," *American Political Science Review* 94, no. 1 (2000): 59–72.

20. Steven Balla et al., "Partisanship, Blame Avoidance, and the Distribution of Legislative Pork," *American Journal of Political Science* 46, no. 3 (2002): 515–525.
21. George Will, "A Loss's Silver Lining," *Washington Post,* November 9, 2006.
22. Ibid.
23. Peter Eisler and Kathy Kiely, "Democrats: Identify Pork Sponsors; Pelosi Plans to Target Anonymous 'Earmarks,'" *USA Today,* November 13, 2006.
24. George W. Bush, State of the Union Address, January 23, 2007.
25. Jim Abrams, "Sen. McCain Leads Effort to Cut Earmarks," *Associated Press,* February 9, 2006.
26. Ibid.
27. CNN.com, "CNN Transcript: Republican Presidential Debate; New Hampshire," June 5, 2007, http://transcripts.cnn.com/TRANSCRIPTS/0706/05/se.01.html (accessed June 20, 2007).
28. Washington Briefing 2007, "Administration Forecasts $4.3 Billion Trust Fund Deficit," July 13, 2007, www.washingtonbriefing.com/Washington-07-13-07.htm.
29. Judy Keen, "Minneapolis Bridge Warning Issued in 1990," *USA Today,* August 7, 2007.
30. Ibid.
31. Quoted in ibid.
32. Federal Highway Administration, *Status of the Nation's Highways, Bridges, and Transit: 2006 Conditions and Performance Report,* March 14, 2007; www.fhwa.dot.gov/policy/2006cpr/es03h.htm (accessed August 7, 2007).
33. Susan Saulny and Jennifer Steinhaur, "Bridge Collapse Revives Issue of Road Spending," *New York Times,* August 7, 2007.
34. Ibid.
35. Evans, *Greasing the Wheels.*
36. Ibid.
37. Ibid.
38. Ibid., 173.
39. Charles Cameron, *Veto Bargaining* (New York: Cambridge University Press, 2000).

APPENDIXES

EXAMPLES OF RECONCILED PROVISIONS IN A CONFERENCE COMMITTEE REPORT

EXAMPLE 1

SEC. 1104. EQUITY BONUS PROGRAM

House Bill
Sec. 1104.

This section retains the Minimum Guarantee program that was created in TEA–21.

Senate Bill
Sec. 1104.

This section strikes and replaces the Minimum Guarantee Program under Section 105 of Title 23, United States Code with the Equity Bonus Program.

The Secretary shall ensure that the percentages of apportionments of each State is sufficient to ensure that no State's percentage return from the Highway Trust Fund is less than 92 percent in each of the fiscal years 2005–2009. The rate of return shall include from each State, the total apportionments made for the fiscal year for the Interstate Maintenance Program, the National Highway System Program, the Bridge Program, the Surface Transportation Program, the Congestion Mitigation and Air Quality Improvement Program, the Highway Safety Improvement Program the Appalachian Development Highway System Program, the Recreational Trails Program, the Infrastructure Performance and Maintenance Program, the Metropolitan Planning Program, and the Equity Bonus Program.

Special rules protect the calculations for States with a population density of less than 20 persons per square mile, a population less than 1 million, a median household income less than $35,000, or a State with a fatality rate during 2002 on Interstate highways greater than 1 fatality per 100 million vehicle miles traveled on Interstate highways. Further, no State receives apportionments less than 110 percent of the average annual apportionments for specified programs during 1998–2003. There is a cap on the Equity Bonus such that no State may receive apportionments more than a specified percentage of their average for 1998–2003. The scope, or percent funding included in the Equity Bonus program, remains the same as TEA–21 at 92.5 percent.

Conference Substitute

The conference adopts the Senate structure with modifications. The Secretary shall ensure that the percentages of apportionments of each State is sufficient to ensure that no State's percentage return from the Highway Trust Fund is less than 90.5 percent in fiscal year 2005 and 2006, 91.5 percent in 2007, and 92 percent in 2008 and 2009. The rate of return shall include from each State, the total apportionments made for the fiscal year for the Interstate. Maintenance Program, the National Highway System Program, the Bridge Program, the Surface Transportation Program, the Congestion Mitigation and Air Quality Improvement Program, the Highway Safety Improvement Program, the Appalachian Development Highway System Program, the Recreational Trails Program, the Safe Routes to School Program, the Metropolitan Planning Program, the High Priority Project Program, the Railway-Highway Crossings Program, the Coordinated Border Infrastructure Program, and the Equity Bonus Program.

Special rules protect the share of apportionments to be provided to any State meeting any one or more of the following criteria: total population density of less than 40 persons per square mile, as reported in the decennial census conducted by the Federal Government in 2000, having at least 1.25 percent of its total acreage in Federal ownership based on GSA's "Federal Real Property Profile, as of September 30, 2004" report; or a population less than 1 million as reported in that census; or a median household income less than $35,000 as reported in that census; or a State with a fatality rate during 2002 on Interstate highways greater than 1 fatality per 100 million vehicle miles traveled on Interstate highways; or a State with an indexed, state motor fuels excise tax rate higher than 150 percent of the Federal motor fuels excise tax rate on the date of enactment of this Act.

Further, no State receives apportionments less than certain percentage above their TEA–21 average annual apportionments for specified programs during 1998–2003. (FY 2005—117 percent; FY 2006—118 percent; FY 2007—119 percent; FY 2008—120 percent; and FY 2009—121 percent)

EXAMPLE 2

SEC. 1107. METROPOLITAN PLANNING

House Bill

Sec. 1816.
This section requires the States to distribute planning funds to the metropolitan planning organizations within 30 days of receipt of such funds from the Secretary.

Senate Bill
No comparable provision in Senate bill.

Conference Substitute

The Conference adopts the House provision with a modification to increase the set-aside for metropolitan planning funds from 1 percent to 1.25 percent.

HOUSE CONFEREES (COMPLETE LIST, 108TH CONGRESS)

TRANSPORTATION AND INFRASTRUCTURE COMMITTEE

Chairman Don Young (R-Texas), ranking member James L. Oberstar (D-Minn.), and Reps. Tom Petri (R-Wis.), Sherwood Boehlert (R-N.Y.), Howard Coble (R-N.C.), John J. Duncan (R-Tenn.), John L. Mica (R-Fla.), Peter Hoekstra (R-Mich.), Vernon Ehlers (R-Mich.), Spencer Bachus (R-Ala.), Steve LaTourette (R-Ohio), Gary Miller (R-Calif.), Dennis Rehberg (R-Mont.), Bob Beauprez (R-Colo.), Nick Rahall (D-W.Va.), William O. Lipinski (D-Ill.), Peter A. DeFazio (D-Ore.), Jerry Costello (D-Ill.), Eleanor Holmes Norton (D-D.C.), Jerry Nadler (D-N.Y.), Robert Menendez (D-N.J.), Corrine Brown (D-Fla.), Bob Filner (D-Calif.), and Eddie Bernice Johnson (D-Texas)

BUDGET COMMITTEE

Chairman Jim Nussle (R-Iowa), ranking member John Spratt (D-S.C.), and Rep. Christopher Shays (R-Conn.)

WAYS AND MEANS COMMITTEE

Chairman Bill Thomas (R-Calif.), ranking member Charles Rangel (D-N.Y.), and Rep. Jim McCrery (R-La.)

SCIENCE COMMITTEE

Chairman Wayne Gilchrest (R-Md.), ranking member Bart Gordon (D-Tenn.), and Rep. Randy Neugebauer (R-Texas)

RULES COMMITTEE

Chairman David Dreier (R-Calif.), ranking member Martin Frost (R-Texas), and Rep. Pete Sessions (R-Texas)

RESOURCES COMMITTEE

Chairman Richard Pombo (R-Calif.) and Reps. James Gibbons (R-Nev.), and Ron Kind (D-Wis.)

JUDICIARY COMMITTEE

Chairman F. James Sensenbrenner (R-Wis.), ranking member John Conyers (D-Mich.), and Rep. Lamar Smith (R-Texas)

GOVERNMENT REFORM COMMITTEE

Chairman Tom Davis (R-Va.), ranking member Henry Waxman (D-Calif.), and Rep. Edward Schrock (R-Va.)

ENERGY AND COMMERCE COMMITTEE

Chairman Joe Barton (R-Texas), ranking member John Dingell (D-Mich.), and Rep. Charles Pickering (R-Miss.)

EDUCATION AND THE WORKFORCE COMMITTEE

Ranking member George Miller (D-Calif.), Reps. Cass Ballenger (R-N.C.) and Judy Biggert (R-Ill.)

HOUSE AND SENATE CONFEREES (COMPLETE LIST, 109TH CONGRESS)

HOUSE CONFEREES

House Transportation and Infrastructure Committee

Reps. Young (R-Alaska)), Petri (R-Wis.), Boehlert (R-N.Y.), Coble (R-N.C.), (Duncan (R-Tenn.), Mica (R-Fla.), Hoekstra (R-Mich.), La-Tourette (R-Ohio), Bachus (R-Ala.), Baker (R-La.), Miller (R-Calif.), Hayes (R-N.C.), Simmons (R-Conn.), Brown (R-S.C.), Graves (R-Mo.), Shuster (R-Pa.), Boozman (R-Ark.), Oberstar (D-Minn.), Rahall (D-W.Va.), DeFazio (D-Ore.), Costello (D-Ill.), Nadler (D-N.Y.), Menendez (D-N.J.), Brown (D-Fla.), Filner (D-Calif.), Johnson (D-Texas), Taylor (D-Miss.), Millender-McDonald (D-Calif.), Cummings (D-Md.), Blumenauer (D-Ore.), Tauscher (D-Calif.), and Del. Norton (D-D.C.)

House Budget Committee

Reps. Nussle (R-Iowa), Mario Diaz-Balart (R-Fla.), and Spratt (D-S.C.)

House Education and the Workforce Committee

Reps. Kline (R-Minn.), Keller (R-Fla.), and Barrow (D-Ga.)

House Energy and Commerce Committee

Reps. Barton (R-Texas), Pickering (R-Miss.), and Dingell (D-Mich.)

House Government Reform Committee

Reps. Tom Davis (R-Va.), Platts (R-Pa.), and Waxman (D-Calif.)

House Homeland Security Committee

Reps. Cox (R-Calif.), Lungren (R-Calif.), and Thompson (D-Miss.)

House Judiciary Committee

Reps. Sensenbrenner (R-Wis.), Smith (R-Texas), and Conyers (D-Mich.)

House Resources Committee

Reps. Pombo (R-Calif.), Walden (D-Ore.), and Kind (D-Wis.)

House Rules Committee

Reps. Dreier (R-Calif.), Capito (R-W.Va.), and McGovern (D-Mass.)

House Science Committee

Reps. Ehlers (R-Mich. (Reichert (R-Wash.), and Gordon (D-Tenn.)

House Ways and Means Committee

Reps. Thomas (R-Calif.), McCrery (R-La.), and Rangel (D-N.Y.)

SENATE CONFEREES

Sens. Inhofe (R-Okla.), Warner (R-Va.), Bond (R-Mo.), Voinovich (R-Ohio), Chafee (R-R.I.), Murkowski (R-Alaska), Thune (R-S.D.), DeMint (R-S.C.), Isakson (R-Ga.), Vitter (R-La.), Grassley (R-Iowa), Hatch (R-Utah), Shelby (R-Ala.), Allard (R-Colo.), Stevens (R-Alaska), Lott (R-Miss.), Jeffords, (I-Vt.), Baucus (D-Mont.), Lieberman (D-Conn.), Boxer (D-Calif.), Carper (D-Del.), Clinton (D-N.Y.), Lautenberg (D-N.J.), Obama (D-Ill.), Conrad (D-N.D.), Inouye (D-Hawaii), Rockefeller (D-W.Va.), Sarbanes (D-Md.), Reed (D-R.I.), and Johnson (D-S.D.)

KEY TRANSPORTATION POLICY CHANGES IN SAFETEA-LU

TOLLING

The most progressive changes in SAFETEA-LU were in the area of tolling. A provision in the U.S. Code prohibits the tolling of interstate highways under most circumstances. Previous surface transportation bills created pilot programs to allow variable tolling on interstates where it could reduce congestion. SAFETEA-LU continued and expanded those programs. For example, under the new Interstate System Construction Toll Pilot Program, a state or compact of states can collect tolls if it is for the purpose of constructing interstate highways. The program is limited to three projects in total (nationwide). Similarly, the new Express Lanes Demonstration Program will allow a total of fifteen demonstration projects through 2009 to permit tolling to manage high levels of congestion, reduce emissions in a nonattainment or maintenance area, or finance added interstate lanes for the purpose of reducing congestion.

FINANCE

SAFETEA-LU also advanced the concept of providing alternative financing sources outside the typical federal government grants. Private Activity Bonds (PABs) already existed under TEA-21, but SAFETEA-LU expanded bonding authority for them by adding highway facilities and surface freight transfer facilities to a list of other eligible activities. PABs make private financing more attractive by providing private bonds with the same tax breaks as bonds issued by government bodies. SAFETEA-LU also created

State Infrastructure Banks (SIBS), which allow states to enter into cooperative agreements to establish infrastructure revolving funds that can be capitalized with federal transportation funds authorized for fiscal years 2005–2009. The program gives states the capacity to increase the efficiency of their transportation investment and significantly leverage federal resources by attracting nonfederal public and private investment.

ENVIRONMENTAL

SAFETEA-LU changed the environmental review process for highway, transit, and multimodal projects with the intention of streamlining the process. A new category of "participating agencies" was added to allow more state, local, and tribal agencies a formal role and rights in the environmental process. After providing an opportunity for public and interagency involvement, the Department of Transportation (DOT) will define the project's purpose and need, and establish a plan for coordinating public and agency participation. As early as practicable in the process, DOT will provide an opportunity for a range of alternatives to be considered for a project. If any issue that could delay the process cannot be resolved within thirty days, DOT must notify Congress. A 180-day statute of limitations for lawsuits challenging federal agency approvals was provided, but it requires a new step of publishing environmental decisions in the *Federal Register.*

SAFETEA-LU also allows states to assume responsibility for certain environmental review responsibilities under certain circumstances. Five states (specified as Alaska, Ohio, Oklahoma, Texas, and California) can also apply to USDOT to assume *all* USDOT environmental responsibilities under the National Environmental Policy Act (NEPA) and other environmental laws (excluding the Clean Air Act and transportation planning requirements). This delegation authority is limited to highway projects.

SAFETEA-LU also made some changes to the controversial "4(f)" provision, which is often seen as a roadblock to construction. Section 4(f) of the DOT Act prohibits projects on publicly owned parks, recreation areas, wildlife and waterfowl refuges, or historic sites unless there is no feasible and prudent alternative and all possible mitigation is used. Under SAFETEA-LU, DOT has some flexibility to allow an exemption from 4(f) requirements if a program or project will have a "de minimis" impact on the area—i.e., there are no adverse effects of the project and the relevant state historic preservation officer or other official with jurisdiction over a property concurs. DOT must also conduct a study evaluating the impact of the "de minimis" finding and report to Congress no earlier than four years after enactment. Also, the interstate system is exempted from being treated as an historic resource under Section 4(f), unless the secretary of transportation determines that individual elements possess national or exceptional historic significance and should receive protection.

SAFETEA-LU established a new program, authorized at a total of $100 million through 2009, called the Nonmotorized Transportation Pilot Program. The idea of this program is to construct a network of nonmotorized transportation infrastructure facilities in four designated communities. The purpose is to demonstrate the extent to which walking and bicycling can represent a major portion of the transportation solution in certain communities. Similarly, SAFETEA-LU established the Safe Routes to School Program, which is intended to enable and encourage more primary and secondary school children to walk or bicycle to school. Both infrastructure-related and behavioral projects in the program are supposed to be geared toward providing a safe, appealing environment for walking and biking that will improve the quality of children's lives and support national health objectives by reducing traffic, fuel consumption, and air pollution in the vicinity of schools.

HIGHWAY CONSTRUCTION

SAFETEA-LU created the Highways for LIFE Pilot Program, which intends to foster the use of new technologies and more efficient ways of building highways. Under the program, DOT is supposed to provide leadership and incentives to demonstrate and promote state-of-the-art technologies, elevated performance standards, and new business practices in the highway construction process that result in improved safety, faster construction, reduced congestion from construction, and improved quality and user satisfaction. A total of $75 million was authorized through 2009 for incentive grants, to fund up to 20 percent but not more than $5 million of the total cost of a qualifying project. A maximum of fifteen projects may receive incentive funds in a given fiscal year, but the goal is to approve and provide funds to at least one project in each state by 2009. SAFETEA-LU also encourages the use of design-build contracting, wherein the same entity, usually a private one, designs and builds a transportation facility. SAFETEA-LU eliminates the $50 million floor on the size of eligible design-build contracts, which had curtailed the number of possible projects. Also, the secretary has to issue revised regulations that will allow transportation agencies to proceed with certain actions prior to receipt of final NEPA approval. This change will encourage public-private partnerships by allowing private sector partners to be involved in the project definition process.

STUDIES/COMMISSIONS

SAFETEA-LU created three separate studies and commissions to examine the future of transportation. The most prominent was the National Surface Transportation Policy and Revenue Study Commission, which is conducting a study of current conditions and future needs of the surface transportation system. They are authorized to develop a conceptual plan with alternatives to ensure that the surface transportation system will continue to serve the nation's needs. The Road User Fees Study authorizes a total of $12.5 million to fund a long-term field test of an approach to assessing highway use fees based on actual mileage driven by a specific vehicle on specific types of highways by use of an onboard computer. The study is to be performed by the Public Policy Center of the University of Iowa. Finally, the National Surface Transportation Infrastructure Financing Commission will complete a study on Highway Trust Fund revenues and the impacts of these revenues for future highway and transit needs. Among the considerations will be alternative approaches to generating revenues for the Highway Trust Fund (HTF). The commission will develop a report recommending policies to achieve revenues for the HTF that will meet future needs.

INDEX

ABOUT THE AUTHORS

Costas Panagopoulos is assistant professor of political science and director of the Center for Electoral Politics and Democracy and the Master's Program in Elections and Campaign Management at Fordham University. He is also a research fellow at the Institution for Social and Policy Studies at Yale University. He served as an American Political Science Association Congressional Fellow in the office of Sen. Hillary Rodham Clinton, D-N.Y., from 2004 to 2005. His academic research, focusing American politics with an emphasis on campaigns and elections, voting behavior, public opinion and Congress, has appeared in the *American Journal of Political Science, Public Opinion Quarterly, Presidential Studies Quarterly, Electoral Studies,* and *PS: Political Science and Politics.* Panagopoulos was part of the Decision Desk team at NBC News in 2006 and has provided extensive political analysis and commentary for various print and broadcast media outlets, including the *New York Times, Los Angeles Times, Newsday,* CNN, *NBC Nightly News,* Fox News, and BBC Television. Panagopoulos holds an undergraduate degree in government from Harvard University and a PhD in politics from New York University.

Joshua Schank is director of transportation research at the Bipartisan Policy Center, where he is directing a national transportation policy study. He was a consultant with PB Consult, the management consulting arm of Parsons Brinckerhoff, one of the world's leading transportation planning and engineering firms, and a senior associate with ICF International, an environmental consulting firm; he was a consultant to federal and local government agencies on transportation issues for both firms. Schank advised Sen. Hillary Clinton on federal highway and transit legislation from 2002 to 2005. He has also been an analyst for the U.S. Department of Transportation Inspector General, and he worked as a transportation planner for the Permanent Citizens Advisory Committee to the Metropolitan Transportation Authority in New York City. Schank is president of the Washington, D.C., chapter of the Transportation Research Forum, one of the oldest professional transportation organizations. In addition to a PhD in urban planning from Columbia University, Schank has a master's degree in city planning from the Massachusetts Institute of Technology.